Institutional Translation for International Governance

Enhancing Quality in Multilingual Legal Communication

Edited by Fernando Prieto Ramos

BLOOMSBURY ACADEMIC
LONDON • NEW YORK • OXFORD • NEW DELHI • SYDNEY

BLOOMSBURY ACADEMIC
Bloomsbury Publishing Plc
50 Bedford Square, London, WC1B 3DP, UK
1385 Broadway, New York, NY 10018, USA

BLOOMSBURY, BLOOMSBURY ACADEMIC and the Diana logo are
trademarks of Bloomsbury Publishing Plc

First published 2018
Paperback edition first published 2019

A catalogue record for this book is available from the British Library.

Library of Congress Cataloging-in-Publication Data
Names: Prieto Ramos, Fernando, 1975- editor.
Title: Institutional translation for international governance: enhancing quality in multilingual legal
communication/edited by Fernando Prieto Ramos.
Description: First edition. | New York: Bloomsbury Academic, An imprint of Bloomsbury Publishing,
2018. | Series: Bloomsbury advances in translation | Includes bibliographical references and index.
Identifiers:LCCN2017036097(print)|LCCN2017044878(ebook)|ISBN9781474292306(ePDF)|
ISBN 9781474292313 (ePub) | ISBN 9781474292290 (hardcover)
Subjects: LCSH: Law–Translating–European Union countries. |
Court interpreting and translating–European Union countries. |
Courts–European Union countries–Translating.
Classification: LCC KJE5306 (ebook) | LCC KJE5306 .I57 2018 (print) | DDC 341.242/2014–dc23
LC record available at https://lccn.loc.gov/2017036097

ISBN: HB: 978-1-4742-9229-0
PB: 978-1-3501-2665-7
ePDF: 978-1-4742-9230-6
ePub: 978-1-4742-9231-3

Series: Bloomsbury Advances in Translation

Typeset by Deanta Global Publishing Services, Chennai, India

To find out more about our authors and books visit
www.bloomsbury.com and sign up for our newsletters.

Institutional Translation for International Governance

Outline of the book

This book provides a state-of-the-art overview of institutional translation issues related to the development of international law and policies for supranational integration and governance. These issues are explored from various angles in selected chapters by guest specialists and in the findings of a large-scale research project led by the editor. Focus is placed on key methodological and policy aspects of legal communication and translation quality in a variety of institutional settings, including several comparative studies of the United Nations and the European Union. The book offers a unique combination of perspectives drawn together through a multilayered examination of methods (e.g. corpus analysis, comparative law for translation and terminological analysis), skills and working procedures. The chapters are organized into three sections: (1) contemporary issues and methods, (2) translation quality in law- and policy-making and implementation, and (3) translation and multilingual case-law.

Contents

Institutional Translation for International Governance

Also available from Bloomsbury:

How to Analyze Talk in Institutional Settings, edited by Alec McHoul and Mark Rapley
Quality in Professional Translation, Joanna Drugan
Translation Solutions for Many Languages, Anthony Pym

List of Figures

List of Tables

About the Contributors

Łucja Biel is Associate Professor and Head of the Corpus Research Centre of the Institute of Applied Linguistics at the University of Warsaw (Poland). She is deputy editor of the *Journal of Specialised Translation* and Secretary General of the European Society for Translation Studies. She holds a PhD in linguistics (University of Gdańsk, Poland), a diploma in English and EU law (University of Cambridge, UK), and a School of American Law diploma (Chicago-Kent School of Law, USA; and University of Gdańsk, Poland). Former visiting lecturer on the MA in legal translation at City, University of London (2009–2014), her research interests focus on legal and EU translation, translator training and corpus linguistics. She has published over forty papers and a book (*Lost in the Eurofog. The Textual Fit of Translated Law*, Peter Lang, 2014) in this area. She has been involved in a number of nationally and internationally funded projects, including *Understanding Justice* (European Commission action grant, Middlesex University, UK); the *Eurolect Observatory* (UNINT, Italy); and the *Eurofog* and *Polish Eurolect* projects (National Science Centre, Poland).

James Brannan has been working for over ten years as a senior translator at the European Court of Human Rights (Council of Europe). He had a similar post at the International Court of Justice and, before that, was a self-employed translator/interpreter in Lyon, in particular for the courts and police as *expert judiciaire*. He has also taught legal English. He studied languages in the UK (BA degree), then law in France (Diplôme de l'Institut de droit comparé de Lyon; DEA de droit communautaire, Université Jean Moulin Lyon 3). He has lectured and published other articles on translation in international courts and on the implementation of Directive 2010/64/EU. He is currently an associate member of Transius and EULITA.

Agnieszka Doczekalska is Assistant Professor at the Kozminski University's Law School in Warsaw (Poland). She holds a doctorate in law from the European University Institute (Italy) and diplomas in translation from the Centre for Modern Translation Studies (University of Lodz, Poland) and the Institut de Traducteurs, d'Interprètes et de Relations Internationales (University of Strasbourg, France). She currently conducts research on the language of national legal acts transposing EU directives. She has published papers on comparative law, Japanese law, legal multilingualism and legal translation, especially on legislative drafting and interpretation of multilingual law in the European Union and Canada. Her research interests also include copyright law subjects.

Jan Engberg is Professor of Knowledge Communication at the Department of German and Romance Languages of the School of Communication and Culture of the University of Aarhus (Denmark). His main research areas are the study of texts and genres in the academic field, cognitive aspects of domain-specific discourse and the relations between specialized knowledge and text formulation, as well as basic aspects of communication in domain-specific settings. The focus of his research is communication and translation in the field of law. He is co-editor of the international journal *Fachsprache* and member of the editorial or advisory boards of a substantial number of international scholarly journals.

Mathilde Fontanet is Associate Professor at the University of Geneva's Faculty of Translation and Interpreting (FTI), where she teaches several translation and revision courses, including in technical and literary translation. She worked as a translator and reviser at the European Organization for Nuclear Research (CERN) between 1991 and 2013, including ten years as head of its French Section. She holds a PhD in translation Studies and has published a number of papers on translation theories and various aspects of the translation process. Her main research interests are translation strategies, translator training and issues related to the translator's creativity and subjectivity.

Diego Guzmán holds a primary degree in French literature from the National Autonomous University of Mexico (UNAM) and two MAs in translation from the University of Geneva's FTI. He has worked as an assistant for the FTI's Centre for Legal and Institutional Translation Studies (Transius) since 2012. He is conducting his doctoral research on legal institutional translation as part of the LETRINT project ('Legal Translation in International Institutional Settings') under the supervision of Prof. Fernando Prieto Ramos. As a practitioner, he completed translation internships at the United Nations Office at Geneva (UNOG) and the South Centre translation services, and he has worked as a freelance translator since 2007.

Anne Lafeber is a senior reviser in the English Translation Service and adviser on testing for the Documentation Division at United Nations Headquarters in New York. She is also the Deputy Secretary of IAMLADP, the international forum of managers of international organizations employing conference and language service providers. After graduating from the University of Oxford (England) with a BA and MA in Modern Languages, she spent several years working in Latin America as a freelance translator for different international organizations before joining the United Nations. She has also taught translation at university level in Mexico and Switzerland. She obtained her PhD in translation and intercultural studies at Rovira i Virgili University (Spain). Her doctoral thesis explored ways to improve the validity and reliability of recruitment tests, and she continues to research and pilot innovations in the testing not only of translators but also of other types of language professionals.

Lucie Pacho Aljanati holds two primary degrees in translation and interpreting (Instituto Superior San Bartolomé, Argentina, and Pompeu Fabra University, Spain); a double MA in European law, area of freedom, security and justice (Toulouse 1 Capitole University, France) and European integration (Autonomous University of Barcelona, Spain); and a dual PhD in translation studies and international relations and European integration (University of Geneva and Autonomous University of Barcelona), co-supervised by professors Fernando Prieto Ramos and Antoni Milian i Massana. She has extensive experience as a translator, interpreter and project manager, and has participated in the first phase of the LETRINT project at the University of Geneva's Transius Centre.

Fernando Prieto Ramos is Full Professor of Translation and Director of the Centre for Legal and Institutional Translation Studies (Transius) at the University of Geneva's FTI. With a background in both translation and law, his work focuses on legal and institutional translation, including interdisciplinary methodologies, international legal instruments and specialized terminology. Former member of the Centre for Translation and Textual Studies at Dublin City University, he has published widely on legal translation and has received several research and teaching awards, including a European Label Award for Innovative Methods in Language Teaching from the European Commission, an International Geneva Award from the Swiss Network for International Studies and a Consolidator Grant for his current project on 'Legal Translation in International Institutional Settings' (LETRINT). He has also translated for several organizations since 1997, including five years as an in-house translator at the World Trade Organization (dispute settlement team).

Colin Robertson worked as legal-linguistic reviser ('lawyer-linguist') at the Council of the EU from 1993 until his retirement in 2013, checking and revising draft EU legislative texts in English. He holds a law degree from Aberdeen University (Scotland) and is a member of the Law Society of Scotland. Apart from English, he has knowledge of several languages, including French, German, Italian, Czech, Slovak and Bulgarian. From 1979 to 1991, he worked as a lawyer in the UK public service, which included two years in the Legal Service of the European Commission on detachment (1982–1983). In 1990, he passed an EU lawyer-linguist competition and subsequently worked as legal translator in the Court of Justice of the EU before joining the Council. He draws on his experience working in the practice of law since 1975 to explore diverse topics of multilingualism in legal language, in particular EU legal language and terminology, legislative drafting and translation. He has published widely in connection with these topics, most recently with his book *Multilingual Law: A Framework for Analysis and Understanding* (Routledge, 2016).

Susan Šarčević is Professor Emerita and former Head of the Department of Foreign Languages at the Faculty of Law of the University of Rijeka, where she taught legal English, legal German and EU terminology. She also taught postgraduate courses on legal translation and terminology at the University of Zagreb, co-chaired a national project responsible for creating Croatian terms for EU legal concepts and headed a project on 'Strategies for Translating the EU *acquis*'. She has published extensively on legal translation, legal lexicography and multilingual communication in the law. Her best-known work is *New Approach to Legal Translation* (1997, 2000). She has co-authored a series of textbooks and edited a number of volumes, most recently *Language and Culture in EU Law* (2015). She has guest lectured worldwide and held keynote addresses and plenary lectures at numerous conferences on law and language. She is research professor at the China University of Political Science and Law in Beijing, and a member of the International Language and Law Association (ILLA), the Multicultural Association of Law and Language (MALL), the University of Geneva's Transius Centre Advisory Board and several editorial boards.

Ingemar Strandvik works as a quality manager at the European Commission's Directorate-General for Translation, where he was formerly a translator. He has a background as a State-authorized legal translator and court interpreter in Sweden, where he also taught translation at Stockholm University and was active for many years as a lexicographer at the publishing house Norstedts. Apart from studies in philology and degrees in translation and interpreting, he has a Master's degree in EU law. He is currently involved in standardization work at different levels and regularly participates in conferences and publications on translation quality, multilingual law-making and terminology.

Aleksandar Trklja holds a PhD in applied linguistics from the University of Birmingham. He is a senior lecturer at the Centre for Translation Studies at the University of Vienna. He presently also works as a research fellow at the University of Birmingham on the European Research Council projects 'Law and Language at the European Court' and 'EU case-law corpus'. His role includes carrying out corpus and discourse analyses of EU jurisprudence and developing a theoretical explanation of relations between law and language in the EU legal order. His research interests lie in the application of corpus linguistics and contrastive linguistic methods to the investigation of lexico-grammatical constructions and discourse organization. He has published on lexicography, translation studies, legal language and multimodality theory.

Susan Wright graduated in law with French from the University of Birmingham and spent two years in Brussels as a documentary analyst at the European Commission, before working for fourteen years as an academic lawyer in the UK, most recently as head of Law at the Department of Linguistic and International Studies of the University of Surrey. She joined the EU Court of Justice in 1998, serving as an English-language lawyer-linguist, then as head of the Court's English-language translation department and, since 2011, as a director in the Court's translation service. She has given guest lectures and conference papers to judges, practitioners, academics and students in a number of European countries in the fields of law and language, the management of multilingualism, and English and French law and legal terminology. She has an active research interest in French constitutional law and has since 1994 been co-rapporteur on France for *European Public Law*, contributing regular reports on the *Conseil constitutionnel*.

Institutional Translation: Surveying the Landscape at International Organizations

Fernando Prieto Ramos

Since Brian Mossop argued that 'translating institutions' were 'an important participant missing in existing models of translation' (Mossop 1988: 65), institutional translation has attracted increasing attention in Translation Studies (TS), particularly after the turn of the millennium. Institutional practices of bilingual law-making had been the subject of earlier work in Canada (e.g. Covacs 1979), driven by practical needs at national level. Systematic research on institutional translation, however, has been slow to develop and has tended to concentrate on case studies. As regards international organizations, the most scrutinized setting of institutional translation has been, by far, that of the European Union (EU) institutions. Substantial insights into this setting were provided by Emma Wagner, Svend Bech and Jesús Martínez's (2002 and second edition in 2012) description of EU translation services; and Kaisa Koskinen's (2008) ethnographic study on Finnish translators at the European Commission. The interest generated by the largest and most multilingual supranational entity in the world partly explains the growing number of contributions on EU discourses and the legal implications of multilingualism (e.g. Derlén 2011; Felici 2010; Kjær 2007; McAuliffe 2011; Šarčević 2013; Biel 2014a). EU enlargements since 2004, as well as the traditional leading role and concentration of TS research in Europe, have also contributed to that heightened interest.

Studies on translation at intergovernmental organizations and on the common features of international institutional translation, however, remain more limited. The most far-reaching attempts at conceptualizing these commonalities have been made in connection with legal translation. This is not surprising considering the legal foundations of all institutional work, which ultimately revolves around the development, implementation and dissemination of policies within international and supranational legal frameworks. In two influential works in Legal Translation Studies (LTS), both Susan Šarčević (1997: 195–228) and Deborah Cao (2007: 134–63) examined the translation of multilateral instruments, drawing parallels between United Nations (UN) and EU legal translation. The first of these two authors referred to the key concept of 'fidelity to the single instrument' (Šarčević 1997: 215), which goes hand in hand with the principle of equal authenticity of international legal acts in all official languages, and challenges traditional source-to-target-text relations in TS. The translation priorities of accuracy and consistency with legal precedents and established discursive conventions derive from the same concept. From a systemic perspective, they are also a matter of institutional normativity, authoritativeness, predictability and legal certainty.

Translation at international organizations is much more than law-making, though. Texts produced in implementation monitoring procedures, in particular, have most often been neglected in the analysis of international institutional translation, despite the large volume of translation in these settings. This category is considered here as one of 'three interrelated contexts of text production that come into play in the development of international and supranational law' (Prieto Ramos 2014b: 315), together with law-making and adjudication processes, as elicited in a comparative analysis of translation work at the UN, the EU and the World Trade Organization (WTO). These core legal functions are supported by other multilingual texts of policy formulation, informative texts on institutional activities for the general public and other administrative documents necessary for the functioning of each organization (at times governed by a restricted procedural language regime). The role of translation is therefore central to achieving wide understanding and implementation of institutional goals, which has recently been described as 'governing by translation' (Koskinen 2014).

The vast scope of multilingual institutional communication is characterized by a high level of hybridity in terms of domains and discourse features (particularly, in English as a *lingua franca*), and by challenges such as terminology management, profile specialization, ambiguity in negotiated texts and court interpretation in cases of interlinguistic divergence. The policies and conventions applied to tackle these issues are manifestations of the normative approach to producing authoritative texts in line with the specificities of each institution. They all have a bearing on quality as the ultimate objective of all institutional drafters and language professionals. This is also the aim of the present volume: enriching our understanding of institutional translation for international governance, in particular with regard to key aspects that contribute to the quality of the core legal communication of international organizations.

These issues are explored from various angles by leading specialists, most of whom have a double academic and applied background, including in translation service management and quality assurance. A diversity of multilateral and EU institutions, perspectives and methods are represented with a view to providing an extensive overview of current issues and research in institutional translation. The volume assembles selected papers from guest authors and outputs of a Consolidator Grant research project[1] led by the editor from the University of Geneva's Centre for Legal and Institutional Translation Studies (Transius), where the analysis of translation practices at international organizations constitutes a primary line of research.

Institutional legal translation is understood here in the broad sense explained above (building on Prieto Ramos 2014b), and the chapters are accordingly organized into three parts. The first one focuses on cross-cutting issues and methods, while the other two address quality-related aspects of multilingual text production in law- and policy-making and implementation (Part II), and in judicial contexts (Part III).

Part I includes three complementary chapters by prominent legal translation scholars. Chapter 1, by Susan Šarčević, elaborates on the challenges to legal translators as transnational communicators in institutional settings, including terminological

[1] 'Legal Translation in International Institutional Settings' (LETRINT), supported by the Swiss National Science Foundation.

considerations. It discusses the central issue of reconciling the translators' multiple fidelities and (sometimes conflicting) priorities, in particular the commonly institutionalized preference for interlingual 'surface-level similarity' to ensure concordance, on the one hand; and the duty to end users and idiomaticity, on the other. The author underlines that interdisciplinary expertise is required to address this issue, without excluding the potential room for translational creativity. In Chapter 2, Łucja Biel highlights the growing relevance and sophistication of corpus-based research in LTS and institutional legal translation in particular, which is illustrated by four other chapters of the book. She provides an overview of advances in corpus use and tools, and their benefits for both practitioners and researchers, especially in identifying translation patterns and generating empirical quantitative data. Jan Engberg closes Part I by exploring an essential method in legal terminology problem-solving in Chapter 3: comparative legal analysis. Building on the view that institutional legal translation is a form of knowledge communication, he uses frames as a tool to describe and assess terminological decisions.

Part II starts with a 'journey' through the evolution of quality assurance policies at the European Commission's Directorate-General for Translation (DGT) in Chapter 4. A quality manager involved in the conception of recent initiatives in this field at DGT, Ingemar Strandvik, explains the rationale behind the increasingly integral, structured and explicit approach to quality, especially since the major EU enlargement of 2004. He presents the key concept of 'fitness-for-purpose', which is at the core of new internal guidelines for the translation of different text categories, quality control, risk assessment and evaluation of outsourced translations. In Chapter 5, Anne Lafeber, a reviser at the UN, focuses on a key aspect of quality assurance: translation competence requirements. Based on a survey of institutional translators and revisers, she compares the skill-sets identified as recruitment priorities for the EU and the UN translation services, and examines the factors that may explain the differences found, including divergent structures, revision practices, working methods and domain specialization.

Chapter 6, by the editor and Diego Guzmán, is one of the outputs of the LETRINT project mentioned above. It applies a corpus-based mixed-method approach that combines lexicometric (quantitative) and acceptability (qualitative) analysis to compare consistency and adequacy levels of translations of an illustrative term (*due process*) into Spanish at the EU, the UN and the WTO over ten years (2005–15). The findings point to correlations between product quality indicators, translation process conditions and thematic specialization. In Chapter 7, Agnieszka Doczekalska also focuses on legal terminological choices from a comparative perspective. As a legal scholar, she pays particular attention to the legal implications of drafting EU multilingual legislation in twenty-four languages as opposed to federal, bilingual and bijural legislation in Canada. The overlap of jurisdictions (i.e. national law and EU law in Member States, and federal law and provincial law in Canadian provinces) and regulated domains proves especially challenging and conditions the techniques applied to express EU autonomous concepts and Canadian bijural concepts.

In the final two chapters of Part II, their respective authors delve into the communicative conditions that shape multilingual text production in the professional settings where they developed their institutional careers. In Chapter 8, Colin

Robertson, former lawyer-linguist at the Council of the EU, outlines the concept of legal-linguistic profiling of organizations as a way of situating their translation work, including legal framework, language regime, specialist terminology domains, and drafting and translation methods. The proposed model is illustrated by the case of the European Aviation Safety Agency (EASA). In Chapter 9, Mathilde Fontanet, also a member of the Transius Centre, analyses how institutional domain specialization actually permeates legal texts at the European Organization for Nuclear Research (CERN) as reflected in a parallel English–French corpus of representative cooperation agreements, safety documents and contract adjudication proposals. She describes the structure and conventions applied to each legal genre, and quantifies the density of technical and legal specialized language in order to compare the hybridity of texts.

Part III assembles four contributions on related aspects of translation and multilingual case-law. The first two focus on the judgments of the EU Court of Justice (CJEU). As a translation manager at this institution, Susan Wright provides a very thorough account of its complex language regime (the 'hour-glass model of multilingual management') in Chapter 10, and she discusses how this regime conditions the drafting of judgments in French and their production in the other official languages. She then raises questions on the challenges that lie ahead for the CJEU's translation service in the light of competing objectives, including the future role of the English language in EU institutions. In Chapter 11, Aleksandar Trklja offers a linguist's insights into one of those key challenges: how to ensure semantic uniformity in the highly multilingual context described in the previous chapter. An investigation of corresponding lexical items in a parallel corpus of all CJEU judgments published in French, English and German until 2011 serves to conclude that one-to-one absolute uniformity is virtually impossible, and that translation-generated lexical diversity could be accepted as part of a more pluralistic view of EU law creation and reception.

Translation policy and practices at the European Court of Human Rights are then described by one of its translation experts, James Brannan, in Chapter 12. The author provides an overview of the challenges deriving from the Court's broad territorial jurisdiction and the interfaces between its two official languages and non-official languages. Among other aspects, he also points to the translators' search for balance between consistency and idiomaticity, as well as to the relevance of internal cooperation with lawyers and judges. The implications of equal authenticity for multilingual law interpretation and translation, a common thread in Part III, are finally addressed in a comparative study conducted by the editor with the support of Lucie Pacho Aljanati (Chapter 13) as part of the LETRINT project. Patterns of explicit comparative interpretation are measured in the case-law of the International Court of Justice, the WTO's Appellate Body and the CJEU. They are discussed in connection with their legal framework, the complexity of the relevant language regimes and other factors quantified in order to nuance our understanding of the differences found in comparative hermeneutic practices: the nature of proceedings, the initiators and motivation of comparison (including cases of divergence between language versions) and systemic factors such as caseload and political considerations. The implications for translators and institutions involved in producing and uniformly interpreting multilingual law are also raised.

These intimately related chapters and perspectives offer a unique snapshot of the dynamic institutional translation landscape, with a clear focus on ensuring quality specialized communication. This book also illustrates the increasing cooperation among institutional and academic actors, and the synergies that can emerge when they exchange approaches, experiences and tools.

Acknowledgements

My gratitude goes to all the authors for their remarkable contributions and commitment. I would also like to thank Diego Guzmán for his technical assistance, as well as the series editor, Jeremy Munday, and all Bloomsbury staff for their support at all stages of the project.

Part One

Contemporary Issues and Methods

1

Challenges to Legal Translators in Institutional Settings

Susan Šarčević

1 Introduction

In retrospect, legal translation has come a long way since the publication of my book *New Approach to Legal Translation* in 1997. At that time, legal translation was regarded merely as one of the many fields of special-purpose translation; today, it is widely recognized as an independent discipline by both comparative lawyers (e.g. Glanert 2014; Jedrzejowska 2011) and translation scholars (e.g. Prieto Ramos 2014b). For his part, Prieto Ramos heralds legal translation not only as 'an independent discipline within general translation studies' but also as one of 'the most prominent disciplines of translation studies' (2014b: 261). Despite the increasing number of scholarly publications in the field, Anne Lise Kjær (2014: 430) still regards my book *New Approach* as 'the most comprehensive study of legal translation'. However, a number of shifts in legal translation have occurred since its publication, especially as a result of what Kjær calls 'changes in the landscape of international law' (2014: 434). Taking account of these shifts, this chapter investigates their impact on legal translators in institutional settings in our age of global governance.

Earlier, I examined legal translation as 'an act of communication in the mechanism of the law' (Šarčević 1997: 55). This time, I zoom in and focus on legal translation specifically as an act of 'transnational communication', enabling institutional multilingualism to operate on a regional and global scale in supranational and international law. While the main emphasis is on the translation of supranational law, here European Union (EU) law and European law in the broader sense, comparisons are made with the translation of treaties, conventions and model laws in United Nations (UN) organizations and agreements of the World Trade Organization (WTO). The purpose is not to compare similarities and differences in translation practices but rather to discuss meta aspects of institutional legal translation and challenges confronting translators in their role as transnational communicators in our interconnected world.

The stage is set by presenting background information on the development of institutional translation and identifying major shifts on the legal scene and their impact on legal languages and translators (Section 2). Thereafter, the spotlight moves to the normative behaviour of institutional translators engaged in multilingual law-making, with special emphasis on challenges to translators participating in the production of equally authentic legislative texts (Section 3). Investigating a specific scenario – multilingual text production in the European Commission – we see that the primary task of translators is to institutionalize uniformity by striving to achieve 'surface-level-similarity' between the authentic texts of a single instrument (Section 4). However, institutional translators also have a duty to the end users to produce multilingual legislative texts that meet the requirements of legal certainty recognized in international human rights law (Section 5). In response to the new challenges, translators are called upon to take an active role as creators of transnational legal languages, especially when deciding whether foreignization should be favoured over domestication in term formation (Section 6). Finally, institutional translators on all continents are encouraged to become effective transnational communicators who dare to go beyond surface-level similarity (Section 7).

2 Institutional legal translation – the pulse of the twenty-first century

Although scholarly interest in institutional legal translation is a relatively recent phenomenon (Kang 2009, 2014),[1] legal translation has been carried out in government institutions at national level for centuries, albeit largely unrecorded. At the international and supranational levels, institutional multilingualism became well established after the Second World War (see Tabory 1980: 6–36), in particular with the founding of the UN and later the European Communities, today the EU, formally ushering in the era of multilingual law-making in the framework of international organizations, where translation is indispensable as the main means of multilingual text production (Prieto Ramos 2014a; Šarčević 1997).

The language policy of intergovernmental organizations, including the selection of official languages, is usually determined by their Member States, taking account of their geopolitical constellation, competences and budgetary concerns. The EU policy of language equality is truly unique (Wagner et al. 2002: 1–7; Šarčević 2012: 86); however, one should keep in mind that the Member States voluntarily surrender some of their sovereign rights upon accession. Nonetheless, it is remarkable that the practice of conferring the status of official language on the major language of each new Member State has remained unaltered despite the increase from six to twenty-eight Member States and from four to twenty-four official languages (on proposals to reduce the number of official languages and contra-arguments, see Šarčević 2013: 17–21). As an embodiment of the principle of democracy (Wagner et al. 2002: 3), all instruments of EU primary and secondary law are 'drafted' in twenty-four equally authentic language versions, and the Court of Justice of the European Union (CJEU) hears cases in all

[1] In 1988, B. Mossop remarked that institutional translation was a 'missing factor' in translation theory (1988: 65); however, it was not until twenty years later that an entry on institutional translation (written by Kang) was included in the *Routledge Encyclopedia of Translation Studies* (2009, 2nd edn).

official languages (see the Official Journal [OJ] and case-law at <eur-lex.europa.eu>). In contrast, the Council of Europe, which has expanded to include forty-seven Member States, operates in French and English. The European Court of Human Rights (ECtHR) hears cases in the two official languages but has begun to publish important judgments in some non-official languages as a means of facilitating the implementation of human rights law throughout Europe (Brannan 2013: 910; see the official website at <hudoc.echr.coe.int>). To ensure a global reach, the UN and its many organizations operate in six official languages, and UN conventions, model laws and other regulatory instruments set out international rules mostly in six equally authentic texts: English, French, Spanish, Russian, Chinese and Arabic (see Zhao and Cao 2013). Nonetheless, the International Court of Justice in The Hague hears cases in French and English only. Responsible for ensuring free trade throughout the world, the WTO continues to operate in English, French and Spanish despite the admission of China and Russia in 2001 and 2012, respectively. The WTO Appellate Body resolves disputes in the three official languages (see Prieto Ramos 2013a).

On the legal scene, the growing need for shared legal standards and rules to manage the economic forces of globalization triggered dynamic processes of transnationalization, giving rise to transnational law in areas regulating cross-border actions and events. According to Cotterrel (2012), transnational law includes international human rights law, international criminal law, international trade law, international financial law, international environmental law, international commercial arbitration practice, EU law and WTO law. The need to interpret and apply new transnational norms has resulted in the proliferation of international courts and tribunals, some of which use sophisticated methods of multilingual interpretation and enjoy increased authority, practising judge-made law by delivering binding precedents and establishing autonomous concepts (see Letsas 2004 [ECtHR], Derlén 2009 [CJEU]).

2.1 Impact of transnationalization on language

Prompting the decline of the nation-state, these developments have also had a notable impact on legal languages, making them less dependent on national legal systems, even in traditional nationally oriented fields such as constitutional law (Jedrzejowska 2011). This shift has occasioned Kjær to regard 'the interdependency of legal language and legal system' as a thing of the past (2014: 431), suggesting that this development foreshadows the end of traditional legal translation as a culture-bound activity (2015: 98). In my opinion, that stage is far in the future, if ever; however, we are gradually moving in that direction. Therefore, Glanert's metaphor of 'translation-in-law as an assemblage in motion' (2014) could be appropriate in this sense as well, although Glanert emphasizes the role of 'glocalization' as a means of bringing the global message to locals (2014: 264). Regardless of the stage in the chain of transnational communication, it is agreed that national law has taken a back seat to supranational and international law (Megale 2015). In our global world, national legal languages are slowly converging as national laws are increasingly harmonized and international standards and norms are recognized worldwide. Today, legal scholars, jurists and practising lawyers from different legal backgrounds and cultures cooperate in 'transnational discursive communities' (Kjær 2014: 431; 2015: 98),[2] communicating mostly in 'neutralized' varieties of supranational and international English.

In the EU, English overtook French as the main drafting language of EU law in the 1990s. Widely regarded as the *lingua franca* of the EU institutions (Pozzo 2012; Felici 2015), English is likely to retain its dominance despite Brexit. An exception continues to be the Court of Justice, where French remains the sole working language and 'Court French' the primary language of judgments and legal opinions (McAuliffe 2013a). Like all euro-languages, EU legal English is not bound to any national legal system but serves as a vehicle language for expressing EU law. In this context, it is worth mentioning efforts by European comparative lawyers to create a common legal language for Europe with a uniform terminology, especially in core areas of private law such as contract law (see Perfumi 2013: 133–9; Pozzo 2012: 199; Šarčević 2010: 33–41).[3]

2.2 Need for effective forms of transnational communication

Long a major objective of international law, uniform law has been most successful in areas of commercial interest such as trade law, dispute resolution, banking and finance, maritime law and civil aviation, all of which are dominated by English. In the twenty-first century, the priorities of the UN and its main legal drafting body, the International Law Commission, have shifted to establishing principles, common standards and rules of law with the aim of promoting cooperation between nations on a global scale for the purpose of combating crime and terrorism, providing aid to the least developed nations, protecting the planet and extending protection to underprivileged and abused individuals (Katz Cogan 2015). Global interdependency has made it necessary for nations to communicate and draft transnational legal instruments in system-neutral varieties of international English that can be understood and implemented worldwide. Paradoxically, the emergence of neutralized varieties of legal English throughout the world has in no way diminished the demand for legal translation, particularly in institutional settings where multilingual law is made and adjudicated. It has, however, created new challenges for institutional legal translators, who can no longer rely on their national legal languages and are under pressure to produce effective instruments of transnational law in their mother tongues.

3 Institutional purpose and normative behaviour

Generally speaking, institutional translation is a 'norm-governed activity' in which the degree of a translator's normative behaviour varies depending on the institutional purpose (Kang 2009: 144; 2014: 472; cf. Koskinen 2008: 20, 147; Biel 2014a: 70).

[2] Cf. Glanert's philosophical reflections on developing common discursive communities at 2014: 262–4 and 2015: 81–8; on the development of an EU legal discursive community, see Paunio (2013).

[3] Reference is made to the Common Draft Frame of Reference (DCFR) and its successor, the Common European Sales Law (CESL). Since the CESL proposal was withdrawn from the agenda of the European Parliament in January 2015, the Juncker Commission has focused on creating a Digital Single Market, which would include remnants of the CESL.

In addition, the institutional purpose determines the criteria for measuring the acceptability of a translation in a particular context (Kang 2014: 472). In multilingual law-making, acceptability is generally measured by the accuracy and reliability of the translated text. As a normative activity, the translation of legislation requires maximum precision and is thus regarded as the most restrictive type of legal translation. This is especially true in the case of equally authentic legislative texts (Glanert 2014: 259; Šarčević 2012: 89; 2001: 87; 1997: 3).[4] Accordingly, it follows that a high degree of normative subordination is expected of legal translators who are responsible for the production of authoritative translations of legislative texts having the force of law in more than one language.

The principle of equal authenticity is crucial for the functioning of multilingual law because it postulates that all authentic texts of a given instrument are 'originals' and enjoy equal status for the purpose of interpretation. From the legal point of view, all equally authentic legislative texts are presumed to have the same meaning, unless alleged otherwise (Šarčević 2013: 7; 1997: 71, 246; Derlén 2009: 23; Prieto Ramos 2013a: 277). Although the presumption of equal meaning is codified in Article 33(3) of the Convention on the Law of Treaties,[5] both lawyers and linguists agree that equal meaning is a fiction rarely achieved in practice. While it is generally accepted that translators cannot be expected to produce authentic texts that are equal in meaning, they are expected to produce texts that are equal in legal effect (Šarčević 1997: 71). Therefore, authoritative translations of legislation, sometimes referred to as 'translated originals' (Pommer 2012: 1248), are generally considered reliable when they produce the same legal effects in practice.

3.1 Fidelity to the single instrument

As an embodiment of the principle of equal authenticity, the main emphasis in institutional legal translation is on the single instrument, leading the way for the old principle of fidelity to the source text to be replaced by the principle of fidelity to the *single instrument*, as I call it in earlier publications (Šarčević 2001: 81; 1997: 112). Accordingly, achieving fidelity to the single instrument is viewed as the dominant principle governing the behaviour of legal translators in institutional settings (Prieto Ramos 2014a; Biel 2014a). Generally speaking, the translator's main task is to preserve the unity of the single instrument with the ultimate aim of promoting its uniform interpretation and application in practice. While the emphasis on achieving fidelity to the single instrument is not new, it has brought about a visible shift in the translator's priorities in the actual translation process. Under pressure to

4 It is common for litigants to contest the accuracy of authoritative translations of legislative texts and court documentation, for example, in the Japan Film case (1998) before the WTO Appellate Body (see Somssich et al. 2012: 31).

5 Pursuant to Art. 33(3) of the Vienna Convention on the Law of Treaties, the terms of a given instrument 'are presumed to have the same meaning in each authentic text'. In cases of an alleged divergence in meaning between the authentic texts, the courts are obliged to compare all language versions in order to reconcile the differences and ascertain the meaning; however, this is not always done in practice.

achieve institutional uniformity, the translator's first priority is to ensure interlingual concordance, that is, consistency of terminology and presentation between each and all the authentic texts of a single instrument (Rosenne 1983: 775; Šarčević 1997: 202; Cao 2007: 152). As a result, ensuring interlingual concordance between the authentic texts of the single instrument has often become the major concern for translators, especially as the number of language versions increases. However, putting too much emphasis on interlingual concordance runs the risk that translators will neglect their responsibility to achieve internal harmonization – the process of ensuring consistency of terminology and presentation within a given text. In my opinion, failure to ensure internal harmonization poses a greater threat to the reliability of translated originals and thus to the uniform interpretation and application of the single instrument. Nonetheless, the yardstick for measuring the accuracy and reliability of the authentic texts of multilingual instruments of international law has long been the degree of their *interlingual concordance*, as it is called in international law (Šarčević 1997: 202).

3.2 Institutional norms in legal translation

The belief that interlingual concordance promotes uniform interpretation reinforces the traditional institutional norm dictating the use of literal translation as the best method for translating equally authentic texts of legislation, treaties, conventions and model laws intended for regional and global usage (Kjær 2014; Prieto Ramos 2014a; McAuliffe 2014). Therefore, as I see it, the challenge for institutional translators today is not whether to endorse literal translation as a viable means of multilingual text production but rather to use their mother tongue effectively to produce accurate and reliable texts of high quality that ensure a sufficient degree of interlingual concordance without putting internal harmonization at risk. But how much interlingual concordance is sufficient? And does the need for institutional uniformity preclude all translational creativity?

Setting the bar at the top, K.-J. Lönnroth (2008: 12), former director-general of the Commission's Directorate-General for Translation (DGT), called upon EU translators to achieve 'absolute concordance'. While absolute concordance, or *exact correspondence*, as it is also called (Guggeis and Robinson 2012: 62), is another legal fiction that cannot be achieved in practice, putting pressure on translators to do so is indicative of the high level of performance and normative subordination required of EU translators who are major actors in the Commission's mission to ensure the unobstructed functioning of multilingual EU law.

It goes without saying that all institutional translators must adhere to the rules set forth in the drafting, translation and editing guidelines of the particular institution, as well as manuals of precedents prescribing standard formats and style manuals for harmonizing language usage. This, however, touches only the surface of the normative behaviour of legal translators, thus implying that there is little to no room for independent decision-making and translational creativity. To see how this plays out in practice, we turn our attention to translating in the European Commission, which is responsible for preparing the base text and initial translations of EU secondary legislation.

4 Translating in the European Commission

The first to investigate ethnographic aspects of institutional translation, Kasia Koskinen, a Finnish scholar of general translation, documented her experiences in the European Commission, where she worked as a translator after graduating from translation school. Her works (2000 and 2008) written after returning to academia provide insight into the translation practices in the DGT and the normative behaviour of institutional translators in general. According to Koskinen (2000: 58), once inside the Commission, 'translators are not free to use just any strategy' but must conform to 'a code of practice' that dictates a literal translation strategy. Despite the EU values of cultural and linguistic diversity, translators are under pressure to forget about the cultural turn in translation studies and to avoid target-receiver culture-specific features, using instead the traditional method of literal translation to achieve a 'surface-level similarity, which is assumed to guarantee that readers of the various translations all get the same message'.

Although EU translators are from different linguistic and cultural backgrounds, Koskinen (2000: 54) acknowledges that their first loyalty is to the institution and its policy of 'acultural communication', a form of deculturalized communication that discourages linguistic diversity. Their primary task is to institutionalize uniformity by striving to achieve 'surface-level similarity', the main characteristic of interlingual concordance in multilingual instruments of supranational and international law. Going a step further, Koskinen concludes that equivalence in EU translation is often taken to mean 'linguistic correspondence, or literal rerendering', reducing the notion of equivalence to a 'mere visual equivalence' without quality requirements: what is important is that all versions look the same' (Koskinen 2000: 54–6; 2008: 33–56, 146–52).

4.1 Surface-level similarity

Koskinen's comments are characteristic of institutional legal translation not only in the EU but also in international organizations where literal translation strategies are preferred and cultural adaptation or domestication is generally avoided to ensure institutional uniformity. Of the many factors contributing to the surface-level similarity of multilingual legal instruments, the main one is undoubtedly their high degree of standardization, ensuring a uniform presentation across languages. To ensure intertextual uniformity, each institution has its own drafting and style guidelines and established format for each type of instrument or document produced within the particular institution. For instance, the *Interinstitutional Style Guide of the Publications Office* and the *Manual of Precedents for Acts established within the Council*,[6] which have been reproduced with equivalent reformulations in all official languages, prescribe the standard formats for all EU instruments (Guggeis and Robinson 2012: 56). Each standard format dictates not only the structure and constituent elements of each part but also the layout on the page, including spacing, paragraphing and even typographic

[6] The *Interinstitutional Style Guide* is available at <publications.europa.eu> under Tools and Manuals; the *Manual of Precedents* at <bookshop. europa. eu>.

characteristics. As a result of mandatory adherence to the standard format, the visual appearance of the authentic texts of a given instrument is basically the same in all languages (Šarčević 2001: 90).[7]

In addition, the formulaic style of EU legislation requires drafters and translators to use standard formulae as a means of achieving terminological consistency, not just within a given language but also across languages (Biel 2014a: 70; in regard to CJEU judgments, see McAuliffe 2013a). For this purpose, individual words, phrases and entire sentences have been standardized to express repetitive actions, especially in the preamble and final provisions, many of which are procedural formalities required as a condition of validity (Šarčević 2001: 91). Stored in templates, the standard formulae are available in all languages and can be retrieved with a mouse click. In light of their mandatory usage, they have taken on the status of precedents and are often referred to as *linguistic precedents* (Kjær 2015: 93, 104; 2007: 77).[8] For the sake of consistency and continuity, the wording of previously translated legislation must be dutifully repeated word for word whenever reference is made to any of its provisions, even if it contains errors and inconsistencies (Prieto Ramos 2014a; Šarčević 1997: 118). Most importantly, as a means of ensuring terminological consistency within a given language, drafters and translators are always obliged to use established equivalents in a given text and in all texts where that concept is used (Šarčević 2015: 199; 2001: 87; Guggeis and Robinson 2012: 63). In this sense, Guideline 6.2 of the *Joint Practical Guide for the drafting of Community Legislation*[9] requires the same terms to be used to express the same concepts, but it also goes a step further by also discouraging polysemy: 'Identical terms must not be used to express different concepts.'

Like EU legislative texts, international conventions and agreements drawn up within the framework of international organizations are negotiated texts; however, their wording has been agreed upon by a considerably larger number of contracting parties from greatly diverse legal, linguistic and cultural backgrounds. Translators of negotiated texts are required to reproduce the wording with maximum accuracy, taking care to preserve any deliberately vague or ambiguous wording that is the result of political compromise (McAuliffe 2014; Prieto Ramos 2014a; Šarčević 2012, 1997) or *droit diplomatique*, as it is called by Guggeis and Robinson (2012: 62). Returning to the question of how much interlingual concordance is sufficient, the answer seems to be 'the more the better' for the sake of institutional uniformity. However, this raises serious questions about the quality and reliability of translated originals. In our age of human rights, translators cannot neglect their professional duty towards the end users.

7 For examples in international law, see the *UN Editorial Manual* at <dd.dgacm.org/editorialmanual/>, the *WTO Editorial Manual* at <telework.wto.org>, and the full text of the revised *Manual for Drafting ILO Instruments* at <ilo.org> via link *Manual for drafting ILO instruments, full text version, 2011.*

8 According to McAuliffe (2013a), the use of linguistic precedents is also a central feature of the drafting and translation of judgments at the CJEU, where the mandatory word-for-word repetition of language and terminology used by the Court in earlier case-law threatens to reduce both the drafting and translation operations to a mere mechanical process of copy/paste.

9 See the *Joint Practical Guide* at <eur-lex.europa.eu/content/pdf/techleg/joint-practical-guide-2013-en.pdf>.

5 Human rights law and the translator's duty to end users

In light of the increasing role of human rights law throughout the world, institutional legal translation has acquired a human rights dimension that intensifies the burden of translators, reminding them of their duty to ensure effective communication for the end users, here the citizens affected by a piece of legislation. It has long been accepted that multilingual law-making can be effective only if the authentic texts of a single instrument guarantee citizens equality before the law, regardless of the language of the text. Now, in addition to equal effect, multilingual legislation should also meet the requirements of legal certainty set out in international human rights law and the case-law of the ECtHR, which is upheld by the CJEU and other courts.

Established case-law of the ECtHR[10] lays down two basic requirements for legal certainty in legislation: accessibility and foreseeability. First, legislation must be accessible so that citizens know their rights and obligations; and secondly, it must be 'sufficiently clear' so that citizens can reasonably foresee the legal effects of a provision and act accordingly. While the criterion of accessibility is a mere formality, the requirement of foreseeability is problematic. From the legal point of view, foreseeability relates to judicial certainty: It is legitimate for citizens to expect to be able to foresee how judges are likely to interpret and apply the provision in court decisions, if need be with the assistance of a lawyer (Schilling 2010: 49). More importantly for our purpose, foreseeability is made conditional on the quality requirement of clarity: The wording of a provision must be 'sufficiently clear', thus allowing litigants to contest the foreseeability of a provision by arguing lack of sufficient clarity.

Generally speaking, a provision is deemed 'sufficiently clear' if it does not raise a problem of interpretation (Schilling 2010: 49), or, as Derlén says, if it is 'unambiguous and free from doubt' (2011: 145). In cases of legal certainty, it is up to the competent court to determine whether the disputed provision is 'sufficiently clear' in the particular circumstances. Since all EU Member States are signatories to the European Convention on Human Rights (ECHR), the ECtHR has not hesitated to rule on the clarity of provisions of national laws of EU Member States reproduced verbatim from European directives.[11] Not concerned with multilingualism, such judgments have only indirect implications for translators of EU secondary legislation. The real threat to legal certainty, at least for now, comes from within the EU itself as a result of conflicting interpretations of multilingual EU legislation.

5.1 Legal certainty in multilingual EU legislation

Recognizing legal certainty as a fundamental principle of EU law, the CJEU has generally upheld the ECtHR's test of legal certainty (Paunio 2013), ruling that 'provisions imposing obligations on individuals or other private parties should be clear

[10] See, for example, *Kokkinakis* v. *Greece*, No. 14307/88, judgment of 25 May 1993 at § 52; also *Sunday Times* v. *the United Kingdom*, No. 1, No. 6538/74, judgment of 26 April 1979 at § 49; *Copland* v. *the United Kingdom*, No. 62617/00, judgment of 3 April 2007 at §§ 45–6.

[11] For instance, in *Cantoni* v. *France*, No. 17862/91, judgment of 15 November 1996.

and precise so that those affected are able to ascertain unequivocally what their rights are and take steps accordingly'.[12] While it is in the interest of the CJEU to support legal certainty, applying the criteria of legal certainty takes on a new dimension in multilingual legislation, raising doubts as to the compatibility of legal certainty and multilingualism. As a corollary of the principle of legal certainty, it is assumed that EU citizens have the right to rely on the authentic text of a provision in their own language without discriminatory effects (Šarčević 2013: 7; Derlén 2011: 145; Schilling 2010: 49). For the most part, provisions of multilingual EU legislation are reliable in this respect; however, problems arise when individuals base their actions on the wording of a provision that diverges in meaning from the other authentic texts, thus resulting in conflicting interpretations.

In cases hinging on linguistic divergences between the various language versions, the CJEU takes the stand that the disputed provision should be interpreted in favour of the individual, especially when the individual would otherwise be subject to criminal liability or suffer economic loss (Paunio 2013; Šarčević 2013; Derlén 2009). However, such favourable interpretation is admissible 'only if it does not distort the purpose of the provision'.[13] Unwilling to put the effectiveness of EU law at risk, the CJEU has consistently sacrificed legal certainty by ruling against an individual's language version that is found to be contrary to the purpose of the disputed provision.[14] As the number of victims of EU multilingualism increases, they are likely to take their cases to the ECtHR if the EU accedes to the ECHR, as it is required to do under the Lisbon Treaty.[15]

5.2 Implications for translators

The fact that legal certainty has become a human rights issue in multilingual legislation should serve as a wake-up call for EU translators and all institutional translators participating in the production of multilingual legislative texts. As the de facto writers of translated originals (Šarčević 1997: 161), it is their responsibility to use 'sufficiently clear' language that will guarantee not only equal effect but also legal certainty. Moreover, translators need to avoid unintended ambiguities and divergences in meaning that could lead to conflicting interpretations, thus enabling citizens to rely on their own language version. Such a task obviously requires a significantly greater degree of translational sophistication and competence than is needed to achieve mere surface-level similarity or formal correspondence. In other words, surface-level

12 Case C-94/05 *Emsland-Stärke GmbH* v. *Landwirtschaftskammer Hannover* [2006] ECR I-2619, § 43. Similar wording is found in Case C-110/03 *Belgium* v. *Commission* [2005] ECR I-2801, § 30; and Case C-143/93 *Gebroeders van Es Douane Agenten BV* v. *Inspecteur der Invoerrechten en Accijinzen* [1996] ECR I-431, § 27.

13 Case C-1/02 *Privat-Molkerei Borgmann GmbH & Co. KG* v. *Hauptzollamt Dortmund* [2004] ECR I-3219, §§ 30–2.

14 See, for example, Case 238/84 *Criminal proceedings against Hans Röser* [1986] ECR 795; Case 173/88 *Skatteministeriet* v. *Herinksen* [1988] ECR 2763; Case C-296/95 *The Queen* v. *Commissioners of Customs and Excise, ex parte: EMU Tabac SARL and others* [1998] ECR I-1605.

15 EU accession to the ECHR has been blocked by the CJEU's Opinion 2/13 of 18 December 2014, in which the Court found the draft agreement for EU accession to the ECHR to be incompatible with EU law (ECLI: EU: C: 2014: 2454).

similarity is not enough; translators are responsible not only for form but also for quality and, above all, for substance.

To master the new challenges of the profession, institutional translators must possess interdisciplinary competence, including subject-matter expertise. To this end, the UN and its organizations encourage their translators to participate in continuous learning programmes to keep up to date on UN policy matters and other issues (Zhao and Cao 2013: 210). Moreover, since translators of authentic sources of law always translate into their mother tongue, excellent native-language competence is a *conditio sine qua non*. This includes acquiring impeccable writing skills, which in itself is a challenge in our age of text messages, tweets and truncated emails. Furthermore, translators must be thoroughly familiar with the institutional text types and established drafting conventions to know where it is advisable to depart from surface-level similarity in order to guarantee uniform legal effects and legal certainty. In such cases, linguistic diversity is not only tolerable but also necessary, for instance, when expressing obligations, prohibitions, permissions, rights and authorizations.

As regards the factor of readability (Koskinen 2008: 147), it is in the interest of both the institution and end users that all authentic texts of a single instrument are readable, thus requiring a proper dose of idiomaticity (Šarčević 2012: 93–4). While legislative texts are not expected to be an easy read, they must be understood by the judges, administrators, practising lawyers and others responsible for interpreting and applying the law. In numerous cases, the fault for reader unfriendliness and lack of clarity lies with the original (Prieto Ramos 2014a; Strandvik 2015). Therefore, as earlier (Šarčević 2012: 102; 1997: 95), I encourage interaction between translators and drafters, the earlier the better, with the aim of identifying and revising any errors, irregularities or unclear wording in the original prior to its finalization, thus making it possible to improve the quality of all authentic texts. Known as *co-revision* in the EU context (Guggleis and Robinson 2012), it is mainly the responsibility of lawyer-linguists.

As a rule, translators of UN instruments do not have this possibility because the translations of treaties, conventions and model laws are usually made by the UN Translation Services after the representatives of the Member States have agreed on the wording of the base text either in the General Assembly or at a conference convened for that purpose (Tabory 1980). However, it is conceivable that a recent shift in the work of the International Law Commission from originator of draft articles to finalizer of important codification projects (Katz Cogan 2015) could make it possible for UN translators to at least have access to the drafters responsible for drawing up the final text, thus enabling them to gain valuable insight into the intended meaning of the particular instrument. Moreover, it is encouraging that some specialized agencies, for instance, the International Labour Organization (ILO), have taken concrete steps to organize 'translation conferences' to agree on the formulation of the other authentic texts after the closing of the conference at which the particular convention, model law or other instrument was adopted (Somssich et al. 2012: 18).

Instruments of EU secondary law are made by the EU institutions but must be incorporated into national law and applied by the national courts of the Member States. Above all, it is the constant interplay between EU law and the national laws of the 28 Member States that makes the translation of EU legislation truly unique but also extremely complex, thus occasioning Kjær to call for an independent research field on EU translation within legal translation studies (2007: 70). The need for EU translators to produce texts that 'fit as seamlessly as possible into the national legal context', as Strandvik puts it (2015: 144), suggests that their responsibility towards the end users is considerably greater than that of their international counterparts. This comes into play in their role as creators of transnational legal languages.

6 Translators as creators of transnational legal languages

Today the pressure to achieve surface-level similarity threatens to reduce the translation of instruments of EU law and international law to mere 'clonism', as Cronin calls 'the reproduction of similarity' in his frequently cited book *Translation and Globalization* (2003). While the use of the metaphor is adequate for our purpose as well, we are reminded that Cronin's concern is postcolonial translation, not institutional legal translation. In my opinion, the purpose of using English as the vehicle language of transnational legal communication is to reach users in as many legal systems as possible, not to 'colonialize' their national languages, as some authors have implied in regard to EU translation (e.g. Biel 2014a: 84).

Generally speaking, EU legal languages are loaded with foreignizing elements; however, this also applies to some extent to EU legal English, which is a mixed and hybrid language. As Robertson reminds us, 'EU legal English started life in translation, mainly from French, and the terminology, syntax, and general structure of EU legal texts derive from a French base' (2012: 1237). For the sake of continuity and legal certainty, the established legal and linguistic parameters are for the most part irreversible. The product of multilingual discussions and amendments, the English in the base text of EU legislation is shaped by the legal and cultural background and even languages of the drafters, who are mostly non-native speakers, thus resulting in a high degree of hybridity, which makes the translator's task even more challenging (Kjær 2015: 93; on the hybridity of EU discourse, see Biel 2014a: 52).

6.1 Terminology considerations

All institutional translators are obliged to use the established terminology available in the institution's term banks; however, these tools are not always up to date and the terms are not always reliable (e.g. IATE (EU), UNTerm and WTOTerm). In particular, EU terminology is in constant flux, with old terms acquiring new layers of meaning either in new legislation or through the case-law of the CJEU (Šarčević 2015: 186; Kjær 2015: 94). Most importantly, the EU legal order is developing at a rapid pace, with new terms and concepts entering the EU lexicon on a daily basis. This presents a major challenge to translators but also offers them an excellent opportunity to take an active role in shaping their own euro-language, a sub-language that exists parallel to the national legal language but must be coordinated with it in order to function properly (Šarčević 2015: 184).

The choice of designations in all languages is crucial, especially for key terms, and can be instrumental in determining the success or failure of an instrument of transnational law.[16] Like drafters and translators of international conventions and model laws, EU drafters and translators are warned to avoid the use of technical terms from a particular legal system and national legal terms in general.[17] In cases where national terms are nevertheless used to designate EU concepts, settled case-law of the CJEU[18] requires them to be interpreted in accordance with their autonomous EU meaning, if such exists. The same applies to terms in the ECHR and judgments of the ECtHR (Brannan 2013: 914; Letsas 2004: 282).

Drafters of supranational and international legislation are encouraged to achieve system neutrality by using neutral terms that can be easily translated into the other official languages without connotational baggage (Germain 2012: 54; Šarčević 2015: 186; 2010: 34). For their part, translators have the task of using neutral terms that will not be confused with terms of national law. Preference should be given to words having the same degree of generality so as not to widen or delimit the intended scope of application. Generic terms are often effective (Brannan 2013: 920). Words of general language are frequently used to express new concepts but must be defined whenever their ordinary meaning is expanded or contracted (Šarčević 2015: 188). As in all translation, it is advisable to choose terms that are semantically transparent. The search for adequate terminological solutions is particularly tedious in international agreements, which must be understood and interpreted uniformly on a global scale by a large number of users of different languages, legal traditions, cultures and socio-economic conditions.

6.2 Terminology harmonization across languages

The harmonization of terminology across languages enhances the effectiveness of transnational legal communication by linking the terms in all languages to the shared concept. As a result, terminology harmonization is a dominant characteristic of institutional legal translation in both supranational and international law (Šarčević 2015: 190). As a rule, institutional translators are encouraged to choose designations with the same or similar roots whenever possible.

[16] For example, the use of the functional equivalent *wilful misconduct* to translate *dol* in a key provision of the Warsaw Convention for the Unification of Certain Rules relating to International Carriage by Air enabled plaintiffs to evade the thresholds of limited liability provided by the Convention, thus resulting in its initial failure. Having learned from mistakes of their predecessors, the drafters of the UN Convention for the International Sale of Goods (CISG) of 1980 made conscious efforts to develop a uniform sales terminology, a major factor contributing to its success; see Germain 2014, also note 23 below.

[17] Guideline 5 of the *Joint Practical Guide* warns EU drafters and translators to avoid using 'terms which are too closely linked to national legal systems'. Since the concept of *faute* 'has no direct equivalent in other legal systems', neutral terms are proposed, such as *illégalité* or *manquement*, depending on the context (point 5.3.2).

[18] For instance, in the landmark *CILFIT* case, the Court stressed that 'Community law uses terminology which is peculiar to itself' (Case 238/81 [1982] ECR 3415, §19).

Despite the advantages of formal correspondence at the level of the term, in keeping with ISO standards,[19] each language unit of the DGT is encouraged to select terms that best suit the morpho-syntactic characteristics of the particular language, taking care not to destabilize the national language. In the absence of written rules dictating methods of term formation, it is up to EU translators and terminologists to decide whether transnational communication is best served by aligning a term on the other language versions, often resulting in foreignization; or by creating a term with domestic roots in the interest of satisfying user expectations (see Šarčević 2015: 189–93, 201).[20]

The choice between foreignization and domestication is particularly challenging when translators must decide whether to translate EU internationalisms with cognates, thus resulting in a high degree of formal correspondence. For example, *cohésion sociale* (fr) is translated as *social cohesion* (en), *coesione sociale* (it), *cohesión social* (es), *coesão social* (pt) and *coeziune socială* (ro). Other language units prefer hybrid terms: *social sammanhållning* (sv), *sosiaalinen yhteenkuuluvuus* (fi), or offer one or more alternatives: *sozialer Zusammenhalt* and *soziale Kohäsion* (de). Based mostly on Latin but also Greek stems, EU internationalisms are particularly difficult to translate into non-Indo-European languages, often resulting in unnatural-sounding terms that are difficult to pronounce, as the Finns discovered when translating the *acquis* for accession in 1995 (Koskinen 2000: 53, 61). Since then, thirteen new languages have been added to the EU discursive community: six Slavic, two Baltic, one Celtic, one Romance and three non-Indo-European languages.

Although the ability to assimilate 'foreign' elements differs from language to language, the language policy of the translator's home country is often the guiding factor when deciding whether to favour domestication over foreignization (Šarčević 2015: 191). Aware of the historical moment of the 2004 enlargement, Lönnroth encouraged DGT translators of the new languages to be 'innovative with language'.[21] While this did not alter preferred methods of the institutional policy on terminology harmonization, it did give them tacit consent to create terms with domestic roots in accordance with language policy back home.

Today, the main rule in EU term formation is to use designations that can be easily recognized as EU terms, thus enabling users to distinguish them from national terms. As earlier, priority is given to literal equivalents (Šarčević 2015: 193; 2001: 83), which has the advantage of making them recognizable as EU terms across languages, regardless of the degree of their domestication. Taking the example of *unitary patent*, which was introduced into EU law in 2012, we see that the literal equivalents chosen have a high degree of domestication: *brevet unitaire* (fr), *brevetto unitario* (it), *patente unitaria* (es), *patente unitária* (pt), *einheitliches Patent / Einheitspatent* (de), *enhedspatent* (da), *enhetligt patent* (sv), *eenheidsoctrooi* (nl), *jednolity patent* (pl), *jednotný patent* (cs) and *jedinstveni patent* (hr) (Regulation 1257/2012/EU in OJ

[19] According to the standard of linguistic correctness in ISO 704: 2009, 'a term shall conform with the morphological, morpho-syntactic and phonological norms of the language in question'.

[20] In the cited article, the terms *conformity* and *creativity* are used instead of *foreignization* and *domestication*.

[21] Lönnroth's video message welcoming DGT staff members from the new Member States in 2004 is no longer available online.

L361/1 of 31.12.2012). A comparison of the terms reveals that each language unit uses the established term at national level[22] for *patent*, which is universal in meaning; note in particular the French (*brevet*), Italian (*brevetto*) and Dutch (*octrooi*). Adjectives from general language are used for *unitary*, with the same or similar roots in each language group – Romance, Slavic and Germanic, with the exception of English. Structural choices vary from language to language according to the respective language usage. As illustrated by this example, the key to effective transnational legal communication is striking a proper balance between foreignization and domestication, keeping the end users in mind as well as the strategic importance of the term.

7 Closing remarks: Going beyond surface-level similarity

Within the framework of this chapter, it has been impossible to touch on all aspects of institutional legal translation and challenges confronting translators in supranational and international law. By now the main message should be clear. Unable to rely on their national legal languages, translators are encouraged by their institutions to achieve surface-level similarity, the traditional yardstick for measuring the acceptability of multilingual legal instruments. However, as indicated above, achieving surface-level similarity is not enough. Moreover, uncontrolled surface-level similarity can be damaging, for example, if foreignizing syntax makes the text unclear or translators resort to cognates that turn out to be *faux amis*. Therefore, as I see it, the greatest challenge to institutional legal translators is learning to go beyond surface-level similarity.

As regards translation management, institutional legal translation is gradually coming of age. Having recognized the vital importance of legal translation for the proper functioning of supranational and international law, institutions are taking steps to improve the quality of equally authentic legislative texts (Strandvik 2015: 146–50; Šarčević 2012: 83, 102). Acknowledging the interdisciplinary nature of legal translation, they now encourage interaction between drafters and translators at an early stage, enabling translators to gain insight into the meaning of individual concepts and the purpose of the instrument as a whole. After all, understanding the base text is a precondition for successful translation (Šarčević 1997: 89). In particular, term formation should be an onomasiological exercise starting at the level of the concept instead of a superficial semasiological approach that starts and stops at the level of the term, as is frequently the case in literal translation (Šarčević 2015: 193). Although the task of translators of supranational and international law is not to compensate for conceptual incongruity between legal systems (Kjær 2014), creating effective system-neutral terms requires considerable knowledge of national laws and legal concepts in order to know which terms could lead to misinterpretations and should therefore be avoided.

22 In cases where two or more national jurisdictions share the same language, a common formulation must be agreed upon to express a new EU concept whenever the established terms at national level differ. The same applies in international law.

At the same time, we are reminded that establishing a uniform terminology on a regional and global scale is an ongoing project requiring decades of dedicated work by institutions and scholars. Choosing the designations of terms is crucial in creating a uniform terminology, but terms alone do not guarantee uniform interpretation. It is up to policymakers and negotiators to reach consensus on the meanings of shared concepts and to formulate the agreed meaning in clear and concise definitions (Šarčević 2010: 35; 1997: 158). Today, specialized courts such as the ECtHR and the CJEU play a decisive role in establishing precedents setting out autonomous concepts and landmark rulings laying the groundwork for the uniform interpretation of disputed concepts and provisions (Kjær 2015, 2014; Derlén 2009, 2011; Brannan 2013; Letsas 2004).[23]

In closing, I encourage translation schools on all continents to provide the interdisciplinary training necessary to motivate future translators to become skilled transnational communicators dedicated to making institutional multilingualism more effective. While translators must be loyal to their institutions, they must also fulfil their duty towards the end users, both the citizens affected by a particular instrument and those who interpret and apply it. Above all, institutional legal translators must be responsible decision-makers who respect the constraints of their profession but also dare to go beyond surface-level similarity, not as a goal in itself but as a means of promoting uniform interpretation and application of the single instrument on a regional and global scale.

[23] In international law, the CISG has made considerable progress in establishing a uniform terminology, gradually resulting in a transnational discourse in international sales law (see note 16 above). In the absence of a specialized court to rule on conflicting interpretations, a number of CISG thesauri and case-law databases have been compiled with the aim of unifying concepts and disseminating cases that may be used as precedents or authorities by other national courts in interpreting the CISG, for example, UNCITRAL's CLOUT Database, the CLOUT Digest, the UNCITRAL Thesaurus and Pace Law School's CISG Database; see Germain 2014: 57–62 (UNCITRAL = UN Commission on International Trade Law).

2

Corpora in Institutional Legal Translation: Small Steps and the Big Picture

Łucja Biel

1 Introduction

1.1 Technological and linguistic turns in Translation Studies

Since the proclamation of its birth in the 1970s, Translation Studies (TS) has grown exponentially as a discipline institutionally, geographically, thematically, theoretically and methodologically. As observed by Snell-Hornby, TS has emancipated itself and is no longer merely a sub-field within Applied Linguistics or Comparative Literature (2012: 371). However, due to the multifarious nature of translation, its links to neighbouring disciplines have inevitably remained strong. It should be remembered, though, that, being an interdiscipline or polydiscipline (cf. Gentzler 2003; Brems et al. 2012), TS has limited autonomy. This claim is especially pertinent to one of its subdisciplines – Legal Translation Studies (LTS), which lies at the intersection of Translation Studies, Comparative Law, Linguistics and Terminology.

The rapid development of neighbouring disciplines has accelerated not only the growth of TS but also its methodological refinement. First, TS experienced the 'linguistic turn' in the 1960s and the 1970s and then the cultural turn in the 1980s and 1990s. It is currently undergoing the 'technological turn' (cf. Cronin 2010) combined with the comeback of linguistic methods, in particular various strands of Functional Linguistics, for example, Neurolinguistics, Sociolinguistics, (Critical) Discourse Analysis, Cognitive Linguistics, Halliday's Systemic-Functional Grammar (cf. House 2013 on the 'linguistic-cognitive orientation of TS'), and last – but not least – Corpus Linguistics.

1.2 Corpus Linguistics as a method in Translation Studies

The combination of technological advancements with the revival of functional linguistic approaches in TS leads us to Corpus-Based Translation Studies (also referred to as Corpus Translation Studies), a branch of TS that applies Corpus Linguistics as a method to study translations.

A corpus is a large representative collection of texts in electronic form, which can be analysed with dedicated software (cf. McEnery et al. 2006: 4–5). Translations are analysed mostly with two types of corpora, referred to as *translation-driven corpora* (Zanettin 2012: 8), that is, comparable corpora and parallel corpora. The former is monolingual and comprises a corpus of translations and a corpus of non-translations in the target language, designed according to the same sampling frame (McEnery and Hardie 2012: 19). The latter – a parallel corpus – is bilingual and comprises source texts aligned with their target texts. It resembles a translation memory in computer-assisted translation tools (CAT tools). More recent approaches require a combination of two types of corpora to account for two fundamental types of relations in translation: that of equivalence (the relation of the target text to the source text), addressing accuracy; and that of textual fit (the relation of the target text to non-translated target-language texts of a comparable genre), addressing the naturalness and acceptability of translations (cf. Chesterman 2004). The relation of equivalence requires the involvement of parallel corpora, while the relation of textual fit requires comparable corpora.

Developing rapidly since the late 1980s, Corpus Linguistics capitalizes on IT opportunities and the reorientation of linguistics towards functional, applied, cognitive, social and communicative aspects of language (de Beaugrande 1996: 511). The main objective of Corpus Linguistics is 'to describe and interpret generalizable patterns of language use' (Biber and Jones 2009: 1287). With a focus on frequency and patterns, corpus methods enable the researcher to see what is 'central and typical, normal and expected'; they show that language use is prefabricated and highly patterned in a way that is cognitively motivated rather than accidental (Stubbs 2004: 111). As a method, Corpus Linguistics can help identify 'differences that intuition alone cannot perceive' (McEnery et al. 2006: 7). It is empirical, inductive and quantitative; its main advantage is the potential to reduce speculation and verify research hypotheses systematically on the basis of more extensive data. However, quantitative data and statistics should not represent 'an end in itself' but rather 'a starting point for continuing richly (re)contextualized qualitative work' and for improving our understanding of translation (House 2011: 206). Thus, corpora are ideally applied in TS as a quantitative-based qualitative approach.

Corpus methods have been applied in TS since the mid-1990s, inspired by Mona Baker's series of papers (1993, 1995, 1996), in which she proposed to study translations against non-translations through corpora in search of translation universals, referred to now more commonly as the typical features, tendencies, patterns or regularities of translations (cf. Olohan 2002: 423; Zanettin 2012: 12). The universals are hypothesized to be inherent in the translation process (Baker 1993: 246) and include, inter alia, explicitation, simplification, normalization/conservatism and levelling out (Baker 1996: 180–5). Research into translation universals has remained central in TS, but there is also work being done on translator styles, contrastive genre analyses and applications of corpora in translator training and practice.

2 Legal Translation Studies: Methodological Development

The emancipation of TS as a discipline combined with its rapid growth contributed to the emergence of subdisciplines that claim autonomy for themselves (can they?).

One such sub-discipline is LTS. In his paper on the historical development of LTS as a discipline, Prieto Ramos distinguishes three phases of development of the field: (1) the initial stage (1970s–mid 1990s), coexisting with the emergence of TS as a discipline; (2) the catalytic stage (mid-1990s to mid-2000s) with the development of conceptual paradigms in seminal monographs; and (3) the current period of consolidation and expansion with a strong emphasis on applied research (2014b: 271–2). Despite growing consolidation efforts, the field is still fragmented both along interdisciplinary lines (law, translation studies, linguistics) and language-specific enclaves – mainly English, French, German, Spanish and Italian – with their own research traditions, and it does require further integration (cf. Biel and Engberg 2013: 2).

Interestingly, the last four years have brought about an unprecedented proliferation of English-language publications on legal translation, especially in the form of special issues of major journals: *Linguistica Antverpiensia, New Series – Themes in Translation Studies* (2013, ed. by Łucja Biel and Jan Engberg); *The Translator* (2014, ed. by Simone Glanert); *International Journal for the Semiotics of Law* (2015, ed. by Anne Wagner and Jean-Claude Gémar); *The Interpreter and Translator Trainer* (2015, ed. by Esther Monzó Nebot); and *The Journal of Specialised Translation* (2017, ed. by Hendrik Kockaert and Nadia Rahab), as well as edited monographs, including this book. This burst of publishing activity attests to the growth of LTS and its expansion phase into new methodologies, new angles and areas of interests. It also attests to the methodological development of the field through an increased methodological rigour and eclecticism, testing and triangulating diverse methods with a shift from qualitative only to empirical, quantitative and mixed approaches.

One such empirical quantitative approach is Corpus Linguistics, which should be regarded as a major methodological advancement in LTS. The objective of this chapter is first to sketch the big picture by discussing recent developments and trends in Corpus Legal Translation Studies with implications for institutional translation practice (Section 3) and research (Section 4). Next, I will discuss steps that need to be taken to improve the functionality of legal corpora for practitioners and researchers.

3 Corpora in Institutional Practice

3.1 The uptake of corpus tools by translators

The uptake of corpora in translation practice is much slower compared to the academia; however, awareness of their existence and the popularity of corpora are growing overall. This is attested to by studies surveying professional translators on the use of translation tools and/or specifically corpora. The European Union (EU)-funded MeLLANGE survey of 1015 translators and interpreters, half of whom were based in the UK, shows that 58 per cent of translators do not use corpora and only 20 per cent use a concordancer to search through texts (MeLLANGE 2006). Four surveys published in 2015, nearly ten years later, report results that vary significantly, depending on the country concerned. At one extreme, Zaretskaya et al.'s survey on the use of translation technologies conducted in 2014 among 736 (mainly freelance) translators from eighty-eight countries shows quite a strong resistance to corpora;

corpora are used by only 15 per cent of respondents, with an even lower percentage of translators compiling their own corpora due to the time-consuming nature of the process and lack of familiarity with tools (2015: 4, 7).

At the other extreme, there are more promising surveys from Spain by Gallego-Hernández (2015) and Alonso (2015), both conducted in 2013. Gallego-Hernández's survey of 526 Spain-based translators (mainly freelancers and only eight employed in institutions) reports that 18 per cent of translators use corpora often or very often, and 30 per cent use them sometimes (2015). Alonso's survey 'The Translator in the Information Society', administered in Spanish with respondents from thirty-two countries (with the majority of respondents having Spanish as their native language or language B), lists corpora among most popular tools and resources used by translators when translating, with as many as 62 per cent of respondents claiming that they almost always or often use aligned or monolingual corpora, including online corpora, and with 20 per cent doing it sometimes. In Alonso's survey corpora ranked third after Google (86 per cent) and online dictionaries (83 per cent of respondents who use them often or very often) as the most frequently used resource during the translation process (2015: 98–9).

While the respondents to those surveys were mainly freelancers, the respondents to Picton et al.'s survey of 2014–2015 were predominantly salaried translators (80 per cent) based in Switzerland. What is worth stressing is the relevance of this survey for institutional legal translation, as 76 per cent of translators in Picton et al.'s survey translated legal texts in the last six months. According to the survey, 40 per cent use corpora often and very often, and 27 per cent use corpora sometimes, mainly to find or check equivalents, to help understand the source text, to check or find idiomatic formulations (e.g. collocations) and to help understand the field (2015). Overall, it can be summed up that the findings are inconclusive.

As part of their study, Picton et al. also conducted semi-structured interviews among in-house translators to ask about major obstacles in the use of corpora. One of the main obstacles indicated by in-house translators was the institutional hierarchy, where decisions are taken at too high a level to respond to actual needs and where the priority is short-term cost-effectiveness. The study also reports resistance of international organizations due to their dependence on the existing tools and long-established habits (Picton et al. 2015).

The relatively slow uptake of corpora in the professional practice is affected by the low awareness of and unfamiliarity with corpus tools among practitioners, agencies and institutions. The surveys have pointed out that translators are often unfamiliar with the terms *corpus* or *concordancer*; for example, 41 per cent of translators in the MeLLANGE survey (2006) had never heard of corpora. It is also unclear whether the term *corpus* was used/understood in a narrow sense or in a broad sense, which may also include a translation memory (TM as 'a specific type of dynamic parallel corpora', Zanettin 2014: 179) or websites based on a parallel corpus, such as Linguee.com, which describes itself as a 'bilingual dictionary'. There seems to be a strong need to continue raising translators' awareness of corpora and to train translators how to use corpus tools in translation work and how to manage documents so that they can be re-used as part of a corpus to optimize work processes.

3.2 Availability of non-institutional and institutional corpus tools

Ready-made corpus tools for legal translators are still underdeveloped for national (intersystemic) legal translation and lesser-used languages. There are few parallel corpora with intersystemic legal translation; however, the number of monolingual legal corpora is growing steadily. Examples of national legal corpora include monolingual corpora – the *BoLC* Bononia Legal Corpus with UK and Italian legislation, the *JuReko* – German Legal Reference Corpus,[1] the *PLC* Polish Law Corpus (Biel 2014) and a multilingual intrasystemic corpus – the *Bilingwis* Swiss Law Text collection (Höfler and Sugisaki 2014) (see also Pontrandolfo 2012 for other types of legal corpora). The existing corpora tend to be skewed towards legicentrism, that is, they are composed of legislation mainly, and it is still quite rare to find corpora with private legal documents due to their confidential nature. Considering limited non-legislative resources, this problem may partly be solved by DIY/ad hoc corpora, also known as *disposable* corpora (Varantola 2002), which are small genre-based corpora built by a translator quickly, for example, in up to 20 minutes, usually by web harvesting, to complete a given assignment (cf. Scott 2012). DIY corpora are useful; however, more structured, representative and integrated resources are needed for professional purposes. As the abovementioned surveys indicate, because of time pressure, translators are willing to use corpora that are available and are free.

The situation is, quite understandably, different in the case of intrasystemic legal translation, because of the availability of large bilingual and multilingual resources and the fact that this type of translation is often institutionalized. It applies both to countries with multilingual law and, above all, to international organizations, such as the EU and the United Nations (UN), with a very large scale of translation activity into twenty-four and six official languages, respectively. Facing pressures to reduce costs (cf. Borja Albi and Prieto Ramos 2013), international organizations invest their time and money in building parallel corpora out of their vast resources, and the main rationale for this is to facilitate the development of machine-translation systems, which will speed human translation (and reduce the need for translation). The interesting development is that the major international institutions with the largest scale of legal translation activity – namely the EU and the UN – provide free access to a substantial part of their resources in the form of parallel corpora.

The UN Parallel Corpus v1.0 is a multilingual parallel corpus released in 2016 and built by the UN from its translation resources in six official UN languages (Arabic, Chinese, English, French, Russian and Spanish) (Ziemski et al. 2016: 1). It comprises official records and other parliamentary documents as well as their translations from a period of twenty-five years (1990–2004) with a total of ca. 800,000 texts and English tokens of 334 million words. The corpus was built mainly for the purposes of the cloud-based statistical machine-translation system (TAPTA4UN), which is integrated with the in-house CAT tool called eLUNa (Ziemski et al. 2016: 1). Earlier UN corpora, for example, the UN Parallel Text Corpus with French, English and Spanish (Graff 1994)

1 https://cal2.eu/core-projects-and-associated-projects/german-legal-reference-corpus-jureko-en.

and MultiUN, released in 2010 in six languages (Eisele and Chen 2010), are unofficial, that is, they were not built by the original data creator and are often incomplete.

The EU corpora are much more extensive and versatile. They include the JRC-Acquis parallel corpus; DGT-Acquis; translation memories of the European Commission's Directorate General for Translation (DGT-TM) and Directorate General for Education and Culture (EAC-TM), and of the European Centre for Disease Prevention and Control (ECDC-TM); the Digital Corpus of the European Parliament (DCEP); and Europarl and the EUR-Lex corpus (Steinberger et al. 2014; Baisa et al. 2016). The EU resources have been available since 2005. This was possible thanks to the EU's commitment to provide its citizens with public access to the documents of the European Parliament, the Council and the European Commission on EUR-Lex (and, later on, on the EU Open Data Portal) by virtue of Article 15 of the Treaty on the Functioning of the European Union and Regulation (EC) No 1049/2001 of 30 May 2001 regarding public access to European Parliament, Council and Commission documents.

The major advantages of EU parallel corpora include their availability in a large number of languages (up to twenty-four), including lesser-used languages; their parallelism; and the broad range of topics covered, which makes them well-suited for training statistical machine-translation systems (Steinberger et al. 2014: 703). The first sentence-aligned EU corpus, JRC-Acquis, was first released in 2006 and now covers twenty-two languages (excluding Irish and Croatian), with English tokens amounting to 55.5 million words (ibid.: 682, 693–94). It comprises the body of EU law, case-law and administrative documents from the period 1958–2006. The most recent and largest resource, the EUR-Lex corpus, contains over 840 million tokens of English; it is available in twenty-four official EU languages and comprises 3.9 million documents available in html format in the EUR-Lex database (Baisa et al. 2016).

The latest development was to move five EU corpora (JRC-Acquis, DCEP, DGT-TM, Europarl and EUR-Lex) into the Sketch Engine, a language corpus management and query system (cf. Baisa et al. 2016: 2799). Even though the access to Sketch Engine is against a fee, this is a major improvement because it caters for the needs of linguists and translators by allowing them to query the EU corpora in a more user-friendly and sophisticated way, for example, to extract collocations and term candidates and to search for parallel concordances. Table 2.1 shows a simple concordance search for equivalents of the term *draft terms of merger* in the English and Polish sections of the EUR-Lex corpus, narrowed down to secondary legislation, while Table 2.2 shows a parallel concordance search for the term *draft terms of merger* with simultaneous criteria for the second language – Polish equivalents that include 'plan' (the Polish term *plan połączenia*). The parallel concordance search also makes it possible to search for equivalents that exclude certain words or phrases.

The next development offered by the EUR-Lex corpus is that, unlike JRC-Acquis, where all document types are mixed in the corpus, the EUR-Lex corpus offers the possibility of selecting a text type out of 113 categories (e.g. a directive, judgment, protocol, proposal, exploratory opinion or common strategy) and to limit the search to selected years, thereby making searches better calibrated. What needs improvement is the relatively long time taken for query processing, and a more accurate match of TL equivalents (e.g. see Table 2.1, where Polish equivalents are not identified and highlighted) is also needed.

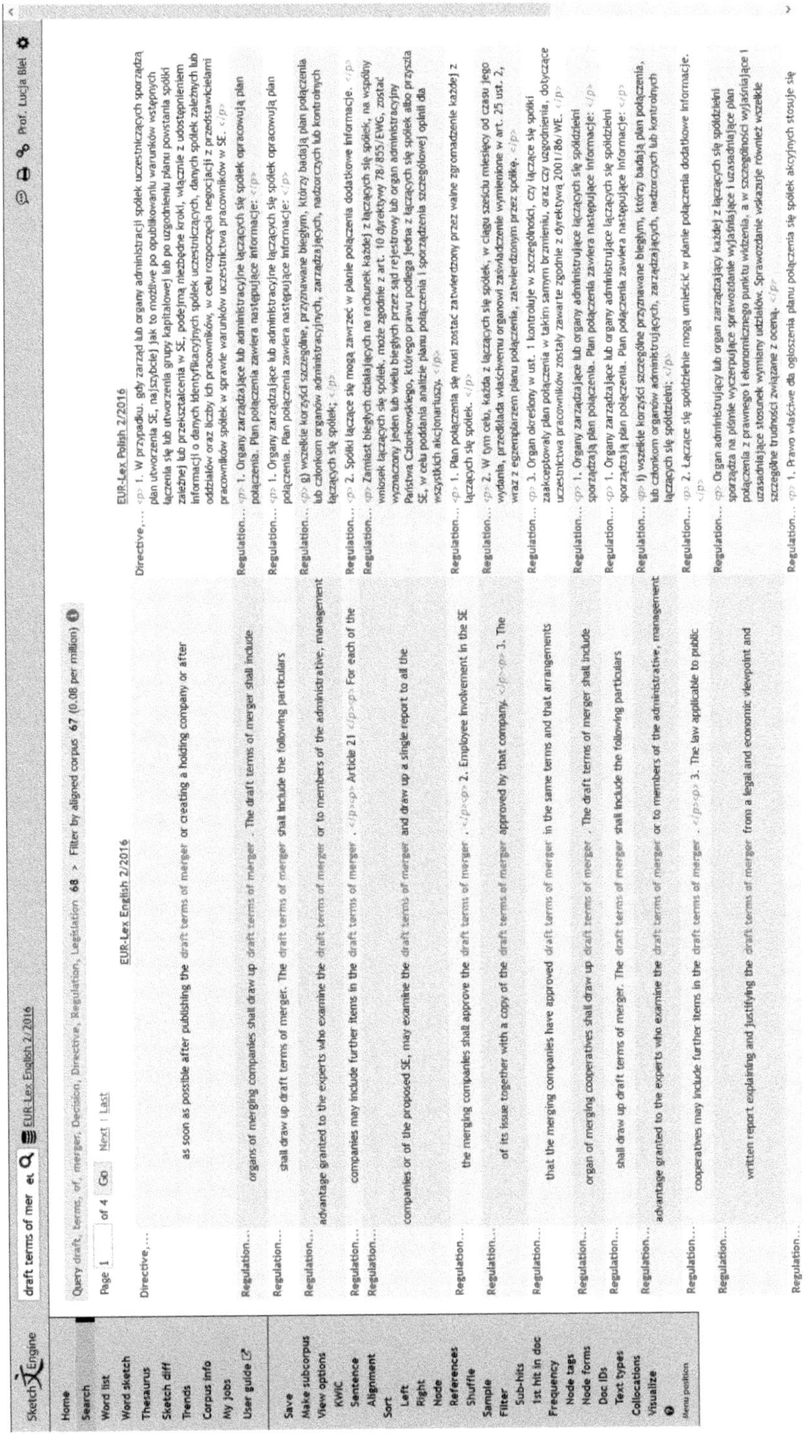

Table 2.1 Simple concordance search in the EUR-Lex parallel corpus.

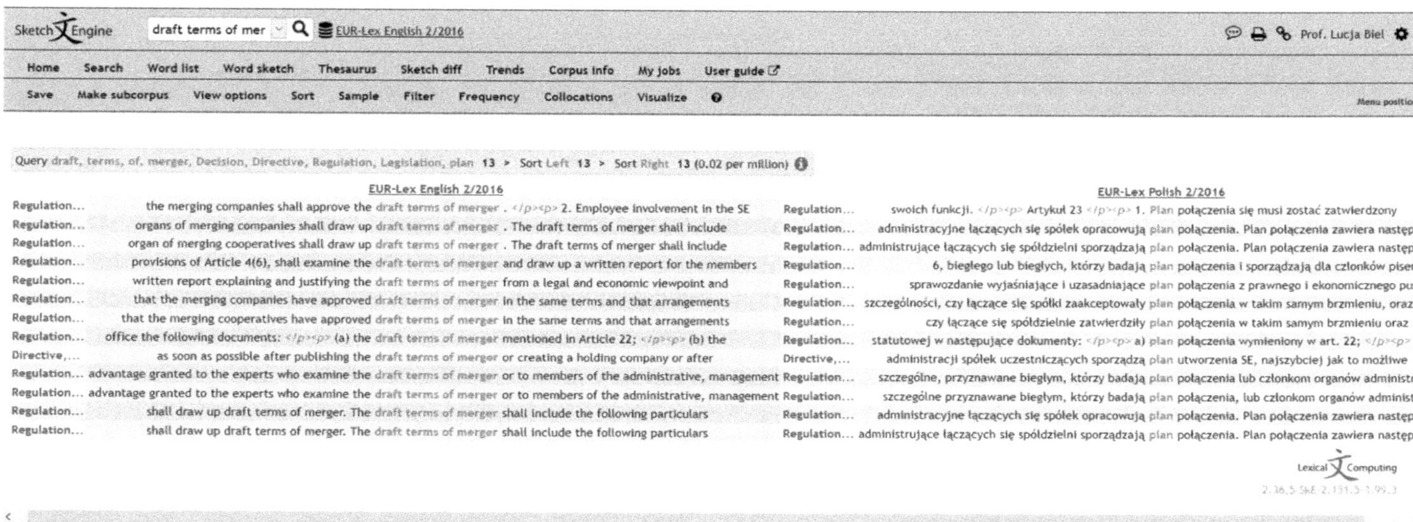

Table 2.2 Parallel concordance search in the EUR-Lex parallel corpus with search criteria for both languages.

The corpus resources described above are mainly prepared to develop derived products, such as translation memories, machine-translation systems and term ontologies (cf. Heylen et al. 2014: 9), rather than to support human translators in their work, which takes a toll on their functionality. In-house institutional translators tend to use corpora in the form of tailor-made translation memories, a type of parallel corpus in themselves. As observed by Pasteur, translators at the World Trade Organization (WTO) may work with large non-validated 'catch-all' memories, which provide not only 'multiple, obsolete or even erroneous translations but also many "translation solutions" that can be useful' (2013: 291). However, as argued by the same author, these are validated quality translation memories ('white' memories), which, being '100 per cent reliable', have an added value and 'must' be prioritized by translators (ibid.). In addition, WTO translators are equipped with smaller, more functional ad hoc memories composed of earlier versions and relevant background documents created at the pre-translation stage and verified by the Translation Support Services (ibid.). It should be stressed, however, that some institutions outsource a percentage of translations to external contractors (e.g. the European Commission's Directorate General for Translation outsourced 27 per cent of its workload in 2015[2]), who do not always have access to tailor-made internal translation memories but only to public resources.

3.3 New functionalities of corpus tools for legal translators

In addition to the abovementioned obstacles, a considerable barrier to the uptake of corpora by professional translators is a lack of integration of corpus tools with CAT and other tools, which slows down the translation process and makes the use of corpora less effective due to the need to switch tools and interfaces. There are, however, some promising initiatives[3] aimed at integrating corpora with other resources to tailor them to legal translators' needs: JudGENTT (Borja Albi 2013) and TermWise (Heylen et al. 2014).

JudGENTT (Borja Albi 2013) is an online multilingual web platform – a knowledge system with documentary, textual and terminological resources for translators of court documents in four legal systems (Germany, Spain, France and the United States). It is developed by the GENTT (Textual Genres for Translation) Research Group based at the Department of Translation and Communication at the Universitat Jaume I in Spain. The platform combines comparable and parallel corpora with more traditional resources, including glossaries, bibliographies and criminal procedure. The major novelty of this system is the integration of different types of resources with a built-in search facility (ibid.).

TermWise is an extension to a CAT tool and cloud-based database known as Term&Phrase Memory, based on a big parallel Dutch–French corpus harvested from the online bilingual *Belgian Official Journal* (1997–2006). It was developed for legal translators at the Belgian Federal Justice Department with statistical knowledge acquisition algorithms. It provides context-sensitive terminological support through a

[2] http://ec.europa.eu/dgs/translation/faq/index_en.htm#6.

[3] See Volk et al. 2014 for the general discussion of innovations in parallel corpus query systems.

one-click access to equivalents of terms and n-grams ranked by relevance according to their similarity to the source text (Heylen et al. 2014). The tool relies on large bilingual data and provides information that is 'highly context-specific' (ibid.: 10). After testing, it is planned that the tool will be integrated into a CAT system.

Corpus tools may improve the efficiency of the translation process thanks to fast information retrieval, precision of searches and contextualization of information with usage preferences. However, in order to improve the uptake of corpus tools by professionals and their functionality, further work is required on compiling comparable and parallel corpus resources (economies of scale), on integrating corpora with other resources and tools, on developing more user-friendly interfaces and on training translators how to use corpus tools efficiently.

4 Corpus research on institutional translation

Until recently, relatively little corpus-based and corpus-driven research has been done in the area of legal translation. Compared to 2009, when I published a paper advocating the use of corpora for legal translation purposes (Biel 2009), one cannot escape noticing harbingers of change in the areas of both applied and theoretically oriented projects and publications. Corpus approaches have become one of the main methodological developments on the quantitative side.

The discussion of applications of corpora in research will be split into practically oriented applied research and theoretically oriented basic research. It should be stressed that, in the case of corpus projects, this division is not clear-cut and is arbitrary to a large extent, as most theoretically oriented projects have practical applications while applied research is often able to pose far-reaching theoretical questions.

Applied corpus research focuses on two broad and interrelated areas – training and practice. Applied research projects oriented at the training of legal translators with the use of corpora are growing in number and sophistication. They include the GENTT (Textual Genres for Translation) Research Group (Monzó Nebot 2008; Borja Albi 2013; Borja Albi et al. 2014) with the aforementioned JudGENTT web platform; the work of Sánchez Ramos and Vigier Moreno (2016) on the application of monolingual virtual corpora in the training of public service translators; and a recent paper by Biel (2017) on the use of comparable corpora as a tool during the translation process and the study of corpora as an analytical resource to reflect on the translation process. In general, the use of corpora in training is an inductive method of data-driven learning with hands-on experience. It ensures an improved knowledge of processes and phenomena in legal translation.

Another track of practically oriented research focuses on developing tools for practitioners. In the context of institutional translation, it can be illustrated by the Qualetra project on training, assessment, certification and accreditation of legal translators in criminal proceedings in the EU, implemented by a consortium led by KU Leuven. The project deliverables include a corpus of essential documents as understood by Directive 2010/64/EU, which was used to carry out a generic analysis of such documents and prepare their templates and the termbase with key terms and phraseology (cf. Kockaert and Rahab 2017). Another example of a practically oriented project, which, however, involves non-institutional legal translation, is the LAW10n project on resources for the translation of software licensing agreements,[4] led from the Autonomous University of Barcelona (Torres-Hostench and Bestué Salinas 2015).

In respect of theoretically oriented corpus research (basic research), Corpus Linguistics offers analytical tools that shift focus from a word to a pattern, and it triggers questions about the patterning of legal language in translation. According to Sinclair's idiom principle, language use is highly patterned and formulaic: 'a language user has available to him or her a large number of semi-preconstructed phrases that constitute single choices, even though they might appear to be analysable into segments' (1991: 110). This certainly extends to legal genres. Compared to other genres, legal genres are highly formulaic, fossilized, petrified, conservative and standardized, which is motivated by the need to ensure certainty of interpretation. The pertinent question is what happens to patterning in translation and whether we can/should achieve a similar degree of patterning (prefabrication) in translation. In general, comparable corpora allow us to study such patterning, its fit to non-translated language and, ultimately, the communicative dimension of institutional translation through identifying overrepresented patterns, underrepresented patterns, atypical patterns and lexical bundles (n-grams). Parallel corpora make it possible to study the relation of equivalence between translations and source texts.

Theoretically oriented projects on legal translation concern, above all, institutional translation with a considerable number of large-scale doctoral and postdoctoral research projects, for example:

- Karen McAuliffe's ERC Starting Grant (*Law and Language at the European Court of Justice*[5]) and ERC Proof of Concept grant to develop an EU Case-Law Corpus EUCLCORP[6] for researching the interaction of national and EU terms;
- Fernando Prieto Ramos's LETRINT project (*Legal Translation in International Institutional Settings: Scope, Strategies and Quality Markers*[7]), supported by a Consolidator Grant, including the design and analysis of several corpora of texts from the UN, the EU and the WTO;
- Laura Mori's *Eurolect Observatory* project[8] to analyse 11 Eurolects through a corpus of EU directives;
- Łucja Biel's *Polish Eurolect*[9] project, involving a genre-based analysis of the Polish Eurolect across four genres (legislation, judgments, reports, websites for citizens) and its impact on administrative Polish;
- Gianluca Pontrandolfo's PhD dissertation on the contrastive analysis of Spanish, Italian and English phraseology in translated EU judgments and non-translated national judgments (Pontrandolfo 2016).

Another project involving institutional translation that is worth mentioning is Aino Piehl's early study (2006) of EU influences on Finnish law.

4 http://lawcalisation.com/.
5 http://llecj.karenmcauliffe.com/.
6 http://llecj.karenmcauliffe.com/index.php/euclcorp-proof-of-concept/.
7 http://p3.snf.ch/Project-157797.
8 http://www.unint.eu/en/research/research-groups/39-higher-education/490-eurolect-observatory-interlingual-and-intralingual-analysis-of-legal-varieties-in-the-eu-setting.html.
9 http://eurolekt.ils.uw.edu.pl/.

There are also – less numerous – corpus-based projects on intersystemic legal translation outside the institutional context, for example, Simmonaes's work on modals and equivalents in the multilingual TK-NHH corpus of translations from the Norwegian National Translator Accreditation Exam (2012), Vanden Bulcke's comparable Dutch and Spanish corpora of articles of association to study deontic modality (2013) and, more recently, Samantha Cayron's PhD dissertation based on a large corpus of private documents – French and Spanish notarial documents related to succession law (Cayron 2017) and the TIPp project analysing court interpreting in criminal proceedings (Orozco-Jutorán, forthcoming).

Interestingly, researchers tend to build their own corpora rather than use existing institutional resources. Due to delicate methodological issues of representativeness, balance and comparability, corpus design is a critical phase in any corpus project. Researchers prefer to work on smaller well-controlled and genre-based corpora, which are carefully adjusted to their research questions, annotated with linguistic information and, above all, practical to work with. Yet, the advantage of large corpora cannot be underestimated, and we need to find ways to work with the vast resources made public by the international organizations.

5 Conclusions

What corpora have to offer to institutional translation is, on the one hand, use as a resource by translators (practical applications) and, on the other hand, use as an analytical tool in product-oriented research, which has some practical applications.

Corpus methods contribute to the methodological development, sophistication and refinement of LTSs, including institutional translation. They raise pertinent questions that break away from traditional foci, focusing on patterns at various levels of discourse organization. Corpus-based and corpus-driven studies into legal translation, combined with the growing number and scale of institutional corpus resources, are small steps that we are taking into the unknown areas of translation. Such studies provide empirical data that allow us to search for patterns of patterns and patterns of translators' behaviour, leading to generalizations about institutional legal translation.

In order to get the big picture, more empirical quantitative data are needed not only from major languages but also from lesser-used languages, various branches of law and translational settings. Corpus data should be interpreted from varied angles and triangulated with qualitative data obtained through mixed methodologies and methodological eclecticism. Finally, the big picture will be incomplete without the integration of practically and theoretically oriented research along interdisciplinary lines and language-specific enclaves. This will help us uncover and better understand the nature of institutional translation.

Acknowledgement

This work was supported by the National Science Centre (NCN) under Grant 2014/14/E/HS2/00782.

3

Comparative Law and Legal Translation as Partners in Knowledge Communication: Frames as a Descriptive Instrument

Jan Engberg

1 Introduction

This chapter is based upon the general assumption that legal translation is a creative process carried out to support a knowledge creation process. It is thus inscribed in the framework of functional approaches to the description of translation, framing the process as one of solving pragmatic formulation problems (Sarcevic 1997; Prieto Ramos 2014b, c: 273). The knowledge creation process supported by the translation takes place when receivers from one or more target (legal) cultural background(s) construct knowledge based on the target text created by the translator from a pre-existing legal text embedded in a source (legal) cultural background.

In this chapter, I want to present a method for comparative legal studies with relevance for legal translation falling under this definition. I want to demonstrate the application of a version of a general analytical tool (frame semantic analysis) that may support translators in the process of building a necessary basis for their creative process, with special emphasis upon finding and categorizing knowledge from comparative legal studies. The tool may be applied irrespective of the number of texts on the source and target sides of the translation process. Consequently, the approach is relevant for traditional 1:1 culture legal translations as well as for translations involving twenty-four different target texts and no real source text, as is the case in the institutional context of European Union (EU) translation, and anything in between. Thus, it is relevant in institutional as well as in non-institutional settings.

Traditionally, legal translation has been seen as being characterized by a limited level of creativity, although a number of researchers have demonstrated that this view is too narrow, even in very documentary kinds of translation like that of legal instruments or contracts for documentary purposes (e.g. Fujii 2013; Pommer 2008; Šarčević 2000a; Vlachopoulos 2013). However, the limits of creativity are certainly narrow in such situations. This is less the case in legal translations carried out for purposes that are more informative. An example is the task of informing legal researchers, which I will investigate in this chapter (cf. Section 3). It is also less the case in the institutional translation of multilingual statutory texts in an EU context with its claim of autonomy for the EU legal system (Engberg 2015a). The claim makes it necessary to find optimal ways of conveying overlaps as well as differences between EU law and national law. The qualitative empirical study to be presented here offers insights into this process that are potentially helpful for supporting the choices of formulation necessary in both of these more creative cases.

The focus of this chapter is on the empirical example presented in Section 3. Before we get to that, however, in Section 2, I will present some basic concepts with relevance for the application of a frame approach to the analysis. Finally, Section 4 contains some concluding remarks.

2 Basic concepts

2.1 Legal translation as an instance of knowledge communication

As a discipline, Legal Translation Studies (LTS) draws upon knowledge from other disciplines and combines this knowledge with a specialized approach. Input comes especially from the field of Linguistics (mainly concerning formal aspects), Translation Studies (mainly concerning methodological aspects) and Law (mainly concerning the content to be expressed, but also Comparative Law as a tool for analysing that content in different legal systems and, hence, a crucial component of legal translation methodologies) (Prieto Ramos 2014b, c: 266). Seeing these disciplines as central for LTS correlates with the fact that legal translators draw upon knowledge from these fields when they solve their formulation problems. For the purposes of this chapter, it is relevant to develop approaches for finding and especially categorizing knowledge generated through comparative legal analysis in order to form a relevant basis for creative translational decisions. The reason is that legal translation produces target texts to be used in legal settings like courtrooms or academic legal settings, and it is therefore translation for legal purposes drawing on legal knowledge (de Groot 1999; Engberg 2013; Prieto Ramos 2014b, c). From here, the specialty emerges that comparative legal knowledge is needed in order to make relevant decisions (Soriano-Barabino 2016: 21–2), as one of the central purposes is to give the receiver access to the legal knowledge underlying the source text. This leads us to the next basic concept: legal translation as an instance of knowledge communication.

In the field of investigating domain-specific discourse, a group of researchers at Aarhus University has been developing a knowledge-oriented approach under the heading of *knowledge communication*. The approach may be described along the following lines.

> The study of Knowledge Communication aims at investigating the intentional and decision-based communication of specialized knowledge in professional settings (among experts as well as between experts and non-experts), with a focus upon the interplay between the knowledge and expertise of individuals, on the one hand, and knowledge as a social phenomenon, on the other, as well as the coping with

> knowledge asymmetries, that is, the communicative consequences of differences between individual knowledge in depth as well as breadth. (Engberg 2016: 37)[1]

According to this approach, what centrally characterizes domain-specific discourse is the fact that specialized knowledge is communicated, either among experts or between experts and non-experts. This knowledge is carried by individual experts (*knowledge and expertise of individuals*), but they also share it with other experts in communities (*knowledge as a social phenomenon*). The community contributes heavily to the specialist status of the knowledge. Consequently, both aspects are equally relevant when describing specialized knowledge. Furthermore, knowledge asymmetries (i.e. differences between the knowledge stocks of different individuals) are central for communication in domain-specific discourse (Jacobsen 2012; Kastberg 2011). Such asymmetries may clearly exist between experts and non-experts, but they also exist among experts, not least if they have different national origins and/or professional cultures. To sum up, the knowledge-communication approach investigates expert communicative situations with a focus upon the processes of acquiring and adjusting personal knowledge in communicative interactions characterized by differences in knowledge stocks.

Legal translation falls under this categorization. In the previous work, I have related the approach to the translation of terms in legal documents: 'Translating terms in legal documents consists in strategically choosing relevant parts of the complex conceptual knowledge represented in the source text in order to present the aspects exactly relevant for this text in the target text situation in order to enable a receiver to construct the intended cognitive structure' (Engberg 2015b: 5).

According to this definition, translating legal terms consists in making a number of choices among possible alternatives, that is, the communication-centred creative process already mentioned. Central among the choices, the translator must select parts of the knowledge connected to the legal concept according to relevance in terms of target as well as source situation. Finally, the goal of the translation is to enable individual readers to construct an intended cognitive structure. Translation is not simply about making a target text. Instead, translation is about creating opportunities for individuals in a target situation to construct knowledge relevantly similar to knowledge normally constructed by individuals in the source situation.

2.2 Frames as analytical approach in Translation Studies

Following the functionalist idea of legal translation as a creative and problem-solving process makes it relevant to employ analytical approaches focusing upon meaning more than form, especially cognitively oriented approaches like frame semantics (Svejcer 2004: 238). This idea is not new; frame approaches have been applied to the analysis of translation products before.[2] However, the approach is relatively new to legal translation.[3]

1 For an overview of literature and the characteristics of the knowledge-communication approach, cf. Porup Thomasen 2015: 57–117.

2 For an overview with a focus upon frame semantics and dictionaries for translation, cf. Boas 2013. For empirical applications of a frame approach, cf. Rojo López 2002; Snell-Hornby 1995: 79–85.

3 For a concept approach to legal translation processes, cf. Griebel 2013.

When translating concepts between two or more cultures according to standards of functional translation, translators need a relevant knowledge base, that is, insight into what knowledge is relevant in order to understand a concept in the way it is understood by the members of the legal field (Busse 2015: 44–5; Engberg 2009b). This means that translators must build up a knowledge base from domain-internal sources like encyclopaedias, statutes and the like. Within the field of legal semantics, the German scholar Dietrich Busse in particular has introduced the idea of *Verstehensrelevantes Wissen*, that is, knowledge relevant for the conforming understanding (Busse 1987). This idea is central for work on knowledge communication in a legal context and ensuing ideas about relevant kinds of translators' comparative legal work.

A relevant way to work analytically with this kind of knowledge is to apply the concept of the frame, drawn from frame semantics, in order to analytically collect and structure the needed basis (Busse 2015; Engberg 2009a). The central advantage of a frame approach is that it models connections between elements of a concept along relevant dimensions and therefore is less tied to specific languages than mainly lexical approaches: 'the frame-semantic approach to lexical organization makes it possible to relate words across languages in a systematic way' (Boas 2013: 152). Due to the limited space of this chapter and its focus upon the qualitative study of an empirical example, I will not go deeper into a description of the frame concept. Instead, I will limit myself to presenting the central aspects of the approach (cf. Busse 2015: 46):

- Frames are structures of knowledge elements, presumed to exist in the long-term memory of individuals but dependent upon agreement with the frames held by other individuals for their function in communicative settings.
- The basic building blocks of the structures are slots, that is, not fully specified attributes or dimensions with central relevance for the understanding of the concept.
- On their part, slots contain or gather knowledge elements of a more concrete kind, which prototypically are used to fill the slots. Such elements are called *fillers* in the frame semantic terminology.

In Section 3.3, an example of a frame will be developed as a basis for the following analysis.

3 Empirical example: Assessing suggested solutions to translation task

3.1 Translation task

To demonstrate how a knowledge-communication approach to comparative legal work with relevance for translation may be fleshed out, I will present a qualitative analysis of different solutions devised by students for a translation task given in the context of an MA course in legal translation at Aarhus University. Focus is upon assessing different creative solutions to a practical translation and knowledge-communication task.

The basis of the translation task is a German court decision (*Bundesgerichtshof, Beschluss vom 10.1.2012 – 4 StR 632/11*). Behind this case lies a situation in which a person has been accused of driving away from several petrol stations without paying for the petrol he put into his car. The central legal question is what kind of legal offence the defendant may be said to have committed: theft (*Diebstahl*), fraud (*Betrug*) or misappropriation (*Unterschlagung*). The outcome of this argumentation has repercussions for the punishment of the perpetrator. The decision reports the deliberations of the German Supreme Federal Court in a special appeal case, a *Revision* (*Bundesgerichtshof*). We will see next some of the characteristics of this type of legal procedure.

The translation brief is to produce a target text aimed for a Danish lawyer who needs the translation for a comparative law project with a view to writing an article for a law journal on the legal status of the act of driving away without paying for petrol in different jurisdictions. In this context, the lawyer is interested in knowing the situation in Germany as reflected in selected parts of the decision. Translating the legal concept into Danish is a challenge, as neither the term nor the concept in a more informal manner exists in the Danish legal context. Consequently, a knowledge asymmetry arises.

Based upon these characteristics, I see the following two interests as central for the translators' decisions:

- To understand the German framework and the German argumentation (as these form the basis of the knowledge that the receiver needs for his article writing).
- To present the key concepts considering goal and the pre-existing knowledge of the intended receiver.

Due to space limitations, I will focus upon the translation of the following sentence in the source text: 'Gegen das Urteil richtete sich die auf *eine Verfahrens- und Sachrüge* gestützte Revision des Angeklagten'[4] (emphasis added). Emphasis will be on the legal concept indicated by the term *eine Verfahrens- und Sachrüge*. As opposed to my earlier work on translations of this concept (Engberg 2015b, 2016), here I will apply a frame-oriented analysis spanning a number of translations.

3.2 Source-culture frame

In the first step, we establish the *Verstehensrelevantes Wissen* (cf. above). It is important to use textual material inherently from the actual domain (here: German legal procedure) in order to avoid restricting oneself to, for example, statutory definitions of concepts. For the relevant meaning of a legal concept does not reside in the words of the statute, but in the knowledge about the concept expressed in different texts of the domain. A full and systematic investigation of the knowledge relevant for a conforming understanding is almost limitless, as it would have to include so many

[4] Against the court decision was directed the appeal of the defendant based on *a procedural and material law objection* (author's interlinear translation).

texts that we are confident that including further texts would not bring additional slots (dimensions) or fillers (actual characteristics) to the structure resulting from the analysis.

However, in practical work, limits may be imposed from the point of view of the degree of understanding relevant for the situation at hand and from the point of view of some of the characteristics of different genres in the domain. In our context, genres like dogmatic commentaries and encyclopaedia articles are central. This is due to the fact that both genres aim at showing the contemporary state of development of legal concepts and often the interpretive history, background and details of this. Both genres can be regarded as points of crystallization where knowledge developments occur through scholarly discussions in academic genres and through adjudication. A key difference between the two is the fact that the dogmatic commentary is much more detailed and is thus a great source for specific characteristics and deeper understanding, whereas the encyclopaedia article aims at giving an overview of the central characteristics of legal concepts. Consequently, encyclopaedia articles are important sources for the construction of a relevant translators' knowledge base for creative solutions. In the practical example that follows, I limit myself to using an encyclopaedia article as basis for my knowledge collection and the structuring of the frame for reasons of practicality and due to the aforementioned characteristics of the genre.

In a legal encyclopaedia compiled and authored by four German legal scholars, and thus most likely reflecting the knowledge needed to understand the concept in accordance with the general legal understanding of the concept, we find definitions of the terms *Rüge*, *Sachrüge* and *Verfahrensrüge*, of which I present the central aspects at the beginning of the entry:

1. **Rüge**: Im Verfahrensrecht die Behauptung einer Partei, eine Handlung der Gegenseite verletze Verfahrensvorschriften oder das Gericht wende das Recht falsch an.[5] (http://www.rechtslexikon.net/d/ruege/ruege.htm)
2. **Verfahrensrüge** ist die Rüge verfahrensrechtlicher Fehler durch die strafprozessuale Revision. Die Anforderungen an die Begründung der auf Verfahrensrügen gestützten Revision sind im Vergleich zur Sachrüge erheblich höher: Gemäß § 344 Abs. 2, S. 3 StPo müssen die den Mangel enthaltenden Tatsachen angegeben werden.[6] … (http://www.rechtslexikon.net/d/verfahrensrüge/verfahrensrüge.htm)
3. **Sachrüge**: Rüge der Verletzung des materiellen Rechts durch die Revision im Strafprozess. Möglich ist die Geltendmachung der Rechtsverletzung als allgemeine Sachrüge, also ohne nähere Bezeichnung des Rechtsfehlers, oder als ausgeführte

[5] Objection: In procedural law, the claim by a party that an action of the other party breaches procedural rules or that the court applies the law incorrectly (author's translation).

[6] Procedural objection is the objection of errors related to legal procedure by way of appeal to a criminal court (*Revision*). The argumentation requirements to an appeal based upon procedural objections are considerably higher compared to material law objections: According to § 344 II 3rd sentence of the German Statute on Criminal Procedure, the facts containing the error have to be indicated (author's translation).

Sachrüge mit Spezifizierung des Rechtsmangels (vgl. § 344 Abs. 2 S.1, 2. Alt. StPO).[7] … (http://www.rechtslexikon.net/d/sachrüge/sachrüge.htm)

Searches in other German online legal encyclopaedias for entries with *Rüge*, *Verfahrensrüge* or *Sachrüge* as headword were unsuccessful, so I limit myself to the above definitions for the construction of the slot system to be used in the analysis.

The definition of *Rüge* states that two sub-types exist, that is, *Verfahrensrüge* and *Sachrüge*. From the point of view of the structure of the frame, the second issue means that for the frame *Rüge*, it is relevant to set up a slot (= dimension) with the denomination 'Type' and with two fillers: *Verfahrensrüge* and *Sachrüge*. In other words, it belongs to the knowledge relevant for understanding the concept as German lawyers do to know that *Rüge* is a superordinate concept, covering two sub-types. On this basis, it is relevant to work here with a frame on *Rüge* and to see all three entries as input to the same frame. As we shall see subsequently, this view is supported by overlaps in the description of the two sub-types.

Concerning the central content characteristics of *Rüge*, the definition starts out by stating that it is a type of claim (*Behauptung*). In the two definitions of the subsequent terms, we are told that this claim in the case of *Verfahrensrüge* must mention the facts (*Tatsachen*) leading to the error (*Mangel*) underlying the claim. We thus see a kind of causal chain reflected in the text: Specific facts lead to the existence of an error, which justifies stating a claim in the form of a *Rüge*. We find the same chain reflected in the description of the *Sachrüge*, albeit in a somewhat more indirect form. There is a distinction between a general form, which is just a claim without explicit substantiation; and a specified form, where the underlying error (and thus probably also the facts leading to the error) is specified. Therefore, I propose a slot with the denomination 'Internal causal chain' and the fillers *Tatsache*, *Mangel* and *Behauptung*.

Finally, from both definitions of subordinate types, we can see that these types of *Rüge* are connected to appeals in criminal court. The appeal is presented as the instrument for performing the objection (*durch die Revision*). This justifies proposing a slot 'Instrument' with the filler *Revision*. It is part of the relevant knowledge that *Revision* is a special kind of appeal, which can only aim at objecting to errors in the application of the law. A renewed evaluation of evidence, for instance, is not possible in this type of appeal (cf. http://www.rechtslexikon.net/d/revision/revision.htm).

Based upon these deliberations, I propose the following slots for a rudimentary frame of the concept *Rüge*.

3.3 Assessing how frame elements are rendered in translations

In the following analysis, the focus will be on assessing what aspects of the rudimentary frame in Figure 3.1 are rendered by the different solutions of the students. The corpus

[7] Objection of breach of the material law by way of appeal in the criminal procedure. It is possible to claim a breach of rules in the form of a general material law objection, that is, without specific mentioning of the legal error, or as a specified material law objection with a specification of the legal error (cf. § 344 II 1st sentence, 2nd alternative of the German Statute on Criminal Procedure (author's translation)).

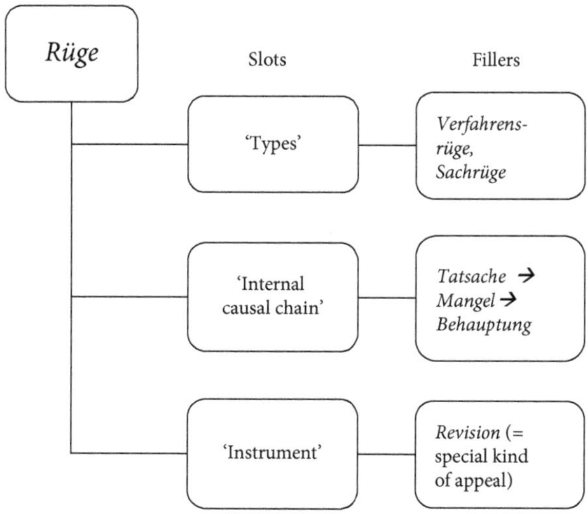

Figure 3.1 Rudimentary frame of *Rüge*.

consists of all solutions by the participants in a course on legal translation as part of the MA programme in International Business Communication at Aarhus University. I will present the five alternatives, before I compare the solutions and their relations to the source-culture frame.

(1) Tiltaltes *revisionsanke*, som var støttet på *en processuel og en materielretlig indsigelse*, rettede sig mod denne dom[8] (Alternative I).

In this alternative, the translator has chosen to use a Danish term (*indsigelse*) as a direct rendering of *Rüge*. The term is a near equivalent to the German term and holds the same procedural note of performing the act of objecting. The translator thus has indicated to the receiver to rely upon a Danish frame with a high degree of similarity with the German frame. Furthermore, the solution presents the distinction between the two types of *Rüge*, again via near-equivalent terms from the Danish context (*en processuel og en materielretlig indsigelse*). Finally, the instrumental appeal is indicated as a specific type (*revisionsanke*), which does not exist in the Danish system. However, the chosen term is the one conventionally used when talking about the German concept in a Danish legal context.

(2) Den tiltaltes *anke* af dommen støtter sig på *påstand om overtrædelse af den materielle ret samt påstand om procedurefejl*[9] (Alternative II).

Here, the translator has chosen to use the Danish term from procedural law for 'claim' (*påstand*). In terms of frame semantics, the translator may be said to have rendered a central aspect in the internal causal chain (*Behauptung*, claim), which in

[8] Defendant's revising appeal, which was based upon *a procedural and a material law objection*, was directed towards this court decision (author's translation).

[9] The defendant's appeal of the court decision is based on *claim of infringement of material law and claim of procedural error* (author's translation).

the definition of *Rüge* in example (1) is presented as a kind of synonym to this term. The claims are characterized relevantly in two ways: First, it is indicated lexically that they refer to problematic behaviour (*overtrædelse, -fejl*) and, secondly, that the problematic behaviour belongs to the procedural and the material field, respectively (*den materielle ret, procedurefejl*). *Revision* is not rendered in its specificity but by the general term *appel*.

(3) Den tiltalte begærede *revision på grund af materielretlige fejl og procedurefejl*[10] (Alternative III).

The central designation of the frame *Rüge* is not rendered in this alternative. Instead, the translator indicates the middle part of the internal causal chain – the error – and presents this as the reason for the appeal. Furthermore, two near-equivalent terms are used to indicate the difference between the two types of reason for the appeal. Thus, the element (*fejl*) is rendered in accordance with its role in the frame and with relevant distinctions (*materielretlige, procedure-*). The translator renders the instrumental appeal with a calque from German (*revision*). Although it is not a term, the word exists in Danish with a related meaning, probably allowing the reader to make relevant inferences.

(4) Tiltalte *ankede* dommen *i forhold til processuelle spørgsmål og i forhold til domsafsigelsen*[11] (Alternative IV).

In this alternative, the translator indicates the kind of facts that underlie the objection instead of the objection as such. Thus, the translator renders the first part of the internal causal chain characterizing a *Rüge*. The distinction between the two types is rendered by the words *processuel* and *domsafsigelsen*. The latter term in particular, which refers to the judgments as such, requires considerable inferences for a reader to reconstruct the relevant knowledge and understand the distinction conformingly. The appeal is rendered by a terminological verb (*ankede*), indicating the process of filing an appeal.

(5) Til prøvelse af rettens dom blev der af den tiltalte *indgivet appel*, der baserede sig på *påtale af procedurefejl og af fejlagtig brug af den materielle ret*[12] (Alternative V).

Finally, in alternative V, we also see the indication of the action of objecting. However, the translator does not use the exact Danish term but a more general one, although one also used in the legal field (*påtale*). The distinction between the two types is indicated by the middle element in the internal causal chain ascribed to the field of procedural and material law by the ordinary Danish terms (*procedurefejl, fejlagtig brug af den materielle ret*). Finally, the act of filing an appeal is indicated, but there is no indication of the special character of the German concept of *Revision*.

Table 3.1 shows how different alternatives render the frame underlying the source text sentence.

[10] The defendant applied for *revision due to material law error and procedural error* (author's translation).

[11] Defendant appealed the court decision *in relation to procedural questions and in relation to the delivered judgment* (author's translation).

[12] In order to test the court's decision, the defendant *filed an appeal*, which was based upon *protest against procedural error and against wrongful use of the material law* (author's translation).

Table 3.1 Rendering of different parts of the frame.[a]

	Special type appeal	Action of objecting	Claim	Error	Facts	Procedural vs. material
Alt. 1	X	X				X
Alt. 2	((X))		X	X		X
Alt. 3	(X)			X		X
Alt. 4	((X))				X	(X)
Alt. 5	((X))	(X)		X		X

[a] In the table, one bracket indicates non-terminological formulation; two brackets indicate superordinate term.

To sum up the analysis as indicated in Table 3.1:

- All alternatives express the appeal instrumental to the objection; three indicate a superordinate term, two indicate the special type of appeal, one uses a term-like solution and one uses a non-terminological formulation.
- All alternatives express the distinction between two types of objection; one uses a non-terminological expression for one of the two types.
- Two alternatives (I, V) indicate the central aspect of the frame, the objection, one with a near-equivalent term.
- In two alternatives (III, V), the error underlying the objection is indicated instead of the objection.
- In one case (IV), the facts underlying the objection are indicated instead of the objection.
- In one case (II), the claim and the error underlying it are indicated together.

These results reflect several strategies. In all cases, the translator chooses to leave parts of the frame for inferencing, as is already the case in the source text. In this text, the author uses the terms *Verfahrens- und Sachrüge*. She thus indicates the frame *Rüge* and the slot 'types' and leaves all parts of the slot 'Internal causal chain' for inferencing, probably because this aspect is not centrally relevant for a German legal reader understanding the sentence and/or because it is seen as knowledge that may be presupposed. In the alternatives, we see the following distribution of strategies:

- Alternative I: Action of objecting expressed (by term); all elements of internal causal chain (and thus the complete slot) left for inferencing.
- Alternative II: Claim and error expressed; action of objecting and facts left for inferencing.
- Alternative III: Error expressed; action of objecting, claim and facts left for inferencing.
- Alternative IV: Facts expressed; action of objecting, claim and error left for inferencing.
- Alternative V: Action of objecting and error expressed; claim and facts left for inferencing.

3.4 Hypotheses about the efficiency of chosen strategies

Seeing legal translation as a type of knowledge communication emphasizes the fact that the success of a translation process has to be measured against the actual reception processes among translation readers (Engberg 2015b). The quality of the translation may thus not be assessed solely through an evaluation of the text as such. Instead, taking the knowledge-communication characteristics seriously means that some kind of assessment of the way the text is actually understood has to be carried out when assessing the quality of the translational choices and strategies. This also applies to practising translators. In this final part, I will establish hypotheses about the efficiency of the chosen strategies that could form the basis of an empirical testing along the lines described above (cf. Section 4 for possible approaches). Especially in the present context, where the intended receiver is known, that is, a Danish lawyer interested in comparative law, it is possible to set up relevant hypotheses.

First, it is likely that the action of objecting may be communicated to the expert receiver by way of the Danish near-equivalent term *indsigelse* (alternative I). The same is probably true about the non-terminological rendition of the action (*påtale*) in alternative V. It is also likely that an expert receiver will construct the relevant frame based on the renderings of parts of the internal causal chain underlying the action of objecting in a court setting. However, the strategy is more relevant for receivers who do not know the terminological expressions. In this case, it expresses details that are not in focus in the source expression but are part of the presupposed knowledge in the source context. Possibly, the alternatives have been chosen because the translators have not found the Danish near-equivalent term and therefore wanted to make sure that they rendered the relevant content. As a creative coping strategy, this solution is very sensible if the parts of the frame rendered are relevant, as it is the case here.

Secondly, the distinction between the two types of *Rüge* is clear in four of the five alternatives. In all these cases, near-equivalent terms are used to indicate the differences. In one case (alternative IV), only one type is indicated by a term (*processuelle spørgsmål*). As the relevant distinction is known in Denmark, the expert receiver will probably be able to infer the correct structure of the slot, but it is hardly the most efficient way to communicate this part of the frame.

Finally, the three alternatives do not convey that the instrumental appeal is of a specific kind. This is not optimal in the present case, as the status of the court case may be relevant for the intended receiver. In other cases, it would be possible to argue that the exact type of appeal is less relevant than the mere fact that an appeal is lodged.

4 Concluding remarks

By way of conclusion, I would like to focus on two aspects: processes for empirically testing hypotheses about understanding, and the competences that are possibly relevant considering strategies analysed in this study.

As regards the first aspect, different approaches that focus on effects as well as on content and knowledge may be useful. Effect approaches have been developed, especially in the field of usability testing of instructions, and in literary translation studies, recent attempts have also been made to establish a basis for assessing the relevance of translational choices (Sinner and Morales Tejada 2015). A content approach based upon the use of think-aloud protocols has been developed and tested by Göpferich (2006a,b), and Luttermann (2010) has presented an approach elaborated especially for assessing the actual understanding of legal texts by establishing knowledge patterns of different reader groups empirically through text analysis and interviews. For the individual practising translator, it will seldom be possible to do such tests, but in institutional settings, it could be relevant and recommendable in high-profiled and very important documents to actually carry out such tests. The practice of including lawyer-linguists when assessing EU legislation can be seen as a way of testing knowledge constructions. It may be relevant to widen the scope in cases where the quality of the target text is very important as a basis for knowledge construction among readers.

Concerning competences, much focus in LTS has recently remained upon assessing what competences are expected of professional translators and must be acquired by translation students. I want to conclude by suggesting what competences we see reflected in the investigated translational choices. Primarily, the choices reflect a strategic competence, that is, the meta-competence to assess actual problems and to choose how to apply and combine other competences in order to solve the problem in a contextually relevant way. The main competences to be combined here are the subject-area competence (insight into legal systems) and the professional, interpersonal and instrumental competence, especially the competence to find and use relevant sources and instruments for comparative legal analysis for accessing unknown subject-area aspects.[13] The creativity mentioned earlier in this chapter would be an integral part of the strategic competence needed to become a good translator. The different analysed solutions may be seen as reflections of the ability to make strategic choices in the absence of sufficient subject-area insight. This ability is relevant in any setting – institutional as well as non-institutional – in which translators must investigate concepts into which they do not possess deep and detailed insights. Thus, creativity as a component of the strategic competence is an important part of performing relevant comparative legal analyses to find and select the most central aspects of a legal concept to be rendered.

We see here a characteristic of the performance of comparative law in translational settings: It is always aimed at solving formulation problems. In order to achieve such solutions, it is essential to be able to perform selective searches that yield insights into relevant details and characteristics and to present them to the reader. As I have shown, this makes it relevant to work with a conceptual and cognitive frame-oriented approach to the comparative legal work in order to make informed decisions. Such a descriptive instrument may prove useful in comparative law for translation, adding to more traditionally legal approaches like the functional approach of Zweigert and Kötz (1996). The requirements for translation are different from those of legal practice. Methods should be different, too.

[13] For an overview of the elaboration of the set of competences by different researchers and for definitions of the competences, cf. Soriano-Barabino 2016: Ch. 10.

Part Two

Translation Quality in Law- and Policy-Making and Implementation

4

Towards a More Structured Approach to Quality Assurance: DGT's Quality Journey

Ingemar Strandvik[1]

1 Introduction: Institutional translation and multilingual law-making

In the European Union (EU), in twenty-three official languages out of twenty-four, translations constitute the interface between the EU and its citizens. A prerequisite for achieving political objectives is that this institutional voice speaks naturally and idiomatically to the addressees (Koskinen 2014). Within the European Commission's Directorate-General for Translation (DGT), we often say that the purpose of institutional translation is to ensure that the institution speaks with one consistent institutional voice in each of the EU's official languages. When institutional multilingualism involves multilingual *law-making*, it should also be borne in mind that formally there are no translations, only equally authentic language versions, *drafted* in all official languages.[2] Once the texts are adopted, there is no 'original' language version with a higher value; all language versions have the same formal status: they create rights and obligations, they *are* the law and they are equally authentic. In such a context, translation quality is of paramount importance – for political reasons, for the correct application of EU legislation and as a matter of fundamental rights and legal certainty.

Translation is largely a question of making choices. As Pym (1992) puts it, there are translation choices that are correct or incorrect (binary errors), but mostly translation issues are not a matter of right or wrong but of making more or less appropriate choices (non-binary errors). Any institutional translation context will therefore necessarily trigger quality concerns and reflections on house style in order to agree on choices that in a number of recurring issues are to be considered preferable, to make the institutional translation possible at all and to ensure consistency over time. This is to

[1] The opinions expressed are those of the author and should not be considered to represent the European Commission's official position.

[2] See Article 4 of Regulation No 1 of 1958 determining the languages to be used by the European Economic Community. *Translation* is not mentioned. This is for a reason, even if, in practice, twenty-three language versions are drafted through translation.

say that quality assurance is always an inherent part of any institutional translation setting. DGT is no exception; quality assurance has always been part and parcel of its operations. This quality assurance, however, has not always been systematic, and it has not necessarily taken place in a structured way across the language departments.

What we have witnessed over the last ten years is a move towards a more conscious, structured and systematic approach to quality assurance. This is what I will describe in this chapter: how quality assurance has evolved over time, with a focus on the impact of some major quality management initiatives on DGT's current structure and work organization. Different aspects of the emerging quality management policy (attempts to define translation quality and guidelines for translation, quality control,[3] risk assessment and evaluation of outsourced translations) and future challenges will then be addressed. When reading the following pages, it is important to bear in mind the scale of DGT's operations; the European Commission's Directorate-General for Translation has around 1500 in-house translators working in twenty-four language departments, producing over two million pages of translation per year, of which almost a third is done through outsourcing.

2 Triggers for change

The need for a more conscious, structured and systematic institutional approach to quality management evolved over time, triggered by a number of interlinked factors, the most important of which are

- extension and deepening of European cooperation and a considerable increase in the number of official EU languages;
- resource constraints;
- increased use of outsourcing.

2.1 Extension and deepening of European cooperation

The EU has evolved over time, from technical cooperation in a restricted number of subject-matter areas to a political union that now covers a wide spectrum of policy fields and affects most areas of the citizens' daily lives. As a consequence, the Commission produces many document types, not only legislation and technical reports but also policy papers, press releases, brochures, web pages and so on. In addition to complying with the legal requirements of multilingualism (Strandvik 2015: 145–6), this text production must contribute to the Commission's political objectives, such as bridging the gap between the EU and its citizens, involving citizens and stakeholders in the political processes at the European level, and convincing them of the added value of European cooperation. Ever since the Danes voted 'no' to the Maastricht Treaty in a referendum in 1992, the Commission has strived to improve the quality of its

[3] In DGT, 'quality control' refers to 'revision and review' (ISO 17100) or 'editing' (ASTM F2575), not post-production assessment, which in DGT is referred to as 'ex-post review'.

communication by addressing quality assurance in an increasingly structured way, for instance by issuing text-type specific drafting guidelines (for legislation, competition inquiries, press material, web texts, etc.[4]).

2.2 Resource constraints

The last ten to twenty years have seen an increasing focus on cost-efficiency in public administrations, also with regard to translation. In the EU context, the addition of thirteen new languages following the 'big bang enlargement' in 2004 and the subsequent accession of Romania, Bulgaria and Croatia, combined with the financial crisis, have underlined the importance of ensuring that the best possible use is made of taxpayers' money. A number of internal and external audits have been carried out (e.g. European Court of Auditors 2006) aiming to ensure that the translation is performed in an efficient way.

With each enlargement, the number of official languages has increased. However, at the same time, every enlargement has triggered reductions in the number of in-house translators per language. For instance, when Swedish and Finnish became official languages in 1995, DGT recruited close to 100 translators for each language. Today, both have around 50 in-house translators. In particular, the enlargement in 2004, which added ten new Member States and nine new official languages in one go, led to a situation where the number of new translators recruited no longer matched the resource needs of the old operational model.

The increasing resource constraints have put DGT under mounting pressure to ensure efficiency by all means and at all times. At the same time, the role of quality and quality assurance in the context of efficiency gains has come to the fore. Processes have been analysed and best practices identified. Technology and tools, and the expectations put on them, have played an important role. As for all sectors of public administration, the buzzword has been to 'do more with less'.

2.3 Increased use of outsourcing

Even if considerable internal efficiency gains have been achieved thanks to the use of IT tools and the streamlining of working methods, they have not been sufficient to cope with the increasing translation demand paired with the successive (and still projected) cuts in the number of in-house translators per language. The solution has therefore been to resort more and more systematically to outsourcing, first for 'less important' documents but gradually also for policy documents and legislation. This, in turn, has led to a need to ensure consistency in quality evaluation and quality assurance so that the outsourced documents are up to the same standards as the documents translated

[4] EU legal acts should comply with drafting rules, formalized formulations and templates in the *Joint Practical Guide* (JPG), the *Manual of Precedents*, the *Joint Handbook for the Presentation and Drafting of Acts Subject to the Ordinary Legislative Procedure* and the *Interinstitutional Style Guide*. Specific guidance for drafting outreach documents can be found in the *Guidelines for Better Press Material*, the *Guidelines on How to Write for the Web* and in the *How to Write Clearly* booklet.

in-house. A precondition for such consistency is a shared understanding across DGT's language departments of what translation quality means.

3 Past initiatives

3.1 The translation strategy

In 2004, nine new official EU languages were added to the eleven that existed at the time. As mentioned above, it was out of the question to almost double the number of translating staff. Therefore, the whole business model had to be rethought and efficiency gains had to be found. The European Commission addressed this issue by introducing structural measures to reduce demand. It did so via the adoption of a series of strategic communications (European Commission 2004, 2005, 2006).

Both supply and demand-oriented measures were taken, including the following actions: A document classification was introduced to establish a prioritization system, restrictions were introduced for the admissible length or a limited language regime of certain documents (some documents do not require translation into all official languages), recommended ways of handling documents (in-house translation or outsourcing) were defined, the editing of originals was intensified and so on. By 2007, while the number of official EU languages had more than doubled, the cost for translation had increased by 30 per cent.

3.2 Quality management in translation

The implementation of this strategy and the integration of nine new official languages required a continuous scrutiny of DGT's practices. In 2006, this led to the creation of a Task Force for Quality Management in Translation and the launch, in 2007, of a quality management project called *Programme for Quality Management in Translation – 22 Quality Actions* (DGT 2009b). It consisted of twenty-two quality-related topics, which were analysed in working groups. This exercise led to a stock-taking of the various processes that were relevant for the quality of the translation services provided. The twenty-two actions, in turn, led to a number of follow-up actions. All in all, some fifty working groups were active during a couple of years in an unprecedented bottom-up initiative. This exercise constituted a qualitative leap in raising awareness of holistic quality management and of the need to ensure quality *before*, *during* and *after* translation – in other words, of the fact that quality is not only about products but also about systems and processes.

A non-exhaustive list of the topics scrutinized included the following: develop a common approach to pre-translation processing; improve translation briefs and feedback for freelancers; develop standards for the evaluation of freelance translations (including specific training, error quantification and tools for evaluation); raise awareness about the nature and purpose of the texts (via service-level agreements, lead translators/file coordinators, info sessions for translators run by the authors, translation briefs and annotated source texts); identify how to establish contacts with experts within and outside the Commission; set up a register for subject-matter competence; improve workflow tools for better capacity monitoring; identify files for a more structured project-based approach; integrate workflow tools; find ways to collect and solicit feedback; and provide a framework for a structured approach to quality management in each language department (with style guides, post-production quality reviews, a quality coordinator/quality manager per language department, etc.).

3.3 Total quality management with the Common Assessment Framework

Almost at the same time, during the first half of 2008, DGT carried out a Total Quality Management exercise applying the Common Assessment Framework (CAF), a European quality management methodology for public sector organizations.[5] This, in turn, involved yet another set of assessment groups, analysing and evaluating all the relevant workflow processes, not just those directly related to the translation but also to the organization as a whole. This exercise resulted in no less than 766 improvement actions proposed by the self-assessment groups, subsequently consolidated into 173, of which ten were selected for implementation. The main lessons from this initiative were in line with some of the basic tenets of modern administrative thinking, such as the importance of a holistic approach to quality, the iterative PDCA cycle thinking (plan, do, check, adapt; plan, do, check, adapt, etc.) and the key role of guidelines to make processes explicit and transparent, and to ensure monitoring and continuous improvement (DGT 2008a,b and 2009a).

3.4 The resulting approach to quality assurance

These ambitious introspection and reflection processes led to an approach to quality assurance that could be described in the following way:

- focus on processes rather than on products;
- quality management seen widely as the management of knowledge;
- emergence of a matrix structure for quality management.

Focus on processes

Process focus leads to the identification of relevant processes, combined with the monitoring and harmonization of these processes. It also contributes to system thinking, paying attention to processes before, during and after translation, that is, both upstream and downstream, not just within DGT but seeing DGT as part of a larger whole. This is highly relevant, not only in terms of international standards (such as ISO 17100, ASTM F2575, ISO TS 11669), but also in that it reflects a shift towards the functionalist paradigm in translation studies. Translation is seen as a purposeful activity involving *goals*, *means* and *conditions* and serving the needs and objectives of

5 For a more detailed description, see http://www.eipa.eu/en/topic/show/&tid=191.

the organization, that is, the Commission as a whole. At the same time, translation products are an integral part of the processes and workings of the Commission, not objects with independent quality attributes on their own (cf. e.g. Nord 1997).

A key issue for quality management in this setting is to strike the right balance with regard to the harmonization of processes. In theory, DGT's twenty-four language departments do the same thing: They translate for the Commission. One of the basic principles of quality management is to harmonize processes. Things should be done in the most efficient way, not in twenty-four different ways. However, if the main objective is to ensure efficiency, experience shows that this basic principle often needs to be nuanced because of the complexity of the workflow processes. Sometimes, there are reasons for different approaches. Let us describe just a few.

One of the consequences of the latest enlargements is that English has become the source language for practically all of the texts produced by the Commission and intended for publication. The English language department therefore has an inverted workflow compared to the other languages: Most documents that the Commission receives from the Member States are translated into English for internal use, and practically all texts produced by the Commission are drafted in English. This leads to a setting wherein the English language department has found itself in a rather unique situation compared to all the other departments in terms of source-language coverage, degree of outsourcing, document types and quality requirements (many translations are for internal use, not for publication).

Because of the technical complexity of legislation and the leaner organization, translators increasingly need to consult national experts on terminology issues. Such contacts depend on the counterparts' preferences and cannot be organized in the same way for large countries, such as Germany, Italy or France, as for smaller countries such as Estonia, Lithuania and Sweden, not to mention Malta. It also matters if a language is official in more than one Member State (as is the case for Dutch, English, French, German and Swedish).

Likewise, the size, nature and maturity of the freelance market are not necessarily the same for languages such as German, French and English as for Estonian, Lithuanian or Maltese. This has consequences for how outsourcing is organized. The competence profiles of the language departments' staff also vary from one language department to another, and they change over time. Such factors necessarily have an impact on work organization.

Quality management as knowledge management

In an institutional setting where twenty-three language departments basically do the same thing – translate the same documents[6] – they are also, in principle, confronted with the same problems. Whenever a problem occurs in one language department, it is highly likely that the same problem occurs at the same time in other language departments too (or that it has occurred before or will occur in future). Therefore, quality management in this context is, to quite some extent, a matter of knowledge

[6] Excluding the English language department for the reasons mentioned above.

management, of sharing good practices and avoiding reinventing the wheel all the time and across the service.

The emergence of a matrix structure for quality management

In the context of an organizational restructuring that was carried out in DGT in 2012 and 2013, the concept of *matrix* was one of the novelties introduced (*Evaluation of DGT's Translation Management System after the 2013 Reorganisation*, DGT 2014a: 16–17). Since the restructuring, focus has been put more on tasks than on persons. Attempts have been made to create communities of practice to foster knowledge sharing among staff appointed to take responsibility for different processes: training correspondents, IT tool correspondents, corrigenda correspondents, freelance correspondents, terminologists and so on. Quality managers have been appointed in each language department as one-stop-shops for quality-related issues, and there are yearly work programmes for quality management at the language department level and also at the DGT level. Portfolio managers have been appointed to create and maintain contacts with the client DGs and to improve customer orientation. Administrative structures for knowledge sharing have been set up. All these instances try to apply matrix thinking as a complement to the traditional hierarchical administrative structure, so that relevant information is shared throughout the complex workflow to ensure efficiency and flexibility, as opposed to working in a linear production chain with closed compartments.

4 Recent developments

Over the last few years, the process of making quality-related processes and principles more explicit and creating quality management structures has given rise to what could be described as a corporate policy for quality management in translation.

4.1 DGT quality management framework

DGT's mission statement reads: 'Our core business is to provide the European Commission with high-quality translation and other language services. Our job is to respect the EU's multilingual character by making sure the Commission produces clearly written documents in all the official languages, and in others as well' (DGT 2016c: 3). Around 2013, attention was drawn to the fact that, while everybody agreed that we should produce high-quality translation, we had no definition of what we meant by 'high quality'. To clarify this, a steering document (DGT 2014b) was drafted, outlining the organization's policy with regard to quality and quality management.

This document, the *DGT Quality Management Framework*, defines key concepts and principles for quality management in DGT and outlines the structure of the quality management–related work, with its main actors and processes. It explicitly builds on the ISO 9000 definition of quality in service provision as compliance with specifications, defining quality as 'the degree to which a set of characteristics fulfils stated or implied needs and expectations' (ibid.: 1). Applied to the delivery of translation services, it defines *fitness-for-purpose* as the key quality concept at the operational level (cf. 'suitability for purpose' in the translation service provision standard): 'A translation is fit for purpose when it is suitable for its intended communicative use and satisfies the expressed or implied needs and expectations of our direct customers (requesting DGs), our partners in the other EU institutions, the end-users and any other relevant stakeholders' (ibid.: 1).

The Framework document explicitly builds on the EN 15038:2006 standard as regards the key processes involved. With this document, DGT officially adheres both to the total quality management principles it already explored in-depth with the CAF methodology in 2008 and to the quality concept of compliance with specifications expressed as fitness-for-purpose. This means that quality is not an absolute value, that it depends on needs and expectations, that it is situation and context dependent and that different actors and stakeholders might have different needs and expectations, which is relevant to bear in mind in a workflow context where there are a number of different stakeholders involved (Strandvik 2015: 142–5).

4.2 DGT translation quality guidelines

What *fitness-for-purpose* meant in practice was still not quite clear at the operational level. 'How do I change the way I translate just because I am now supposed to take into account the purpose of the text?' was a recurring question. To address this – to operationalize the fitness-for-purpose quality concept defined in the Framework – another set of guidelines was developed, in which the documents DGT translates were categorized according to their purpose and the quality-related risks involved: the *DGT Translation Quality Guidelines* (DGT 2015a).

Moreover, for workflow management purposes and to ensure cost-efficiency, there was also a need to ensure that the priorities were set for taking decisions on how much quality control is needed under normal circumstances and what to do when workload peaks will not allow for the usual treatment. In other words, the objective of these guidelines was to increase both quality and efficiency. This was done by

- codifying existing good practices;
- promoting work organization and working methods in line with the standards for professional translation service provision;
- providing workflow managers with guidance on how to carry out risk assessments and how to assign work as cost-efficiently as possible without incurring excessive risks.

The European Commission's institutional drafting guidelines for different text types (cf. 2.1 above) outline how the Commission wants its staff to communicate through different text types to achieve the institution's political objectives and fulfil the legal requirements. Since, in twenty-three languages out of twenty-four, translations constitute the interface between the EU and its Member States and citizens, these political objectives and legal requirements have to be achieved through translation.

The translation quality guidelines therefore draw attention to the fact that the Commission's drafting guidelines outline the Commission's communicative intent for all languages, not just the in-house 'original'. Consequently, with very few exceptions (incoming documents, procedural documents in non-authoritative language versions, etc.), texts should not read like translations in a negative sense but like originals. This bold statement, however, has to be nuanced with 'as far as possible', since twenty-three of the twenty-four language versions *are* translations and *do* depend on a source text. The question is *to what extent*.

To clarify the fitness-for-purpose principle and provide guidance on the concept of 'as far as possible', the guidelines establish a text categorization building on the purposes of the texts and the risks involved:

a. legal documents;
b. policy and administrative documents;
c. information for the public;
d. input for EU legislation, policy formulation and administration.

For each text category, recommendations are given as to which quality aspects should receive special attention and how to apply a safe amount of quality control building on the competence profiles of the persons – translator, reviser – involved (in line with a risk mitigation roster inspired by Prioux [2006] and Prioux and Rochard [2007]). Explicit references are made to the ISO 17100 standard as regards translation, revision and review and competence management.

4.3 DGT guidelines for evaluation of outsourced translations

The effective and projected increases in the use of outsourcing have meant that DGT has had to pay even closer attention to its practices in evaluating freelance translations. The system in place implies that every outsourced translation is evaluated on the basis of a revision of a 10 per cent sample of the text, which is marked on a five-mark scale. The contracts made with the external providers stipulate that translations must be revised before delivery and be usable as delivered. Nevertheless, until recently, the translations delivered rather systematically underwent not just a 10 per cent spot-check but a full in-house revision, despite the fact that over 90 per cent of the translations were marked 'good' or 'very good' (the two highest marks).

This was repeatedly identified as an issue. Either the additional revision was superfluous, as, in principle, translations marked 'good' or 'very good' should have been usable as delivered; or the marking practices were overly lenient, suggesting that evaluators perhaps tended to be compassionate towards their freelance colleagues and their working conditions or wanted to avoid the rather heavy procedures for the follow-up of bad marks. Another explanation was that most documents were actually fully revised in-house, independently of their evaluation marks, as a result of the risk assessment, that is, because they were politically sensitive documents, legislation creating rights and obligations, and/or important for the Commission's image.

To address this issue, a new outsourcing framework was adopted and new evaluation guidelines were issued. The *DGT Outsourcing Framework* (DGT 2016b) emphasizes communication and specifications, aiming to improve the quality of outsourced translations through better freelance briefs and feedback. The new evaluation guidelines, *DGT Guidelines for Evaluation of Outsourced Translation* (DGT 2016a), strengthen the link to the contractual quality requirements as stipulated in the tender specifications, that is, the link between evaluation and the quality levels the freelancers have agreed contractually to deliver. They also explicitly state that decisions on additional quality control (revision or review) beyond the 10 per cent sample should be taken on the basis of the translation quality guidelines, that is, based on a risk assessment taking into account the type and purpose of the document and the risks involved.

5 Future challenges

Against this background, which are the main challenges we are confronted with as regards DGT's quality assurance in future? In a context of ever-diminishing resources, it goes without saying that cost-efficiency is a must. We constantly have to re-think the way we work; we have to learn to do more with less, maybe even to cut some corners here and there. But the question is, where does it stop? Is there a breaking point at which professional working methods become so seriously undermined that we will no longer be in a position to ensure high-quality translation? What will happen if, for instance, as a result of ever-faster technological developments, translators will more and more often have to translate short and disconnected pieces of text with no proper context, and the translation segment becomes the dominant translation unit, instead of the text (cf. Drugan 2013); or if translators more often than not do not have enough time to read through their translations before revision and there is less and less time for revision, even when the risk assessment calls for it? What will happen if the organization becomes so lean that it is no longer possible to maintain any domain specialization? Will we have the competence required to assess quality?

How do we make the European Commission aware of the costs of not factoring in multilingualism sufficiently into the workflow processes? According to the study *Document Versioning and Its Impact on DGT* (DGT 2014c), 17.2 per cent of DGT's translation production in 2013 amounted to modifications of drafts sent for translation before a final version had been established (*versioning*). While nobody questions the need for modifications of drafts in the workflow of a political organization preparing draft legislation, spending a sixth of the resources on it amounts to a lot of money, when every euro counts. In the recent Communication to the Commission (European Commission, 2016), a call is made for better corporate discipline in that respect. However, recent figures show that, since then, the corporate discipline has worsened, and versioning and longer documents have continued increasing.

It is evident that DGT will have to outsource more in the future. But how much can we outsource? Is there a tipping point after which the European Commission will no longer be in control of its communication and legislative drafting, because it no longer has the in-house competence to assess and ensure quality? Does it make a difference if legislation is no longer translated by dedicated in-house staff but by commercial agents following procurement logic under procurement conditions? Is there a risk that a strict application of the procurement principles to institutional translation and multilingual law-making will lead to a situation where the translation work is de-professionalized, as we have seen in other areas, for instance, in relation to the implementation of Directive 2010/64/EU (Buckingham 2014; Professional Interpreters for Justice 2014; APTIJ 2016a,b) or in relation to Finnish audiovisual translation (Abdallah 2012)? If there is such a risk, what are the political and legal consequences?

These questions summarize the quality challenges we face for the future. The way we reply to these questions will determine the resulting organization of our work. And the way we reply depends on our understanding of some conceptual issues: What kind of translation products do the Commission and the EU need in terms of quality and reliability? What is the nature of the work of institutional translators? Is translation intellectual craftsmanship or can it be seen – and treated – as an industrial process?

6 Conclusions

The quality journey described above shows how a quality management system has been put in place, building on principles of modern administration and applying system and matrix thinking, international standards for translation service provision and a functionalist approach to translation. In today's public administration, the cost reduction concerns are real, they are omnipresent and they are here to stay. However, at least for the time being, everybody would seem to agree that cost-efficiency without quality is a no-go when it comes to institutional translation and multilingual law-making for legal, political and reputational reasons. Despite all the technical progress and all the expectations placed on machine translation to date, for the text types DGT translates, human intellectual input is imperatively needed in the process.

At a time when the machine-translation community and industry in general struggle to get away from an overly simplistic quality approach with one-size-fits-all models of quality (see e.g. TAUS 2012), we should not streamline and automate our workflow processes to an extent that distorts working methods specific to the types of texts we translate. If we do, we might soon no longer be able to assess quality.

All in all, in the spirit of the functionalist approach adopted in line with the international standards for translation service provision, to meet the challenges outlined above, the European Commission needs to address the following key questions: What is the European Commission trying to achieve with its texts and their translations? What kind of translated texts does it need to achieve these goals? How can such texts be produced reliably and sustainably? What level of quality is needed for the various translation products, and through what kind of quality assurance procedures and workflow processes can such quality be ensured? What are the risks for the Commission if translation quality cannot be ensured and maintained?

Since the translation industry and the translation profession at large are confronted with the same challenges, useful insights can be provided by the international standards on translation service provision (EN 15038, ISO 17100, ASTM F2575, ISO TC 11669) and the ongoing work on the standardization of translation quality assessment that takes place in ISO, ASTM, TAUS and the EU-funded QT21 project with multidimensional quality metrics (MQM). Building on the accumulated knowledge in the field will help us avoid reinventing the wheel and ensure that the challenges are addressed in an efficient, effective and proportionate manner.

The international standards outline in detail translator and reviser competence requirements and principles for competence management, for work organization, for translation and revision and for project management and communication between the different actors involved. MQM, in turn, sets the foundations for a common approach to quality assessment. Working according to the principles of professional translation service provision is likely to be the best guarantee to ensure reliability and productivity over time and in a sustainable way. Can you even claim to be professional if you do not work according to the standards of the profession?

5

The Skills Required to Achieve Quality in Institutional Translation: The Views of EU and UN Translators and Revisers

Anne Lafeber

1 Identifying the skills most required

In this chapter, we look at the skills that are most important in one particular type of institutional translation – translation at international organizations (IOs) – specifically at two of the largest IOs and largest employers of translators, the United Nations (UN) and the European Union (EU). A method for identifying empirically the relative importance of skills for IO translation was devised as part of a broader investigation into recruitment test design conducted between 2010 and 2013. A survey consisting of two questionnaires was circulated among in-house translators and revisers at over 20 IOs with the support of IAMLADP.[1] One questionnaire was on the impact of forty skills on quality and the other on the scarcity of those same skills among new recruits.

The basis for the list of skills presented in the questionnaires was a review of the scholarly literature on IO translation available at the time, essentially works produced by EU translation service insiders such as Wagner, Bech and Martínez (2002); by outsiders who had managed to gain some access to IOs, such as Koskinen (2000 and 2008); and by those working, if not with IOs, then with large institutions: Mossop from the Canadian Government's Translation Bureau (1988) and Williams (1989), who had

[1] International Annual Meeting on Language Arrangements Documentation and Publications (www.iamladp.org). The exact number of organizations is difficult to determine as the specificity of answers varied, but they included European Bank for Reconstruction and Development, Economic Commission for Africa, Economic Commission for Latin America and the Caribbean, Economic and Social Commission for Western Asia, European Commission, European Committee of the Regions, European Economic and Social Committee, European Patent Office, Food and Agriculture Organization, International Civil Aviation Organization, International Committee of the Red Cross, Inter-American Development Bank, International Fund for Agricultural Development, Inter-American Investment Corporation, International Labour Organization, International Maritime Organization, International Monetary Fund, International Tribunal for the Law of the Sea, International Telecommunication Union, North Atlantic Treaty Organization, Organization of American States, Latin American Economic System, United Nations Headquarters, United Nations Offices at Geneva, Nairobi and Vienna, World Bank and World Trade Organization.

worked with the same Bureau as a consultant. To supplement the scholarly literature, IO publications and statements were also examined (e.g. EMT Expert Group 2009; Hindle 1984; Sekel 2008; Verleysen 2010).

The survey findings were then correlated using the principles of qualitative risk analysis on the premise that skills are important to IO translation services in two ways: not just in terms of their impact on the quality of the product (as they are in any context), but also in terms of their impact on the revision workload (the more scarce they are among new translators, the more revision work they generate).[2] Having translations revised by other, usually more experienced, translators is standard practice in institutional translation. Under the risk-assessment policy of the 'fit-for-purpose approach' (see Chapter 4) to revision at the European Commission, for example, 85 per cent of translations are revised; at the UN Secretariat, all translations are revised, unless they are done by internally officially recognized 'self-revising translators' or 'revisers'.[3] Revision is considered the best instrument of quality assurance, but it is also a major expense. In the IO context, therefore, the most important skills are those that have both a direct positive impact on quality and a direct negative impact on the revision burden. Impact and abundance do not necessarily go hand in hand, however; indeed, the survey findings showed that not all high-impact skills are equally easy to find among new recruits. The ability to ensure the coherence of the target text and knowledge of the source language, for example, were both awarded high-impact ratings (4.75 on the five-point scale), but the former was reported as being far more scarce among new recruits than the latter (mean scarcity ratings of 3.19 and 2.78, respectively, on the five-point scale).[4]

2 The skills required at the EU and the UN[5]

The survey also showed that the relative importance of skills varies from one organization to another. Plotting the ratings awarded in the two questionnaires on a scatter chart produces a skills profile, such as those presented in Figures 5.1a and b, which show the impact and scarcity ratings awarded by in-house language staff at the EU and the UN, the two largest organizational groups in the survey. The most important skills (the most oft-lacking, high-impact skills) are those towards the top right of each figure. Not only does their presence have the most impact on quality;

2 For a detailed description of the methodology, see Lafeber (2013: 47–106).

3 Descriptions of EU working and training arrangements were obtained from the survey responses and through consultations with colleagues at the European Commission in June 2016. Descriptions of those of the UN are based on the author's own experience. The content of this chapter was reviewed by translation service managers at both the EU and the UN for accuracy, but the views expressed are the author's and do not necessarily reflect the views of the UN, and the observations, analysis, inferences and conclusions are entirely the author's own.

4 For a detailed report of the findings for IOs in general, see Lafeber (2012).

5 The ways in which respondents identified the organizations they belong to (some referred to the umbrella organization, others to the specific body) and confidentiality considerations precluded breaking down the survey population by more than broad organization group. The majority of those responding for the EU were from the European Commission, and the vast majority of those responding for the UN were from the UN Secretariat.

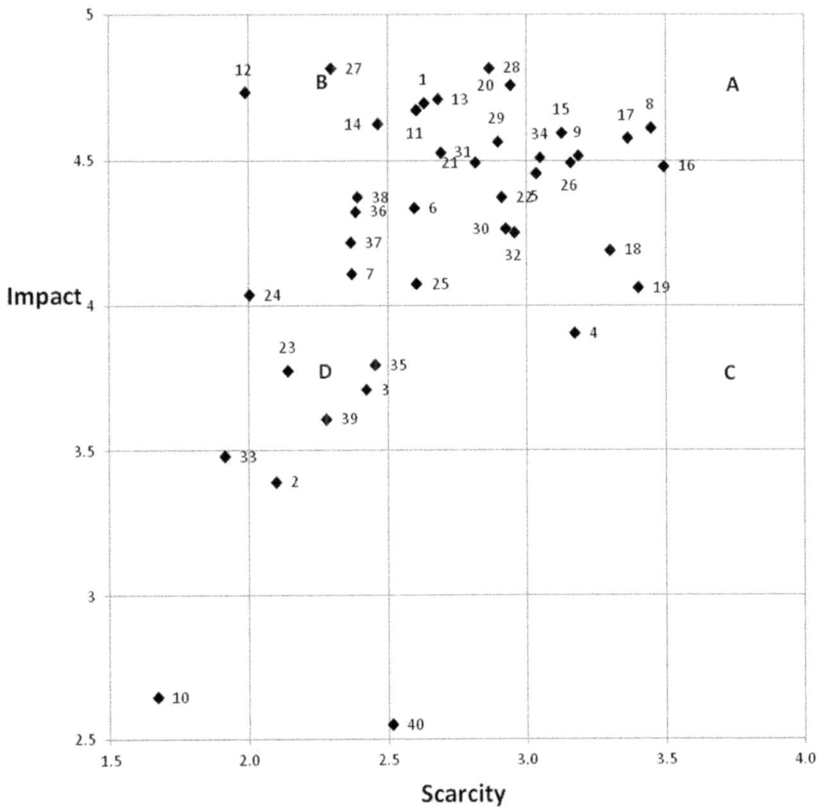

Figure 5.1a Skills by impact on quality and by scarcity among new recruits at the EU.*

*The points in the figures reflect mean impact ratings awarded to a list of forty skills by eighty-three and sixty-five translators of the EU and UN translation services and the mean scarcity ratings awarded by sixty-eight and eighty-two revisers from those same services, respectively.

their absence also generates the most revision work. They are therefore top training and recruitment priorities. We will refer to these as '*A*' skills.

The other important skills for achieving quality are those towards the top left (near the *B* in the figure), the high-impact but less scarce skills: notably, knowledge of the source language, ensuring the completeness of the target text and mastery of grammar, punctuation and spelling. These are the basic comprehension and drafting skills involved in all translation work and are routinely assessed in recruitment tests, which is why they are seldom found lacking among new recruits. To uphold their quality standards and maximize productivity, institutions must continue to test as rigorously as they do at present for these *B* skills, while also trying to find or develop the *A* skills. The *C* skills towards the lower right have less impact on quality, but their absence generates revision work. They are particularly important for the institution if the revision burden is an issue. The *D* skills towards the lower left are the lowest

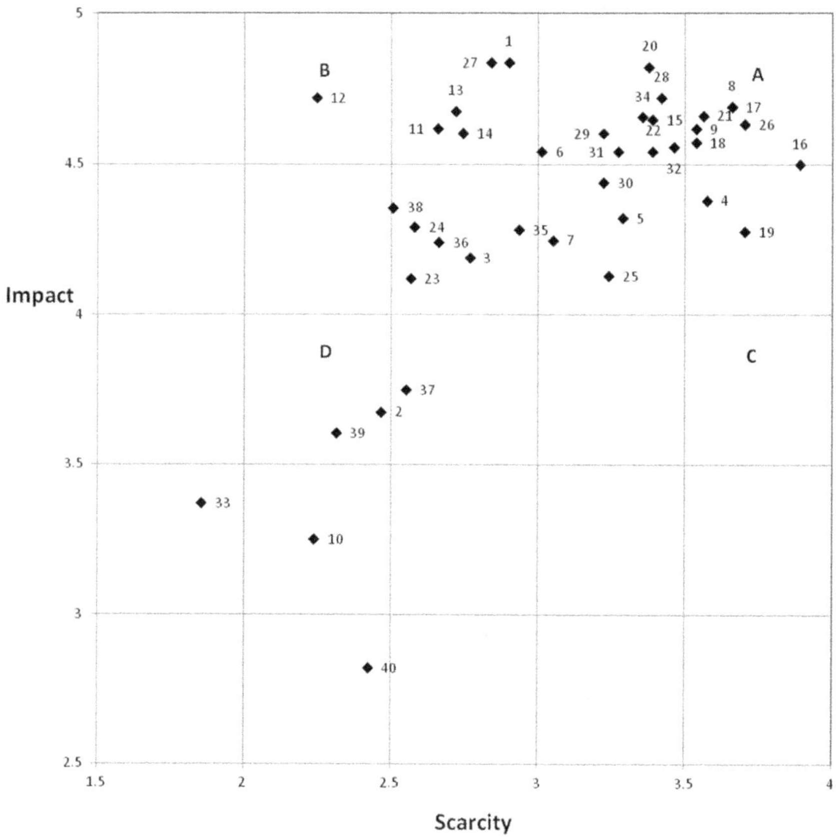

Figure 5.1b Skills by impact on quality and by scarcity among new recruits at the UN.

recruitment and training priorities, having relatively less impact on quality and rarely being found lacking.

It should be noted that skills other than the forty presented for rating in the survey were reported by some respondents as being relatively important. These included interpersonal skills (e.g. team work, receptiveness to feedback, ability to work with authors) or skills that are difficult to assess in recruitment testing (e.g. general knowledge, organization and time management). They are not included in this analysis. Further research is required to see where these skills fit into the ideal candidate profile.

What is immediately striking is that the EU and UN profiles, and hence the EU and UN training and recruitment priorities, clearly differ. When the cut-off points of 3 for scarcity and 4.5 for impact are applied to identify the *A* skills,[6] the number of

[6] Cut-off points chosen on the basis that an impact of 4.5 or over can reasonably be considered high, and a scarcity rating of 3 or more suggests the skill is at least more often than not lacking. The analysis thus treats those close to the cut-off scores in the same way as those that are major outliers. This would not be done if the profiles were being used to prioritize skills for training or recruitment purposes. Strict cut-offs are nevertheless useful for the purposes of comparison here.

such skills is far lower for the EU than for the UN, as shown in Figures 5.2a and b and summarized in Table 5.1.

Key to figures:

Knowledge of

1. the source language (vocabulary, expressions, rhetorical devices);
2. the different varieties of the source language;
3. the source-language culture(s) (history, geography, economic and political situation, customs, value-laden concepts, sensitive issues, etc.);
4. the subject (technical knowledge, e.g. of economics, international law, science, technology);
5. the organization and how it works.

The ability to

6. understand complex topics;
7. master new subjects quickly (i.e. gain more than a layperson's knowledge);
8. work out the meaning of obscure passages in the source text;
9. detect inconsistencies, contradictions, nonsense, unintended ambiguities, misleading headings, etc. in the source text;
10. detect mathematical errors in the source text;
11. exploit an extensive vocabulary in the target language.

Knowledge of

12. spelling rules in the target language;
13. the finer points of grammar of the target language;
14. punctuation rules in the target language.

The ability to

15. produce idiomatic (natural-sounding) language in the target text;
16. produce translations that flow smoothly even when the source text does not;
17. select and combine words in the target language to capture the exact and detailed meanings (nuances) of the source text;
18. recast sentences in the target language (to say the same thing in different ways);
19. produce an elegantly written target text regardless of how elegantly written the source text is;
20. convey the source-text message clearly;
21. convey the intended effect of the source text;
22. achieve the appropriate tone and register in the target text.

Knowledge of

23. target-language varieties;
24. target-language cultures (knowledge of history, geography, economic and political situation, customs, traditions, belief systems, value-laden concepts, sensitive issues, etc.).

The ability to

25. tailor the language of the target text to the readers' needs;
26. adhere to in-house style conventions;
27. ensure the completeness of the target text (i.e. no unwarranted omissions);
28. ensure the coherence of the target text (e.g. consistent terminology use, no contradictions, logical connections of ideas);
29. track down sources of information to check facts;
30. track down sources to obtain a better grasp of the thematic aspects of a text (understand the topic);
31. mine reference material for accepted phrasing and terminology (those used by the organization or in a specialized field);
32. judge the reliability of information sources;
33. type accurately and fast;
34. maintain quality even when translating under time pressure;
35. justify translation decisions and explain translation problems posed by the source text (e.g. to authors, users or revisers);
36. follow complicated instructions about what needs to be done with a text (additions that need translating, parts that need relocating, patching together, revising against new versions, etc.);
37. make effective use of translation memory software;
38. make effective use of electronic terminology tools;
39. work with more than basic Word functions (formatting, macros, track changes, tables, autocorrect, etc.);
40. work with Excel documents and/or PowerPoint presentations.

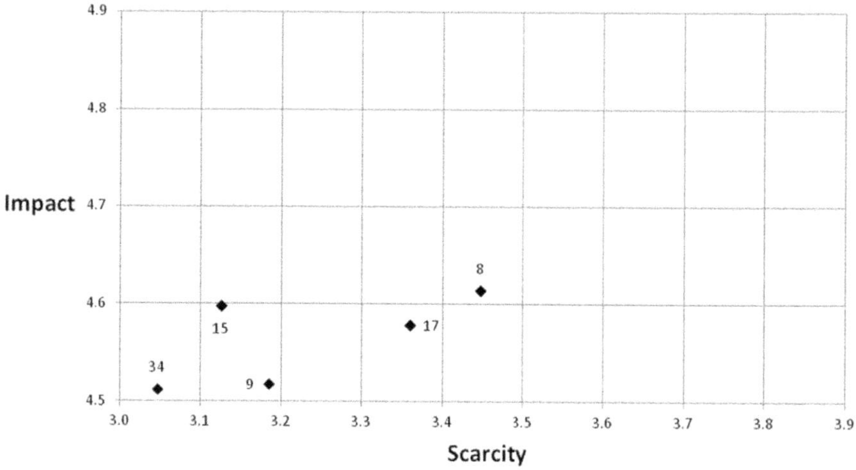

Figure 5.2a Training and recruitment priorities: the high-impact skills often lacking among new recruits at the EU.*

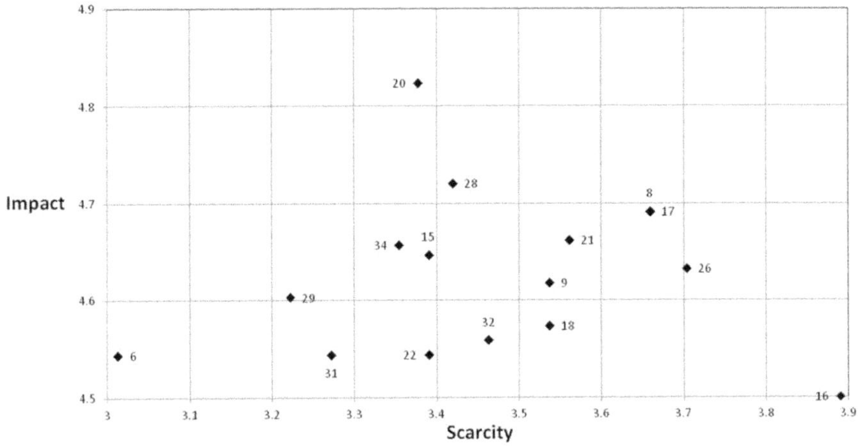

Figure 5.2b Training and recruitment priorities: the high-impact skills often lacking among new recruits at the UN.*

*For a key to numbers used in the figures, see the key for Figures 5.1a and b.

Another point to note is that the views of translators and revisers on the impact of skills differ slightly within the same organization group. For example, if only the revisers' views are considered in drawing up the UN profile instead of theirs and those of the translators together, then the abilities to understand complex topics, achieve the right tone and register, adhere to in-house style conventions and mine reference documents for past usage are no longer *A* skills, while subject knowledge is. This suggests that UN revisers do not think that adhering to style guidelines and mining reference documents have as much impact as UN translators do. It could be that translators, who possibly have yet to master in-house conventions, still spend so much time wading through manuals and reference material that they feel it is an important part of their work, while revisers see it as less important since they have internalized usage rules and spend less time consulting the corresponding reference manuals. Such differing perspectives could also explain why translators rated being able to understand complex subjects highly and revisers did not. With the benefit of experience, revisers see the topics covered not as complex but as requiring specialized knowledge, something they report as (understandably) lacking among new translators. If only translators' opinions are taken into account at the UN, for example, subject knowledge would be replaced as an A item with the ability to track down sources to understand the topic – two sides, in effect, of the same coin. Revisers see a need for specialized knowledge; translators see a need for the ability to find the knowledge required for a particular translation. Again, it may be that translators are more focused on the process, being, as it were, in the thick of it, while the revisers view needs from a loftier end-product perspective. This is mere speculation, however, and the reasons for the differing views require further investigation. For the purposes of this analysis, the opinions of revisers and translators are considered equally valid and both factored into the impact ratings.

Table 5.1 EU and UN: '*A*' (high-impact, oft-lacking) skills, grouped by type

Analytical skills	• Understand complex topics (6)* • Work out the meaning of obscure passages in the source text (8)** • Detect inconsistencies, contradictions, nonsense, unintended ambiguities, misleading headings, etc. in the source text (9)**
Drafting skills	• Ensure the coherence of the target text (e.g. consistent terminology use, no contradictions, logical connections of ideas) (28)* • Produce idiomatic (natural-sounding) language in the target text (15)** • Produce translations that flow smoothly even when the source text does not (16)* • Select and combine words in the target language to capture the exact and detailed meanings (nuances) of the source text (17)** • Recast sentences in the target language (to say the same thing in different ways) (18)* • Convey the source-text message clearly (20)* • Convey the intended effects of the source text (21)* • Achieve the appropriate tone and register in the target text (22)* • Adhere to in-house style conventions (26)*
Research skills	• Track down sources of information to check facts (29)* • Mine reference material for accepted phrasing and terminology (those used by the organization or in a specialized field) (31)* • Judge the reliability of information sources (32)*
Other skills	• Maintain quality even when translating under time pressure (34)**

Notes:
* Indicates *A* skills for the UN only.
** Indicates *A* skills for both EU and UN.

Numbers in parenthesis refer to item numbers used in Figures 5.1a, 5.1b, 5.2a and 5.2b. Full descriptions can be found in the corresponding key.

All the skills listed in Table 5.1 have a particular relevance in the context of IO translation; we will examine each one, grouping them for convenience into analytical, drafting, research and other skills.

3 Key skills for IO translation by type

3.1 Analytical skills

The constant evolution of the international agenda and the intricacies of intergovernmental processes and multilateral negotiations call for a superior ability among IO translators to understand complex topics. Meanwhile, the occasionally opaque and ambiguous language and the rhetoric of international diplomacy and treaties (an issue raised in Prieto Ramos 2014a) could explain the high ratings awarded to the ability to work out obscure passages in the source text. As the former chief of the United Nations English Translation Service, Stephen Sekel, points out, in institutional translation,

> words have a significance beyond their obvious meanings … there is always a political dimension in the work … translators … must always be aware of, and

sensitive to, the positions of the parties to a negotiation, and must ensure that, to the extent possible, all translated versions of a text fully and accurately reflect the meaning and intent of the author or authors. (Sekel 2008: 1)

As noted by Poscher (2012), addressing vague wording is a delicate issue that requires translators to tackle questions of interpretation, not only from a linguistic perspective but also as persons with solid understanding of the context and implications of the text content (Harvey 2002).

More often than not, however, it would seem that the obscurity of passages in the source text is the result of poor writing. The fact that texts are often drafted not only by non-native speakers, but also in haste by multiple authors, some chosen more for their technical expertise than their drafting skills, and then rewritten several times (as noted by Wagner et al. 2002: 70 and Frame 2005: 21–4), calls for another key analytical skill: the ability to detect inconsistencies, nonsense, unintended ambiguities, misleading headings, etc. in the source text. The often poor linguistic quality of the source texts and the challenges they pose prompted numerous unsolicited comments from both EU and UN respondents in the survey. 'What do you do with documents that are incomprehensible because they are drafted by people whose mother tongue is not English!' groaned a French translator at the UN, where the obligation to submit documents in one of only at most six official languages results in many being drafted in English by non-native speakers.

The same situation is apparently common at the EU, where a Portuguese reviser at the Council of the European Union, for example, highlighted the need to be able 'to understand, navigate through and decode the various types of "pidgin" English, which are the result of deficient knowledge of the language or of strong mother tongue interference'. This new type of English is becoming more and more usual within IOs, especially in the EU, due to its very rapid enlargements. According to Frame, an EU Court of Justice lawyer-linguist, writing in 2005, 'linguistic peculiarities' in EU legislative texts are attributable not only to non-native drafters but also to some native speakers of English and to an overreliance on technical experts (2005: 22). Indeed, despite efforts to work with and support author departments, the quality of source texts is an ongoing issue. This means that IO translators need to have the judgment to determine whether a lack of clarity or awkward syntax, for example, is deliberate and politically motivated or a stylistic slip. As noted by a Finnish translator at the Committee of the Regions of the EU, a key component of the skill-set is 'the ability to pinpoint unclear passages'. Having spotted vague wording, the next step is to categorize and assess the seriousness of the ambiguity and decide on which strategy to adopt for translation (Prieto Ramos 2011: 11).

3.2 Drafting skills

The drafting skills listed in Table 5.1 are essential in institutional translation for two equally important reasons: (i) to facilitate high-profile, high-stakes communication; and (ii) to protect the institution's reputation. It is not just a matter of achieving the most detailed level of accuracy by capturing every nuance and emphasis (an *A* skill at both the EU and the UN), as well as the intended effect, but also of conveying the message clearly, maximizing readability (paying attention to idiomaticity and flow, recasting sentences as necessary) and ensuring coherence. All this must be done regardless of the quality of the source text.

Mossop observes that 'experienced translators tend to produce translations whose writing quality is much superior to that of the source text. To accomplish this they engage in what might be called mental stylistic editing and structure/content editing *while they translate*' (2001: 33) (italics in the original). IO translators routinely do this because IOs communicate within themselves and with the world through their translations; they are both 'translating institutions', inasmuch as they produce textual translations, and 'translated institutions' because their ideology is enshrined, captured and conveyed through their translations (Koskinen 2008: 27). High standards of excellence, quality, professionalism and reliability are expected in all aspects of their work, including their translations. This has several implications for the drafting of their translations.

IO translators, like translators in other fields, have to resolve, on a daily basis, the conflict between the need for highest level of accuracy and faithfulness to the source text on the one hand and the need for natural-sounding, well-written target texts on the other. Unlike translators in other fields, however, IO translators do this not just to produce highly readable translations that accurately convey the meaning of the original; they do this also to avoid 'Chinese-whispers-like' distortions occurring further down the line. At the UN, for example, translations (especially English ones) often serve as the source texts for the translations into the other languages. The need to uphold the organization's reputation, meanwhile, makes also achieving the right tone and register and adhering to in-house usage rules of paramount importance. Since translations become official records of the organization's activities and communications, not only excellent writing but also political correctness, consistency and standardization are essential.

3.3 Research skills

The pursuit of consistency and standardization underpins the presence of the research skills in Table 5.1. The ability to track down and judge the reliability of information sources refers not only to internet searches, as in any translation context, but also to finding approved language and figuring out when to trust what the translation memory software churns out. 'It is quite common in many institutional settings to have 'document chains' in the sense that each document is anticipated for (or regulated) in previous documents, and it in turn paves the way for new documents taking the issue further' (Koskinen 2008: 125). Each translation sets a precedent for future language use; hence the insistence on quality and revision, and hence the presence of being good at mining reference material in Table 5.1.

Often, in-house translations, which will have been through the translation service's revision process, are considered superior sources of accepted terminology and phraseology, while source texts, whether drafted in-house or not, are generally considered less reliable. Views on the reliability of translations done by external translators vary according to the degree to which they are subject to in-house revision and the topic covered by the text. Translations are sometimes outsourced deliberately to experts in highly technical subjects, in which case their specialized knowledge is appreciated and tapped.

3.4 Other skills

The pressure on translation services at IOs to improve their productivity or handle ever-increasing workloads calls for translators who can work fast without sacrificing the high quality demanded by the import of diplomatic communication and the archival function of the translations that they produce; hence the high-impact rating awarded to the ability to translate under time pressure. That new recruits lack this ability is unsurprising, given that the documents, tools and methods are unfamiliar to them. Speed in translation is developed with practice and confidence.

4 Why the difference between the EU and UN list of *A* skills?

All the skills listed in Table 5.1 have a particularly significant role to play in achieving quality in the context of institutional translation, but why are there so many more in the category *A* list for the UN than in the list for the EU? Statistical analysis shows that this is overwhelmingly due to differences in the reported scarcity of these skills among new recruits, a situation that generates revision work. In only one case, the 'ability to recast sentences' was category *A* status at the UN and not at the EU due to a statistically significant difference in impact rating (4.55 at the UN vs. 4.18 at the EU).[7] That difference is possibly due to the language combinations of the respondents. Translating from and into Arabic, Chinese and Russian, which, among the sample population, are solely used at the UN, probably requires far more reformulation, for example, than translating from French into Spanish. The high proportion (60 per cent) of legal translation at the EU may also be a factor, given the tendency or need to respect precedent and accepted phraseology.

In the remaining ten cases, category *A* status in the UN but not in the EU skills profile was due to a statistically significant higher scarcity rating. In fact, not only for these ten, but also for another five skills as well (i.e. fifteen of the forty skills rated in the survey and all the items from subject knowledge to the right in Figure 5.3), the UN scarcity rating was statistically significantly higher than that of the EU. And, overall, twice as many skills and knowledge types were reported as at least sometimes lacking (scarcity ratings of 3 or more) among new recruits at the UN (twenty-two items) than at the EU (eleven items). Why? A number of possible factors are considered below.

7 Significant differences reported in this chapter were calculated using t-tests for a confidence level of 95 per cent.

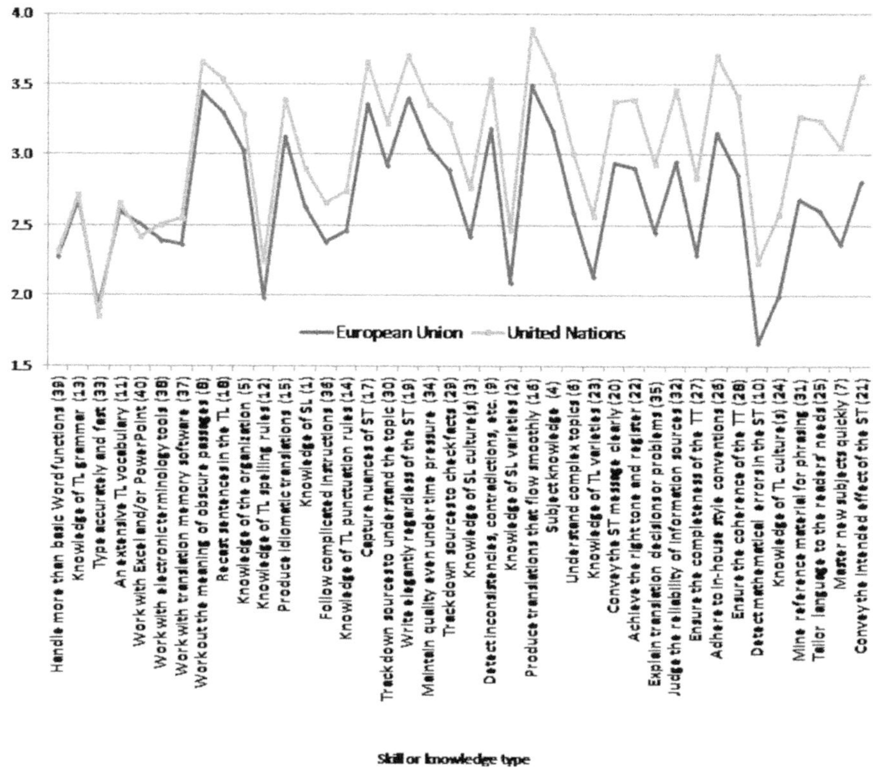

Figure 5.3 EU and UN: average frequency with which selected skills are found lacking among new recruits (rated on a scale of 1–5, where 1= almost never and 5= almost always).*

*Full definition of skills is provided in the key to Figures 5.1a, 5.1b, 5.2a and 5.2b.

Factor 1: Differences in revision practices and arrangements. Revision is about bringing translations up to standard, and differing notions of quality could be behind the difference in scarcity ratings awarded by EU and UN revisers. The idea that UN revisers are generally fussier is supported by the fact that they rated thirty-five of the forty skills presented in the questionnaire as more frequently absent among new recruits than their EU counterparts. EU revisers might simply be more tolerant of slips in style, tone, register, consistency and coherence. This is likely to be the case under the fit-for-purpose policy adopted by the European Commission, for example, especially for certain types of documents. This could explain the discrepancies in the scarcity ratings for drafting skills in particular. Rather than divergent quality standards, however, the general tendency to find new recruits lacking in the skills required probably reflects the radically different ways in which the EU and the UN view and organize revision and the different type of relationship that is established between translator and reviser as a result.

At the European Commission, for example, translation staff are expected to both translate and revise from the outset. Task assignment is based on risk assessment, taking into account the skills profiles of available staff (e.g. experience, domain competence, text-type competence, etc.). So typically, new recruits either revise the work of very experienced translators (to learn from them as well) or start by revising low-risk documents. At the UN, with the exception of the smaller translation services in certain UN bodies, translators are almost invariably not asked to revise until they have been working for the service for several years, have familiarized themselves thoroughly with in-house usage rules and the range of document types translated by the service and have proven their competence as translators of UN documents. In many cases, even if translators have achieved the necessary level of familiarity and competence, they are not given revision work until they are promoted to the rank of 'self-revising translator', 'reviser' and ultimately 'senior reviser', which occurs only as and when these posts become available. And then they have to compete with their peers for the promotion.

As explained by colleagues at the European Commission (see footnote 3): 'The translator is generally deemed responsible for the finished product – that is, the translation that is sent back to the requester. The reviser's role is essentially advisory: he/she suggests changes, (justifying them if they are challenged by the translator) but leaves it to the translator to decide whether or not to accept them and incorporate them into the translation.' This arrangement was adopted mainly to maximize productivity: 'The translator is the person who digs most deeply into the text and who has the final say. If revisers were to assume responsibility (for the final quality of the translation) and have the final say, they would need to dig as deeply into the texts as the translator. That would not be cost-efficient.' Another factor, according to a former European Commission translator, was the sudden incorporation of new languages that accompanied the enlargements of the EU, which made hierarchical structures for some combinations, at least temporarily, difficult to establish. Translators of these languages had to be accountable for the translations since there were no revisers.

The situation is very different at the UN, where the number of languages has remained small and stable and where revisers are held responsible for the quality of the final output. The reviser's role is to check the translation and make it publication ready, and the reviser has the final word. The translation may be sent back to the translator with comments on the relative importance of the changes made, but this is essentially for training purposes and often happens after the translation has been passed on for publication. This could explain the generally higher scarcity ratings awarded by UN revisers to the skills of new recruits. UN revisers are seasoned veterans, removed from the translators by experience, function and rank. They judge the work of subordinates to whom they are officially recognized as being superior in terms of competence. This is likely to incline them to rate more harshly the problems that translators have applying skills that now come easily to them after years of service (see observations on differences between translators' and revisers' perspectives in Section 2).

In addition, UN revisers revise, if not exclusively, far more than they translate. At the EU, by contrast, the scarcity ratings of the skills of new recruits were awarded by colleagues who have the same function and post and who both translate and revise. Differences in position on the pay scale are mostly due to years of service. Attitudes in non-competitive peer-like relationships are probably likely to be more generous, and less constant exposure to the shortcomings of new recruits is likely to result in lower reported incidences of such shortcomings.

The more vertical structure and the correctional nature of revision at the UN and the more horizontal structure and advisory nature of revision at the EU, together with the different degree of exposure to the work of new recruits, could thus explain the difference between the overall satisfaction of UN and EU revisers with new recruits. New recruits at the UN might not generally lack skills more than their EU counterparts do; those who revise them just perceive them as being more frequently lacking due to the experience and functional gap between reviser and translator, the greater proportion of time UN revisers spend revising and, possibly, the fit-for-purpose policy adopted by some EU bodies. However, lowering the cut-off point for scarce/not scarce for the EU (e.g. from 3 to 2.5 on the five-point scale) does not result in the same skills appearing on the A list for both institutions. There are clearly other factors at play as well.

Factor 2: Differences in the effectiveness of recruitment mechanisms. The overall higher level of satisfaction with new recruits among EU revisers might, of course, reflect more effective selection procedures. Both the EU and the UN organize competitive recruitment tests: Could the EU be more successful at finding translators that more closely meet its standards? Or are UN standards and expectations at the time of recruitment higher and hence their disappointment greater? Neither would seem to be the case. A look at the 'Translator profile' posted on the European Commission website,[8] for example, and the requirements listed in the announcements of the examinations for UN translators[9] reveal strikingly similar expectations: superior mastery of mother tongue/main language, excellent knowledge of other relevant languages, thematic knowledge, openness to technology and willingness to learn, and no previous work experience is required. And consultations with UN staff reveal no complaints about the calibre of the new translators recruited through the UN Language Competitive Examinations, only that the examination process does not find more of them.[10] Of course, expectations of the examinations' capacity to find candidates with the *A* skills may be low. As noted earlier, it is the *B* skills that are routinely assessed in recruitment; the analytical and research skills, as well as some of the drafting skills on the UN *A* list (e.g. consistency, coherence, achieving the right tone, register and intended effect) are difficult to assess thoroughly in an examination context.

Factor 3: Differences in degree of specialization. Another, more likely, factor behind the different views of new recruits is the slightly greater specialization of EU translators, especially at the Commission, which has more in-house translators than the other EU bodies. Domain specialization is an effective quality-assurance tool. Working on similar document types or ones on similar topics enables new recruits to be brought up to speed more quickly. Not only is the bulk of the Commission's translation work legislation; traditionally, the Commission has also had a strong subject-matter specialization, with each translator specializing in a few policy areas. And even though its translators today

8 http://ec.europa.eu/dgs/translation/workwithus/staff/profile/index_en.htm (last accessed August 2016).

9 For a recent example: https://careers.un.org/lbw/jobdetail.aspx?id=57602 (last accessed August 2016).

10 Results of a survey of twenty-two chiefs of translation services conducted by the author at UN Headquarters and the three main UN duty stations in May 2015.

cover more policy areas than those in the past, under the risk assessment guidelines, the domain competence profile of translators is to be taken into consideration in translation task assignment. At the UN, subject specialization has never been systematic or structural, and the organization's mobility policy, which encourages movement between duty stations that each handle very different topics and document types, works against it. There are, of course, translators who, by virtue of extended experience in a given subject or duty station, end up as the de facto specialists in that area, and some translation managers encourage this, but it is not established practice.

Factor 4: Differences in induction training. New recruits at the EU are also possibly brought up to speed more quickly thanks to more intense and structured induction training. There is a 'newcomer's package' and an explicit 'path for newcomers'; professional development includes training in law, economics and science, and requesters of translations are increasingly systematically invited to give presentations to translators to clarify the policy issues and political background involved. Induction includes formal training as soon as possible after arrival in the use of CAT tools, terminology databases, etc., and guidance on how to optimize internet searches and consult EU legislation online (essential for most translation assignments). This could explain why problems adhering to in-house style, tracking down sources and mining reference documents for standard phrasing and terminology are less commonly seen by EU revisers among their new translators. There is no standard induction programme for new translators at the UN; new recruits generally familiarize themselves with the subject matter and the tools and procedures used as they go along, receiving guidance and feedback for each assignment from more experienced colleagues. Some translation services have a mentoring scheme, but this is not the case across the board, and there is no regular or systematic training in UN subjects for translators. The skills and knowledge are acquired, but possibly not as quickly as at the EU, where greater domain specialization makes arranging such training easier and more cost-effective. These differences could in part explain the greater frequency with which deficiencies in the research, drafting and analytical skills specific to IO translation listed in Table 5.1 are apparent among new UN recruits.

Factor 5: Differences in working methods. The gaps in the scarcity ratings between the two organizations could also reflect fundamental differences in their working arrangements. The more often particular skills are needed, the more often their absence will be noticeable in the work produced by new recruits. Questions on the responsibilities of translators within the document production chain and the provision of background material were included in the survey to contextualize the findings on the relative importance of the components of the skill-set. The supposition was that if translators are not responsible for fact checking, for example, then research skills will be less important; or if the organization has an army of editors, then translators will not have to detect inconsistencies or nonsense in the source text.

The results clearly showed the influence of working arrangements on the skills required. A direct (negative) correlation was found, for example, between how often revision work was attributed to a lack of ability to work out the meaning of obscure passages (Pearson correlation coefficient is 0.974) and to detect inconsistencies, contradictions, nonsense, etc. (Pearson correlation coefficient is 0.982) and the frequency with which source texts are edited. Similarly, the frequency with which poor research skills account for revision work was found to vary in relation to the provision of reference material. They all affect the volume of revision work to the greatest extent under the two extreme situations: when no reference material is provided, which means that the research is left to the translators; and when translators work with reference material all the time. This shows how the scarcity ratings reflect both how much and how often a skill is required.

Since both the EU and the UN awarded statistically similar high scarcity ratings to the ability to work out the meaning of obscure passages and the ability to detect inconsistencies, contradictions, nonsense, etc., it would seem that translators and revisers at both organizations are spending an equal proportion of time compensating for poor-quality source texts. The fact that the scarcity ratings for mining reference material and judging the reliability of sources are statistically higher in the UN than in the EU, meanwhile, suggests that (i) either background documents are provided more often or more effectively at the EU or (ii) working with reference material is more often part of the job in the UN.

Consultations with EU colleagues in 2016 suggest that it could be a combination of both these factors. At the European Commission, for example, 'requesters of translations ... are generally conscientious about indicating background documents and other reference materials when submitting a request'. Moreover, translations have been produced with the organization's formidable memories and databases since the early 2000s, while the UN started working with translation memory tools far more recently (and far more extensively since the survey was conducted in 2010).[11] Another consideration is that a sizeable portion of UN translators' work is to translate reports and opinions submitted by 193 Member States on a multitude of subjects. Background documents in such cases are rarely provided, and translators can end up spending copious amounts of time fact checking and hence also judging the reliability of resources.

The differences between the ranking of the skills required to achieve quality at the EU and the UN would thus seem to be the result of a combination of factors. The more hierarchical structure of the translation services at the UN and the differences in revision practices and specialization between the two institutions probably explain the greater number of skills on the UN A list, although expectations of recruitment tests and their effectiveness may also come into play. The differences in rankings in some cases probably reflect differences in the need to exercise the skills in question (e.g. fact checking) or the amount of induction training provided (e.g. mining reference material). And, of course, the skill-set required at each institution might be influenced by other factors not considered here.

[11] The UN has developed a suite of customized CAT tools in-house: a translation memory tool (eLUNa), a statistical machine-translation tool (TAPTA4UN), a repository of bilingual parallel texts and an automated referencing tool connected to the global terminology base UNTERM. Their use has been introduced and expanded in stages. All relevant language staff had been trained in their use by the end of 2015, and they are expected to be fully implemented at all duty stations by the end of 2016.

5 Conclusions and implications

In short, at both the EU and the UN, the skills required for achieving quality are more than just language skills; they include analytical and research skills, as well as procedural and substantive knowledge. The ideal candidate profile varies from one organization group to the other (and presumably, within them, between their different bodies – although such finer distinctions were not analysed here) and seems to be influenced by the languages involved and the nature of the source texts, as well as in-house training arrangements and provisions for domain specialization. The challenge for training institutions that offer courses in institutional translation is to not only raise awareness of, but also actually foster, the priority skills that are common to their graduates' target markets. The challenge for translators aspiring to work for IOs is to master and demonstrate them in IO selection processes. The challenge for IOs is to assess them in recruitment and impart the missing skills and knowledge as fast and efficiently as possible.

By spotlighting the roles that revision and thematic competence play in translation quality, the analysis also raises translation quality management issues facing IOs. In the pursuit of greater cost-efficiency, both the EU and the UN are seeking to create more flexible workforces, since having staff who can perform multiple tasks makes it far easier to optimize resource and job allocation. However, when tasks are assigned using a fit-for-purpose approach in which the minimum combined level of expertise is expended for the sake of cost-efficiency, as at the EU, quality is dependent on the existence of sufficient expertise among the team to offset the lack of it in some of the players. As one EU quality manager put it, 'If the reviser doesn't have relevant domain competence or text-type convention competence, revision might not add value at all and could even lower the quality.'

Having translators cover more policy areas than they did in the past runs the risk of turning them into jacks of all trades and masters of none, making it increasingly difficult to find ideal translator–reviser combinations for given translation projects. Achieving expertise in multiple subjects and types of documents takes longer than achieving expertise in a few and therefore means that only translators with considerably more experience in the institution can effectively revise (this is the logic behind the UN revision structure). Diminishing the subject-area specialization of EU translators could thus undermine the feasibility of its fit-for-purpose task assignment mechanism and the cost-effectiveness of the accompanying advisory revision practices.

The challenge at the UN is slightly different. Specialization there is along functional lines, and quality assurance is based on highly experienced translators revising the work of other, less experienced ones. The pursuit of cost-efficiency has focused on monitoring and increasing staff productivity and injecting flexibility by having translators self-revise (i.e. not be revised) and revise as soon as they are able. Having less experienced translators assume revision work could, however, affect quality, and an increased focus on translator productivity in a hierarchical structure can actually reduce cost-efficiency. This is because the pursuit of productivity targets tends to encourage translators to prioritize speed over quality, which effectively creates more work for the revisers, whose time is more costly to the institution. Gains in translator productivity run the risk of producing losses in reviser productivity. And if those revisers are increasingly less experienced, those losses will be even greater. Alternatively, if the revisers aim to meet their own productivity targets, quality could suffer. To mitigate the risks outlined above, both the EU and the UN are working to provide more effective training, especially early on and in revision.

Translation quality assurance at IOs, therefore, depends not just on translators having the skills identified in the survey and examined in this chapter but also on translation managers having the skills to find translators with those skills (or the potential to develop them) and to get the balance right between training, specialization, risk assessment, workload standards and revision arrangements. As pointed out by Prieto Ramos (2015), quality assurance in institutional translation depends on the process and the product and on the competence of both the translators and the quality controllers involved.

6

Legal Terminology Consistency and Adequacy as Quality Indicators in Institutional Translation: A Mixed-Method Comparative Study

Fernando Prieto Ramos and Diego Guzmán

1 Background

As a key aspect of legal discourses and translation competence, legal terminology constitutes a prominent theme in Legal Linguistics and Legal Translation Studies. It is 'the most visible and striking linguistic feature of legal language as a technical language, and it is also one of the primary sources of difficulty in translating legal documents' (Cao 2007: 53). However, decision-making on legal terminology at international organizations, despite its relevance for institutional translation quality, remains largely unexplored. There is a particular need for more empirical evidence on the relationship between decision-making patterns (process) and the adequacy of the resulting translations (product) in the light of the relevant communicative conditions and the various factors that may have an impact on quality, such as working procedures, translator profiles, revision practices and time constraints. In that vein, the focus of this chapter will be on the consistency and adequacy of terminological decisions in international legal texts and their correlation with recommendations found in the corresponding institutional terminological databases at three representative organizations: the European Union (EU), the United Nations (UN) and the World Trade Organization (WTO).

The comparative analysis will concentrate on patterns of translation of an illustrative term (*due process*) into Spanish over fifteen years (2000–2015). It is part of a large-scale project, 'Legal Translation in International Institutional Settings: Scope, Strategies and Quality Markers' (LETRINT),[1] which covers the same period and adopts the abovementioned holistic approach to quality (encompassing process, competence and product [see Prieto Ramos 2015]) for the analysis of terminological adequacy. This kind

[1] Supported by the Swiss National Science Foundation through a Consolidator Grant.

of integral analysis provides the relevant ground to investigate, among other aspects, the factors that contribute to inappropriate terminological decisions, especially when such decisions are recurrent. This has been illustrated by two preliminary studies on the translation of national court names at different international organizations and the assessment of legal entries in terminological databases (Prieto Ramos 2013b, 2014c). The same integrative decision-making model will be used here for the qualitative analysis of translation adequacy, in conjunction with substantial quantitative analysis. This mixed-method approach will be explained in more detail in the next section, before the results of its application are presented and discussed.

2 Mixed-method approach

The combination of methods emerges as the most appropriate approach for identifying and interpreting translation patterns in our ten-year corpus of institutional texts. Lexicometric (quantitative) analysis and acceptability (qualitative) analysis are combined to address our research questions: How was the term *due process* translated into Spanish in the three organizations under examination between 2005 and 2015? What are the levels of consistency and adequacy found in each institution? To what extent are translation solutions in line with recommendations in the relevant institutional terminological resources? What implications for institutional translation decision-making may be derived from the triangulation of findings? While translation decision-making is intrinsically qualitative in nature, the search for regularities and the measurement of quality variables inevitably calls for the integration of statistical analysis in exploiting our corpus. In other words, both types of analysis complement each other.

2.1 Corpus description

The corpus for this study is composed of three parallel sub-corpora of texts translated from English into Spanish and published in institutional repositories of the UN, the EU and the WTO[2] in 2005, 2010 and 2015. This means that texts were translated by multiple institutional teams in the case of the UN and the EU (including the European Commission, the Council of the EU and the European Parliament, all of them involved in the ordinary legislative procedure, as well as the Court of Justice of the EU [CJEU]), whereas WTO translations were produced by a single team per target language. In the three contexts, a proportion of translations is outsourced, but the responsibility for their revision (where appropriate) and final quality lies with the same institutional language services.

In order to build the parallel bilingual sub-corpora, all texts featuring occurrences of *due process* in English were first retrieved and filtered to exclude documents in which the term did not refer to the concept under scrutiny (see Section 3), for instance, texts that were translations from third languages or where the English text

[2] Texts were retrieved from EU's EUR-Lex, UN's search.un.org and WTO Documents Online, using each year of the corpus and 'due process' as search criteria.

was a back translation from Spanish (e.g. the case of *due process* as translation of *debido proceso* in the Report of the High Commissioner for Human Rights on the situation of human rights in Colombia, E/CN.4/2005/10). However, in the case of bilingual originals or multilingual texts, the Spanish versions were considered if the English term referred to the relevant concept and this was clearly the 'master version' for translation (or co-drafting, if any). In the case of the UN, for example, in bilingual originals on the situation of human rights in particular countries (e.g. Somalia or Nigeria), occurrences of *due process* referred to international obligations with the sense studied here and were validated for the analysis of their translations into Spanish.

The EU sub-corpus demanded special attention, as there is officially no 'original version' of EU texts. Nonetheless, in practice, English is the predominant language of originals for EU law-making and monitoring procedures,[3] and this was the starting point for the verification of the idiomatic use of the English term in context. The presumption was confirmed through the preliminary semantic validation. In the case of the CJEU, the reverse was presupposed, since French is the internal working language of the Court, and only instances involving English as the language of the case were considered. Again, the verification of meaning in context was the ultimate test to validate each occurrence. Overall, *due process* was used with its prevalent procedural sense in English as original language in the overwhelming majority of texts initially retrieved; only in the case of the CJEU were a more significant proportion of cases excluded (ten out of sixteen documents initially retrieved).

A total of 1179 documents were confirmed as corpus components after the semantic verification process (see Table 6.1). They contain a total of 2579 occurrences of *due process*. For ease of reference, each occurrence was assigned a unique code that identifies the institution and the year of text publication, for example, occurrence 1210_UN_2010. The UN parallel sub-corpus is the largest, with 946 English texts and their Spanish versions, followed by the WTO sub-corpus (175 documents) and the EU sub-corpus (58 documents). The texts compiled were produced for various institutional purposes, including policy and law-making (e.g. EU legislation), implementation monitoring (e.g. compliance reports of UN human rights treaty bodies) and adjudicative procedures (e.g. WTO dispute settlement reports and CJEU judgments).[4] The most prominent text groups at each institution (see Table 6.2) are

Table 6.1 Documents compiled per year and organization

	2005	2010	2015	TOTAL
EU	17	22	19	58
UN	237	333	376	946
WTO	70	45	60	175
ALL	324	400	455	1179

3 As confirmed by internal statistics provided by the European Commission, the Council of the EU and the European Parliament for the period under examination.

4 The UN's main judicial body, the International Court of Justice, is excluded from this study because its official languages are limited to English and French.

Table 6.2 Origin of corpus documents

		Number of documents	% of compiled docs for the organization	% of compiled documents
EU (58; 4.92%)	Council of the European Union	15	25.86%	1.27%
	European Commission	13	22.41%	1.1%
	European Parliament	13	22.41%	1.1%
	Council of the European Union/ European Parliament	6	10.34%	0.51%
	Court of Justice and General Court	6	10.34%	0.51%
	Other bodies[a]	5	8.62%	0.42%
UN (946; 80.24%)	Human rights bodies	418	44.19%	35.45%
	General Assembly	321	33.93%	27.23%
	Security Council	144	15.22%	12.21%
	ECOSOC	32	3.38%	2.71%
	Programmes, funds and specialized agencies	16	1.69%	1.36%
	Procedures or bodies related to other UN legal instruments	12	1.27%	1.02%
	Other bodies or procedures	3	0.32%	0.25%
WTO (175; 14.84%)	Dispute settlement panels	33	18.86%	2.8%
	Appellate Body	25	14.29%	2.12%
	Committees[b]	24	13.71%	2.04%
	Working parties on accession	24	13.71%	2.04%
	Other negotiating groups[c]	23	13.14%	1.95%
	Negotiating Group on Rules	19	10.86%	1.61%
	Other bodies[d]	27	15.43%	2.29%
	Total compiled documents	1179		

[a]European Data Protection Supervisor, European Economic and Social Committee, and European Court of Auditors.

[b]Committee on Anti-Dumping Practices, Committee on Regional Trade Agreements, Committee on Safeguards, Committee on Subsidies and Countervailing Measures, Committee on Technical Barriers to Trade, Committee on Trade and Development, and Committee on Trade-Related Investment Measures.

[c]Negotiating Group on Market Access, Negotiating Group on Rules and Negotiating Group on Trade Facilitation.

[d]Council for Trade in Goods, Council for Trade in Services, Council for Trade-Related Aspects of Intellectual Property Rights, General Council, Working Party on Domestic Regulation, ministerial conferences and other Dispute Settlement Body documents.

documents produced in the framework of human rights treaty body procedures in the case of the UN (44.19 per cent); WTO dispute settlement documents, including texts produced by panels, the Appellate Body and the Dispute Settlement Body (40 per cent); and EU legal acts (37.93 per cent).

As regards the breakdown of language services responsible for translations at the UN and the EU, in the first case, the UN Office at Geneva takes the largest share with 48 per cent of the UN sub-corpus (as it deals with the majority of texts of human rights bodies), closely followed by the UN Headquarters in New York at 46.5 per cent (all occurrences in Security Council documents and most occurrences in General Assembly documents) and other duty stations (5 per cent of the sub-corpus translated in Vienna and less than 0.5 per cent in other offices). As to the EU sub-corpus, the documents originated from the Commission, the Council and the Parliament in similar proportions, followed by the CJEU (six documents). Only five documents of that sub-corpus were issued by other bodies: two from the European Data Protection Supervisor, two from the European Economic and Social Committee, and one from the European Court of Auditors.

2.2 Quantitative and qualitative analysis

All occurrences of *due process* and its translations were extracted from the corpus using XBench, a quality assurance and terminology management tool. The resulting database was used for the analysis of the relevant variables, starting with translation consistency, by measuring the variability of terminological decisions (Section 4). Lexicometric methods of frequency analysis and cooccurrence analysis were applied to generate comparative statistics. Reformulations were grouped by lexical clusters in Spanish, which facilitated the dissection of semantic nuances during the acceptability analysis of translations. Finally, the adequacy levels resulting from this qualitative analysis were quantified for further statistical comparison between periods and organizations, and also, subsequently, between extracted translations and recommended reformulations in terminological database entries (Section 5). As pointed out by Mattissek (2010: 318), with the help of lexicometry, particularly 'systematic comparisons and the calculation of similarities between different sub-corpora (e.g. comparisons over time)', the researcher can reveal discursive phenomena that would be difficult 'to discover through the mere use of reading and interpretation due to large quantities of text'.

As for the key acceptability (qualitative) analysis used to determine adequacy levels, as already mentioned, it was based on a previously tested integrative decision-making model in legal translation, presupposing that the evaluation of adequacy of terminological decisions depends on the same communicative parameters that condition these decisions. Such conditions are defined at macro- and microtextual levels, starting with the analysis of the translation brief, the source text (ST) and the target text (TT) communicative situations, and the legal contextualization of the translation (see Figure 6.1). This provides the background for the translation-oriented analysis of the original term in context and for the actual acceptability analysis of possible reformulations through comparative legal and linguistic analysis

1. Definition of **adequacy strategy at macrotextual level**
   - *Translation brief* (type and conditions of translation) + *ST and TT communicative situations*
   - *Legal contextualization*: legal systems + branches of law + legal genres

2. **Analysis of ST term** in context

3. **Acceptability analysis of TT formulations at microtextual level**
   - *Microtextual priority* (prioritization of formal / conceptual / functional ST-TT correspondence) considering function and relevance of text segment, legal constraints and receivers' needs and expectations
   - *Acceptability of possible TT formulations* identified through comparative legal and linguistic anlaysis considering type and degree of ST-TT correspondence

Figure 6.1 Outline of decision-making model.

in the light of the microtextual priority for adequacy (e.g. in the case of system-bound terms, identification of the legal singularity, pre-eminence of 'system-neutral' conceptual solutions or functional renderings) (for more details, see e.g. Prieto Ramos 2014c).

The proposed methodological triangulation ultimately aims to illustrate the benefits of multi-method research design to empirically capture and assess institutional translation patterns beyond the qualitative analysis of selected examples, which is the most common approach in the field (see e.g. Jopek-Bosiacka 2013 on the assessment of the translation of five common law terms into Polish in CJEU judgments). Before delving into the quantitative results, the analysis of the source term and its possible reformulations into Spanish for the three contexts at hand will be summarized in the next section.

3 Analysis of source term and possible reformulations

In line with the decision-making model outlined above, the *general elements of the adequacy strategy* were defined to guide the translation-oriented analysis and the evaluation of terminological decisions. In the institutional contexts scrutinized, three elements take priority in the light of the principle of equal authenticity of the various language versions and the need for interlinguistic concordance: accuracy, semantic univocity and consistency, particularly in the case of key concepts and established names.

As for our *illustrative term*, *due process*, all uses validated in the corpus conform to the meaning traditionally found in common law, as defined by Garner (2014: 610): 'The conduct of legal proceedings according to established rules and principles for the protection and enforcement of private rights, including notice and the right to a fair hearing before a tribunal with the power to decide the case'. The doctrine of procedural due process is particularly developed in the United States, where the Constitution enshrines this principle in its Fifth and Fourteenth Amendments. In its substantive sense, 'due process of law' entails protection against arbitrary or unreasonable legislation. In our corpus, most occurrences refer to procedural provisions or guarantees in adjudicative or administrative proceedings (e.g. WTO dispute settlement or UN human rights reviews). In the case of the EU, references are often made to procedural obligations under international law rather than specific EU or national provisions.

In the *acceptability analysis* of possible reformulations into Spanish, the microtextual priority is conceptual correspondence for an international Spanish-speaking audience in the case of UN and WTO texts, and the Spanish legal system in the case of EU texts. In the comparative legal analysis, emphasis is therefore on finding common denominators that can facilitate understanding of the original concept while avoiding functional renderings that might refer to national singularities or specific procedures or branches of law. Based on a mapping of related procedural concepts in constitutional, civil and criminal law in the most populated Spanish-speaking countries (see Table 6.3), we can conclude that *debidas garantías procesales* (and its variants) is the most suitable rendering to meet both the adequacy strategy and the microtextual priority. The concept of *garantía procesal* conveys the essence of the original term and is the most widespread in the Spanish-speaking world, including Spain. The concept of *debido proceso* is also an accurate conceptual rendering that

Table 6.3 Related procedural concepts in most populated Spanish-speaking countries

	CONSTITUTION	CRIMINAL PROCEDURE LEGISLATION	CIVIL PROCEDURE LEGISLATION
MEXICO	*formalidades esenciales del procedimiento; garantía del debido proceso legal*	*garantías*	
COLOMBIA	*debido proceso*	*garantías procesales*	*debido proceso*
SPAIN	*tutela efectiva*	*garantías procesales*	*tutela judicial efectiva; garantías procesales*
ARGENTINA	*juicio previo fundado en la ley*		
VENEZUELA	*debido proceso*	*debido proceso; garantías del debido proceso*	*garantías procesales*
PERU	*debido proceso; tutela jurisdiccional*		*igualdad efectiva de las partes en todas las actuaciones del proceso*
CHILE	*proceso previo legalmente tramitado; garantías de un procedimiento y una investigación racionales y justos*	*juicio previo y proceso legal*	
GUATEMALA	*derecho de defensa*	*garantías procesales*	
ECUADOR	*debido proceso; garantías básicas*	*juicio previo; garantías previstas*	

can be easily recognized in the Spanish-speaking world; it is actually used in various Latin American national legal systems (e.g. Mexico, Colombia, Venezuela, Ecuador, Uruguay), which reflects the influence of the original common law concept in Spanish-speaking legal systems.

Finally, the concept of *tutela judicial efectiva* as established in the Spanish legal system (also found as *tutela jurisdiccional* in Peru) may be an adequate translation in EU texts when used in connection with judicial contexts. Otherwise, as would be the case for texts that refer to international obligations within the EU, it might prove more appropriate to use an internationally oriented conceptual rendering than a term bound to a specific national legal system.

Reformulations including *garantías procesales* and *debido proceso* are also the common denominator between recommendations in institutional terminological resources (EU's IATE, UNTERM and WTO's dispute settlement glossary), while *tutela judicial efectiva* also features in an IATE entry (see Table 6.11).

4 Translation consistency

4.1 Intertextual variability

A total of 123 translations of *due process* in Spanish were found among the 2579 occurrences of the term (see the list in the Annex). In order to draw a precise picture of each indicator, the total number of occurrences ('TO') and the number of occurrence categories per document ('OD', i.e. counting each translation variant once in each text, regardless of its repetitions in the same text) were quantified separately for each sub-corpus (see Table 6.4).

Terminological variants were bundled into clusters according to their lexical core, resulting in ten lexical clusters (*derecho, garantía, juicio, legalidad, norma, procedimiento, proceso, regularidad, salvaguarda* and *tramitación*) and a miscellaneous group ('other') composed of twenty-six different reformulations (with three or fewer instances in each variant) and six omissions.

Table 6.4 Total occurrences and occurrence categories per document

		2005	2010	2015	TOTAL
EU	TO	27	27	40	94
	OD	21	25	32	78
UN	TO	488	631	711	1830
	OD	329	425	462	1216
WTO	TO	187	284	184	655
	OD	112	80	89	281
TOTAL	TO	702	942	935	2579
	OD	462	530	583	1575

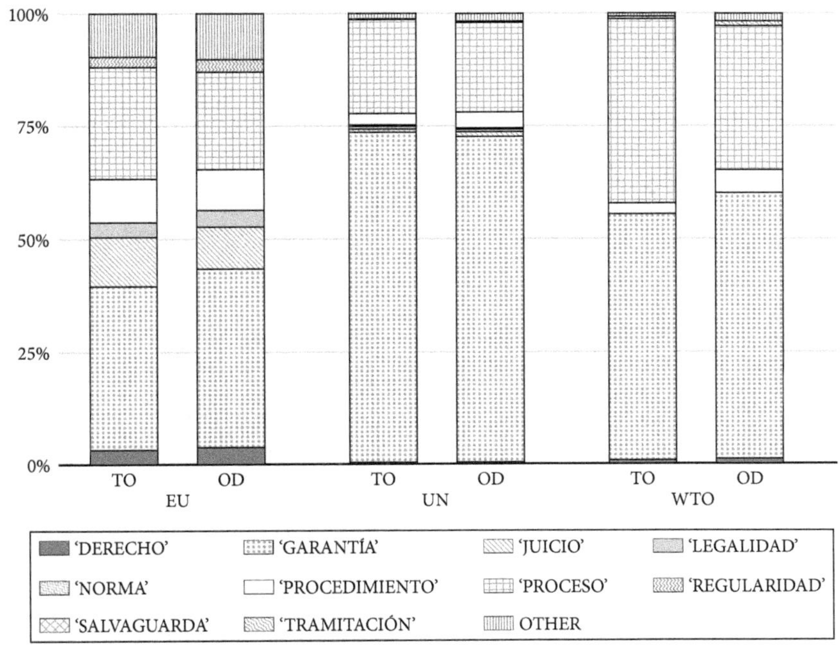

Figure 6.2 Lexical variability in each organization.

Figure 6.2 presents the overall distribution of these clusters in each organization. The results show a markedly higher degree of intertextual variability in EU documents despite the significantly lower number of occurrences found in this sub-corpus. The most frequent cluster (*garantía*) accounts for 36.56 per cent of this sub-corpus, as opposed to 73.27 per cent and 54.5 per cent in the UN and the WTO sub-corpora, respectively. When combined with translation variants including *proceso*, the TO share of the two most frequent clusters exceeds 90 per cent (94.09 per cent at the UN and 95.57 per cent at the WTO), whereas a similar figure (93.54 per cent) is only reached by combining the five most frequent clusters (*garantía, proceso, juicio, procedimiento, derecho*) and other reformulations in EU texts.

4.2 Intratextual variability

Intratextual inconsistencies (i.e. different translations of the term within the same document) range from 28 per cent of WTO texts to 12.47 per cent of UN texts and 15.52 per cent in EU texts for the entire period. They show very different trends over the decade analysed: They declined from 30 per cent to 22.85 per cent at the WTO; they remained mostly stable at the UN, between 17.3 per cent and 15.18 per cent; and they registered a very significant increase at the EU, from 5.88 per cent to 35.29 per cent (see Table 6.5).

A closer examination reveals that many of these texts are compilations where previous translations are reproduced in literal quotations, or long documents whose translations tend to be divided between different translators. For example, compilation documents represent one tenth of UN sub-corpus texts, including,

Table 6.5 Proportion of texts containing inconsistencies at each organization

	2005 (%)	2010 (%)	2015 (%)	Total (%)
EU	5.88	11.76	35.29	15.52
UN	17.3	12.31	9.57	12.47
WTO	30	17.14	22.85	28

Table 6.6 Translation variants identified in Council Decision (CFSP) 2015/555

1725_EU_2015	Responsible for grave violations of the right to **due process**.	*Responsable de graves violaciones de* ***las garantías procesales****.*
1726_EU_2015	He is, therefore, complicit in a grave violation of the right to **due process**, contributing to the excessive and increasing use of the death penalty.	*Es, por tanto, cómplice de grave violación del derecho a un* ***proceso justo****, contribuyendo así al uso excesivo y en aumento de la pena de muerte.*
1728_EU_2015	They were arrested, tortured and hanged without **due process**.	*Estas personas fueron detenidas, torturadas y ahorcadas sin* ***proceso previo****.*
1729_EU_2015	The five were arrested without charge for over a year, tortured and sentenced without **due process**.	*Las cinco personas mencionadas habían sido detenidas durante un año sin ningún cargo, siendo luego torturadas y sentenciadas sin el* ***debido proceso****.*
1731_EU_20155	He is complicit in a grave violation of the right to **due process**, contributing to the excessive and increasing use of the death penalty and a sharp increase in executions since the beginning of the year.	*Cómplice de una grave violación del derecho a un* ***juicio justo****, contribuyendo así al uso excesivo y en incremento de la pena de muerte que ha desembocado en un grave aumento de las ejecuciones desde principios de año.*

for instance, document E/CN.4/2005/L.11/Add.5 of 2005, in which occurrences 560_UN_2005 (*debido procedimiento legal*) and 561_UN_2005 (*debido proceso*) are reproduced from resolutions 2005/30 and 2005/32 of the Human Rights Commission, respectively. Official, provisional and summary records, half of which originate from the UN Security Council, are usually divided between several translators and represent 31.9 per cent of the UN documents containing intratextual inconsistencies.

In the WTO sub-corpus, intratextual inconsistencies are mostly found in dispute settlement reports (67.35 per cent), which also constitute the largest group of documents from this organization (see Table 6.2). Here, divergence is most often detected in footnotes and citations referring to other documents. At the EU, up to five translation variants were found in *Council Decision (CFSP) 2015/555 of 7 April 2015 amending Decision 2011/235/CFSP concerning restrictive measures directed against certain persons and entities in view of the situation in Iran* (see Table 6.6).

5 Translation adequacy

5.1 Adequacy levels

As part of the acceptability analysis (see Section 3), all translations of *due process* were cross-checked in context in order to grade their adequacy levels in a scale from 1 (highest level) to 3 (lowest level). Level 1 solutions (dark grey colour in Figures 6.3 to 6.6) reflect all conceptual nuances mentioned in Section 3. Examples given in Table 6.7 illustrate this group. They all meet adequacy requirements in their contexts. Occurrences 1210_UN_2010 and 678_WTO_2005 convey the meaning of *due process* with conceptual formulations that can be recognized in all Spanish-speaking countries, while 1738_EU_2015 is adapted to the Spanish audience within the EU.

Level 2 translations (grey colour in Figures 6.3 to 6.6) are acceptable in context but are not the most adequate in terms of accuracy. They tend to be generic formulations that lose some nuance of the original concept, such as *procedimiento establecido*, *procedimiento adecuado*, *procedimiento correspondiente* or *aspectos de procedimiento* (see examples in Table 6.8). In the case of *procedimiento establecido* (back-translated as *established procedure*), for example, the concept might be acceptable when referring to the relevant procedural rights, but such procedures might not have been established, in which case the translation may be misleading. These level 2 generic solutions or hypernyms might be the result of a deliberate decision to avoid a more specific concept, a simple oversight or insufficient awareness of the legal content of the

Table 6.7 Examples of level 1 (highly adequate) translations

678_WTO_2005 WT/DS290/R	43. The European Communities is also of the view that the "deficiencies" of the requests for establishment of a panel seriously prejudice its **due process** rights as a defending party, notably, to know the case it has to answer.	*43. Las Comunidades Europeas opinan también que las "deficiencias" en las solicitudes de establecimiento de un grupo especial perjudican gravemente su derecho a gozar de las* ***debidas garantías procesales*** *en su condición de parte demandada, y en particular al derecho a conocer los argumentos a que han de responder.*
1210_UN_2010 A/65/44	(25) The Committee regrets the complaints alleging a systematic failure to comply with the principle of 'non-refoulement' and with the right of access to **due process** and information for refugees and potential asylum-seekers, and the failure to provide proper safeguards against persons being placed at risk when returned to their country of origin.	*25) El Comité lamenta las alegaciones de que no se respeta sistemáticamente el principio de "no devolución", acceso al* ***debido proceso*** *y acceso a información para los refugiados o potenciales solicitantes de asilo, ni se garanticen plenamente los mecanismos que impidan poner en riesgo a las personas devolviéndolas a su país de origen.*
1738_EU_2015 02011R0359-20150409	The restrictive measures should target [...] persons complicit in or responsible for directing or implementing grave violations of the right to **due process** [...].	*Las medidas restrictivas deben dirigirse [...] contra las personas implicadas o responsables de la dirección o ejecución de violaciones graves del derecho a la* ***tutela judicial efectiva****, [...].*

Table 6.8 Examples of level 2 (acceptable) translations

537_UN_2005 CCPR/C/USA/3	Specifically included are the Fourth Amendment's proscription against unreasonable searches and seizures (including seizing a person's body), the Fifth Amendment's proscription against depriving one of life, liberty or property without **due process**, and the Eighth Amendment's proscription against the infliction of cruel and unusual punishment.	*Concretamente esto se refiere a la prohibición, prevista en la Enmienda IV, de la entrada y registro arbitrarios en lugar cerrado (incluida la aprehensión de una persona), la prohibición contenida en la Enmienda V de privar a una persona de la vida, la libertad o los bienes, salvo por los* ***cauces legales establecidos****, y la prohibición contenida en la Enmienda VIII de infligir castigos crueles e inusitados.*
1480_WTO_2010 WT/ACC/SYC/10	transparency and **due process** requirements, including circulation for review and comment of all standards, technical regulations, and conformity assessment provisions prior to implementation	*Requisitos en materia de transparencia y requisitos de* ***procedimiento****, incluida la distribución de todas las normas, reglamentos técnicos y disposiciones de evaluación de la conformidad con miras a su examen y a la formulación de observaciones al respecto, antes de su aplicación*
1749_EU_2015 52014IE5356	1.4 Apart from the principle of 'Most Favoured Nation' (MFN), and the cover normally included by the Commission to deal with compensation in cases of war, revolution and so on, the Committee urges that investor protection under an IIA and therefore open to the use of ISDS, must be restricted to cover the four substantive protections, namely [...] prompt, adequate and effective compensation when expropriation occurs (not discriminatory and with **due process**); [...]	*1.4 Aparte del principio de «nación más favorecida» (NMF) y la cobertura que la Comisión incluye habitualmente para hacer frente a las compensaciones en caso de guerra, revolución, etc., el Comité pide que la protección de los inversores en el marco de un AII – que, por consiguiente, puede incluir el recurso a la RCIE – esté claramente restringida y abarque únicamente los cuatro tipos de protección sustantiva, a saber: [...] compensación rápida, adecuada y efectiva en caso de expropiación (que debe ser no discriminatoria y seguir* ***los procedimientos adecuados****), [...]*
1750_EU_2015 52015AA0001	This exception to the basic rights of **due process** must be more closely managed.	*Esta excepción a los* ***derechos fundamentales de defensa*** *debe regularse de forma más limitativa.*

original notion. A smaller group of reformulations that refer to specific procedural guarantees within the scope of *due process*, but convey the concept only partially, were also included in level 2 (e.g. *derechos fundamentales de defensa* in 1750_EU_2015).

Finally, level 3 translations (striped bars in Figures 6.3 to 6.6) are considered 'unacceptable'. Most failed to reflect the content of the term because the sense conveyed was too broad or diverted from the original concept (e.g. *atestado en regla*, *riguroso proceso*, *diligencia debida*), or they were unjustified omissions (see examples in Table 6.9). For example, *principio de legalidad* was considered inaccurate as it referred to the broader (related) concept of rule of law. Only one typographical error was spotted: *las garantías procesarles* (1446_UN_2010). In another case, the European Commission corrected a mistranslation found in a previous EU Council Decision on the same

Table 6.9 Examples of level 3 (unacceptable) translations

737_WTO_2005 WT/REG198/1	Neither Party shall expropriate or nationalize an investment of an investor of the other Party in its Area either directly or indirectly through measures tantamount to expropriation or nationalization (hereinafter referred to as 'expropriation') except: (a) for a public purpose; (b) on a non-discriminatory basis; (c) in accordance with **due process** of law and Article 60; and (d) on payment of compensation pursuant to paragraphs 2 through 5 below.	*1. Ninguna Parte expropiará o nacionalizará una inversión de un inversionista de la otra Parte en su Área, ya sea directa o indirectamente mediante medidas equivalentes a expropiación o nacionalización (en lo sucesivo referido como "expropiación") salvo que sea: a) por causa de utilidad pública; b) sobre bases no discriminatorias; c) con apego al* ***principio de legalidad*** *y al artículo 60; y d) mediante indemnización conforme a los párrafos 2 a 5 siguientes.*
760_EU_2010 52010IP0310	Urges the Iranian authorities to eliminate, in law and in practice, all forms of torture and other cruel, inhumane or degrading treatment or punishment, and to uphold **due process** of law and end impunity for human rights violations;	*Insta a las autoridades iraníes a que supriman, de hecho y de derecho, todas las formas de tortura y penas o tratos crueles, inhumanos o degradantes,* ***hagan respetar la ley*** *y pongan fin a la impunidad en caso de vulneración de los derechos humanos;*
2244_UN_2015 A/70/35 [Omission]	12. Not all the occupation-related costs can be measured in monetary terms; for example, no dollar value can be assigned to the distress and agony of the loss and destruction of life, community, culture, shelter or a homeland, or the detention of a human being without **due process** and legal justification.	*12. No todos los costos derivados de la ocupación pueden medirse en términos monetarios; por ejemplo, no se puede tasar en dólares lo que cuesta la angustia y la agonía de la pérdida y la destrucción de la vida, la comunidad, la cultura, la vivienda o una patria, o la detención de un ser humano sin justificación legal.*

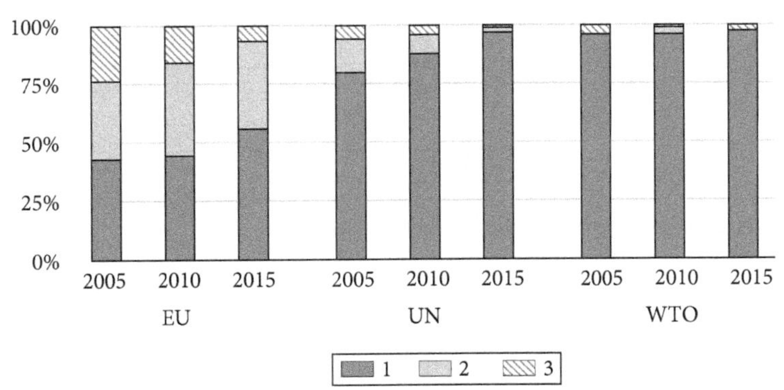

Figure 6.3 Adequacy levels in the three organizations (quantified in OD).

matter. The sentence reproduced in English and rectified in Spanish was: 'STRESSING the common values governing privacy and the protection of personal data . . ., including the importance which both Parties assign to **due process** . . .'; in which *due process* was translated as *tratamiento que corresponda* in Council Decision 2010/16/CFSP/JHA as opposed to *tutela judicial efectiva* in Commission Proposal COM(2010) 316 final.

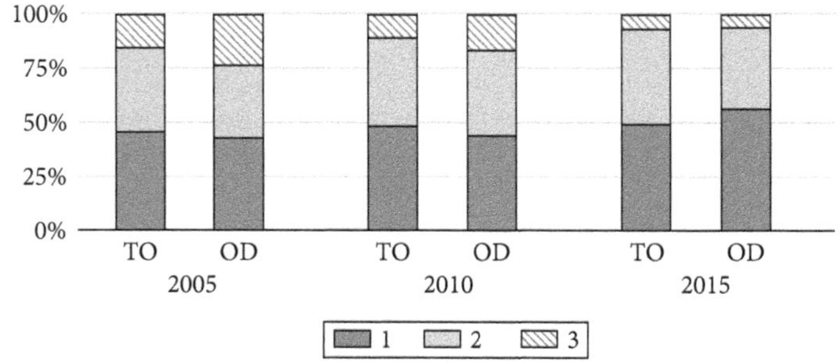

Figure 6.4 Adequacy levels in the EU sub-corpus.

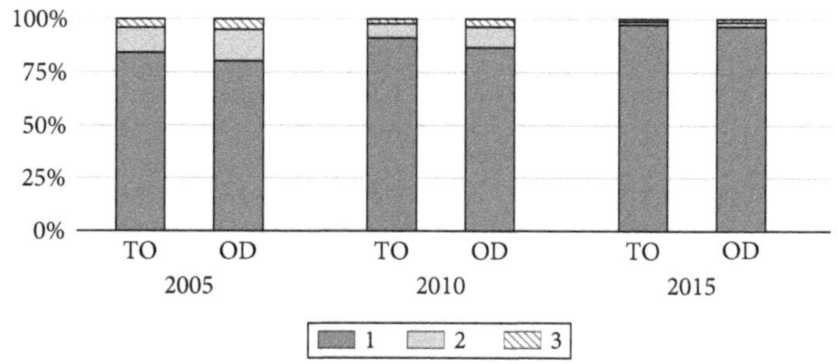

Figure 6.5 Adequacy levels in the UN sub-corpus.

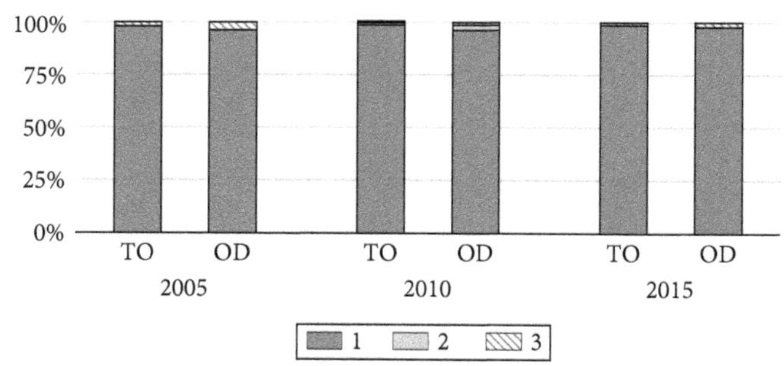

Figure 6.6 Adequacy levels in the WTO sub-corpus.

The adequacy grading results (see comparative levels of OD in Figure 6.3) show that level 1 scores are predominant at the WTO (96.44 per cent of OD) and at the UN (88.73 per cent), but account for less than half of translations at the EU (48.72 per cent). The reverse applies to level 3: 15.35 per cent as average for the whole period at the EU (with a peak of 23.81 per cent in 2005), compared to 3.67 per cent at the UN (with a highest annual score of 5.47 per cent in 2005) and 2.65 per cent at the WTO (highest annual score of 4.46 per cent in 2005). Finally, the proportion of level 2 translations is increasingly low at the UN (14.59 per cent in 2005 and 2.38 per cent in 2015) and negligible at the WTO (except for 2.5 per cent in 2010), as opposed to a share of 37.18 per cent evenly distributed through the EU sub-corpus.

Overall, the general trend observed at the three institutions in terms of adequacy levels between 2005 and 2015 is positive, particularly so where there was more room for improvement, that is, in EU translations. Level 3 scores dropped from 23.81 per cent in 2005 to 6.25 per cent in 2015 in that sub-corpus, and level 1 scores increased in a similar proportion from 42.86 per cent to 56.25 per cent. At the UN, level 1 translation scores improved from 79.94 per cent to 96.32 per cent, while level 3 translations registered the opposite trend, down from 5.47 per cent to 1.3 per cent. Finally, the situation at the WTO remained stable over the same period, with a high global average of 96.51 per cent of level 1 translations and negligible fluctuations between levels 2 and 3 in the remaining portion of the sub-corpus.

5.2 Adequacy of most frequent translations

In order to draw a comprehensive overview of terminological decision patterns, the quantitative results on translation frequency and adequacy are now examined conjunctly. In particular, this section zooms in on the adequacy levels of the five most recurrent translations in each organization. Table 6.10 lists the 'top five' translations and their share of each sub-corpus, while Figure 6.7 presents their combined adequacy levels. In the first breakdown, the translations recommended in the respective institutional terminological resources are underlined.

The five most recurrent translations account for less than 60 per cent of occurrences at the EU, as opposed to shares close to or above 90 per cent at the UN and the WTO. In these two organizations, the two most frequent translations represent more than 60 per cent of total occurrences and occurrence categories per document, which doubles

Table 6.10 Five most recurrent translations in each organization

	EU	UN	WTO
TO	1. ***garantías procesales*** (22.58%) 2. *proceso justo* (11.83%) 3. *juicio justo* (10.75%) 4. *debido proceso* (7.53%) 5. *debidas garantías procesales* (5.38%)	1. ***garantías procesales*** (37.81%) 2. ***debidas garantías procesales*** (28.20%) 3. ***debido proceso*** (16.56%) 4. ***debidas garantías*** (3.06%) 5. *garantías legales* (1.58%)	1. ***debido proceso*** (40%) 2. ***debidas garantías procesales*** (32.06%) 3. ***garantías procesales*** (13.13%) 4. ***debidas garantías de procedimiento*** (6.87%) 5. ***procedimiento con las debidas garantías*** (1.68%)
	58.07% of TO	**87.21% of TO**	**93.74% of TO**
OD	1. ***garantías procesales*** (24.36%) 2. *proceso justo* (8.97%) 3. *juicio justo* (8.97%) 4. *debidas garantías procesales* (6.41%) 5. *debido proceso* (6.41%)	1. ***garantías procesales*** (33.63%) 2. ***debidas garantías procesales*** (29.11%) 3. ***debido proceso*** (14.06%) 4. ***debidas garantías*** (3.78%) 5. *garantías legales* (1.89%)	1. ***debidas garantías procesales*** (29.54%) 2. ***debido proceso*** (29.54%) 3. ***garantías procesales*** (16.73%) 4. ***debidas garantías de procedimiento*** (7.83%) 5. ***procedimiento con las debidas garantías*** (2.85%)
	55.12% of OD	**82.47% of OD**	**86.49% of OD**

the corresponding proportion found in the EU sub-corpus. Likewise, in terms of adequacy, level 1 scores for the entire period are higher in the two intergovernmental organizations (approximately 98 per cent at the UN and 100 per cent at the WTO) than in the EU (approximately 65 per cent). The remaining occurrences ranked at level 2 (acceptable), and none of the most frequent translations were unacceptable at any of the institutions (see Figure 6.7).

Interestingly, the four most recurrent translations at the UN and the five most frequent ones at the WTO are also found in their institutional terminological resources, which means that there is a very high consistency between the actual terminological

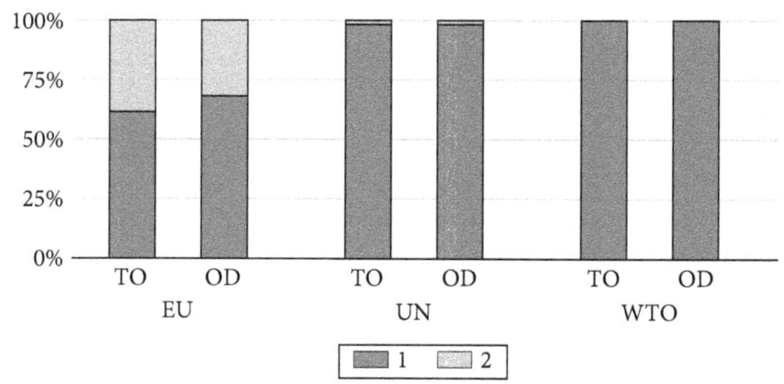

Figure 6.7 Adequacy levels of the five most frequent translations in each organization.

Table 6.11 Translations recommended in institutional terminological resources

	IATE	UNTERM		WTO dispute settlement glossary*
Entry	**910481**	**315858**	**897163**	
EN	*due process*	*due process*	*due process of law*	*due process*
EN	*due process of law*			*due process of law*
ES	*tutela judicial efectiva (3.23%)*	*garantías procesales (37.81%)*	*debidas garantías procesales (28.20%)*	*debido proceso (40%)*
ES	*respeto de las garantías procesales (22.58%)*	*debido proceso (16.56%)*	*debido procedimiento legal (0.27%)*	*debidas garantías procesales (32.06%)*
ES	*conformidad con las garantías procesales (22.58%)*	*procedimiento reglamentario (1.20%)*		*debidas garantías de procedimiento (6.87%)*
ES		*procedimiento previsto en la ley*		*procedimiento con las debidas garantías (1.68%)*

*The Spanish translations of *due process* found in this glossary, a priority resource for legal terminology at the WTO, are also found in the relevant entry of the WTOTERM database, except for *debido proceso*.

decisions and the relevant database recommendations. This contrasts with less than 25 per cent of occurrences matching an IATE recommendation, *garantías procesales*, which is the most frequent translation in the EU sub-corpus (see Table 6.11, where the frequency of recommended translations found in our corpus is indicated between brackets).

6 Discussion and conclusions

The triangulation of results of quantitative and qualitative analyses points to a series of correlations. In sum, the highest intertextual consistency and adequacy levels found at the WTO are systematically coupled with a highly prominent text group in that institution (40 per cent of occurrences were found in dispute settlement texts) and, more significantly, the most centralized translation service and the highest degree of adherence to internal terminological resources. At the opposite end, the lowest levels of consistency and adequacy of *due process* translations in EU texts (albeit improving from 23.81 per cent of inappropriate term reformulations in 2005 to 6.25 per cent in 2015) can be associated with the greater multiplicity of EU translation services (including in the case of the most prominent text group, legal acts) and the low adherence to the relevant IATE terminological recommendations. Finally, the UN sub-corpus shows patterns that are increasingly closer to the WTO's, despite the large volume of texts including *due process* and the division of most of their translations between two major duty stations. In other words, evidence suggests that terminological harmonization is facilitated by thematic coherence and language service concentration, and may be hindered by the fragmentation of texts and translation teams.

While the translation consistency and adequacy patterns identified cannot be extrapolated to all legal terminological decision-making in each organization, they provide the empirical ground required for further investigation of the factors that may influence product quality variables in the translation process, including not only the reliability and use of term bases but also time constraints, quality control practices and profile specialization. For instance, all texts tend to be revised at the WTO, whereas this is not necessarily the case at EU institutions.[5] In the latter context, the remarkable proportion of generic reformulations found in Spanish (between 35 per cent and 40 per cent of level 2 adequacy translations throughout the period analysed) and the low rate of adherence to IATE recommendations enable us to hypothesize that the legal nuance of *due process* was not detected and the term was translated 'at face value' in many cases.

Variations between EU institutions are also worth exploring. For example, inappropriate translations reach 19.35 per cent of total occurrences in texts of the European Commission, 14.29 per cent of occurrences in texts exclusively translated at the European Parliament and less than 7 per cent of occurrences in texts exclusively translated at the Council of the EU, while no mistranslations were detected in texts

[5] All references to revision levels, internal practices and profiles mentioned in this chapter have been cross-checked with institutional informants.

translated by CJEU's lawyer-linguists. Although the EU sub-corpus is much smaller in size than the other two, the different patterns elicited can shed light on legal translation specialization and working methods in specific cases.

Text groups within the UN and the WTO sub-corpora do not show any significant divergence from the overall institutional adequacy trends, except for texts of the WTO's working parties on accession, which account for most of WTO's low rate of inaccuracies at 8 per cent of level 3 adequacy translations within that group. This contrasts with the total absence of mistranslations in Appellate Body texts, among other groups. As opposed to WTO texts on accession, the Appellate Body texts are systematically assigned to translators specializing in WTO law and are scrupulously revised.

These findings illustrate how mixed-method corpus-based research can be useful to identify textual patterns and relate translation quality indicators to translation process and competence components from an institutional perspective. By considering various factors through multiple lenses, this kind of empirical approach can enrich our global understanding of institutional practices and support adapted quality enhancement measures such as coordinated consistency checks, thematic screening and training, updating of terminological resources and discrimination of univocity levels and revision needs.

Annex: List of translations of *due process* by lexical cluster

DERECHO
derecho a la defensa
derecho a la jurisdicción
derechos de defensa
derechos procesales
[garantizar] todos sus derechos

GARANTÍA
debidas garantías
debidas garantías de procedimiento
debidas garantías del procedimiento
debidas garantías fundamentales
debidas garantías judiciales
debidas garantías legales
debidas garantías procesales
garantía de un proceso imparcial
garantía(s) del debido proceso
garantía jurisdiccional
garantías
garantías adecuadas
garantías adecuadas del debido proceso
garantías constitucionales

garantías de un juicio
garantías de un juicio imparcial
garantías de un proceso legal
garantías del debido proceso legal
garantías elementales del debido proceso
garantías esenciales de defensa
garantías judiciales
garantías judiciales del debido proceso
garantías legales
garantías previstas en la ley
garantías procesales
garantías procesales debidas
garantías procesales del derecho
garantías procesales legales
garantías procesarles [sic]
garantías sustantivas

JUICIO
[juicio] con arreglo a derecho
juicio con las debidas garantías
juicio imparcial
juicio justo
juicio regular

LEGALIDAD
legalidad
legalidad de las actuaciones
legalidad de un proceso
legalidad del proceso
legalidad procesal

NORMA
debidas normas procesales
normas fundamentales que rigen los procesos
normas procesales
normas procesales legales

PROCEDIMIENTO
debido(s) procedimiento(s)
debido procedimiento legal
preceptivo procedimiento
procedimiento(s)
procedimiento con las debidas garantías
procedimiento con las debidas garantías procesales
procedimiento con todas las garantías
procedimiento correspondiente
procedimiento de recurso

procedimiento debido
procedimiento justo
procedimiento reglamentario
procedimientos [que] siguen plenamente los cauces jurídicos adecuados
procedimientos adecuados
procedimientos legales vigentes
procedimientos pertinentes
procedimientos reglamentarios
procedimientos reglamentarios debidos

PROCESO
correspondiente proceso judicial
debido proceso
debido proceso judicial
debido proceso jurídico
debido proceso legal
pertinente proceso legal
proceso
proceso adecuado
proceso apropiado
proceso con garantías
proceso con las debidas garantías
proceso con todas las garantías
proceso con todas las garantías de la ley
proceso con todas las garantías jurídicas
proceso conforme a derecho
proceso [que] debe contar con todas las garantías
proceso debido
proceso equitativo
proceso establecido
proceso imparcial
proceso judicial apropiado
proceso judicial ordinario
proceso justo
proceso legal
proceso legal con todas las garantías
proceso previo
proceso previsto en la ley
procesos justos
procesos plagados de irregularidades
riguroso proceso

REGULARIDAD
regularidad del procedimiento
regularidad del proceso

SALVAGUARDA
salvaguardas previstas en la ley
salvaguardias procesales

TRAMITACIÓN
tramitación ajustada a derecho
tramitación correcta

OTHER
ajustarse a derecho
aplicación conforme a derecho de los procedimientos
aplicar la ley debidamente
atestado en regla
cauces legales establecidos
curso debido a los procedimientos judiciales
de conformidad con la ley
debida protección procesal
debido mandamiento judicial
diligencia debida
hacer respetar la ley
igualdad ante la ley
ilegalmente
integridad del proceso
justicia equitativa
Omission
perceptivamente [oír]
prácticas procesales
principio de legalidad
procesar con arreglo a derecho
reglas del juego
requisitos procedimentales
resguardos procesales
respeto de sus formas
tratamiento que corresponda
tutela judicial efectiva

Comparing Multilingual Practices in the EU and the Canadian Legal Systems: The Case of Terminological Choices in Legislative Drafting[1]

Agnieszka Doczekalska

1 Introduction

It is not easy to communicate legal norms in a legislative text so that those who are subject to it can correctly understand their rights and obligations and predict the legal consequences of their actions. The challenge is even greater when the legislative text must express the same norms, rights and obligations in more than one language. The difficulties are both linguistic (especially, the task of finding equivalents in two or more languages) and legal (particularly, the task of guaranteeing equal status of all authentic language versions of a legal act). In Canada, co-drafting of English and French versions of federal legal acts was introduced in the 1970s to ensure the high quality of both language versions. The method applies the following pattern: two co-drafters – each responsible for one language version – write the English and the French text of a legal act independently on the basis of instructions from the sponsoring ministry. Co-drafting has ensured that the same idea is successfully conveyed in two versions, while respecting the spirit of both French and English (see, for example, Gémar 2013). Moreover, by providing the two high-quality versions, with equivalence and consistency between them, and by guaranteeing that neither version is a translation, this method overcomes legal challenge.

The European Union (EU) also struggles with ensuring the quality of twenty-four language versions of EU legal acts and ensuring the equality between them. The Canadian co-drafting cannot be applied to draw up EU laws, mainly due to the number of EU official languages and because the EU legislative process involves more than one

[1] The work of the author has been supported by the Polish National Science Centre funds allocated on the basis of decision no. DEC-20137/11/D/HS5/01822.

institution.[2] Nevertheless, some authors recognize co-drafting elements in the process of legislative multilingual drafting in the EU.[3]

Legislative multilingualism[4] is not the only common challenge for Canadian federal and EU supranational legislative drafting; the application of multilingual law in the territory where a different legal system is already settled is another challenge. In order to properly understand the terminological choices made by legislative drafters, it is crucial to analyse the relation between federal and provincial law in Canada and the relation between EU law and national law of Member States. Finding the differences between the two types of relations should facilitate an understanding of the methods applied to express legal concepts with a proper legal term. Moreover, these findings can help us to appraise whether any methods and practices applied by Canadian drafters can be used by EU translators and vice versa. Hence, after a short description of the EU multilingual and Canadian bilingual legislative practices with the focus on the aspects that influence terminological choices (first part), the chapter compares relations between federal and provincial law in Canada and between EU law and the national law of Member States (second part). With the results of the analyses in hand, in the final part, the terminological practices in Canadian federal and EU legislative drafting are explained and compared.

The focus of the chapter is on the legal terminology of EU secondary law (mainly regulations and directives) and of Canadian federal law that refers to property and civil rights. Although the subject of the chapter is legal terminology, both Canadian drafters and EU translators struggle with specialized terminology from various fields (e.g. technical, chemical, biological).

2 EU and Canadian multilingual legal drafting: Rules and practices compared

This chapter does not offer an exhaustive analysis of multilingual legislative drafting in Canada and the EU;[5] instead, it focuses mainly on similarities and differences in

2 In the search for new drafting methods before the enlargement of the EU in 2004, which almost doubled the number of EU official languages, meetings with Canadian experts were organized. For instance, the European Commission hosted in 2002 André Labelle – head of the Jurilinguists Service in the Canadian Ministry of Justice – at a seminar entitled 'La qualité de la législation: l'expérience canadienne' (information provided by lawyer-linguists of the European Commission). See also http://ec.europa.eu/dgs/legal_service/seminars_en.htm (accessed 1 September 2016).

3 The former head of the Legal Revisers Group of the Legal Service of the Council of the EU, Tito Gallas (2001: 90), and the current head, Manuela Guggeis (2005: 499), describe the revision of language versions of EU legal acts by jurist–linguists in the Council as 'co-drafting'. See also Loiacono (2010: 246), according to whom the EU drafting process resembles the Canadian co-drafting due to the theoretical basis of the political-institutional structure of the EU, which requires legal texts to be drafted collectively in all EU official languages.

4 In this chapter, legislative multilingualism refers to two legal requirements: first, legal acts must be drafted by a legislative body in more than one language; and second, after its enactment, all of the official language versions of a legal act become equally authentic.

5 Extensive literature is available on this subject. To mention just a few works as examples: Bastarache 2004, Creech 2005, Labelle 2000 and 2002, Šarčević 1997, Tosi 2003, Wagner et al. 2002, Wood 1996.

understanding legislative multilingualism and in the legislative drafting processes in Canada and the EU that determine terminological choices.

The number of languages in which law is drafted, which is the most obvious difference between Canadian and EU legislative multilingualism, results in a divergence between Canadian and EU requirements to use precise equivalents in all language versions. In Canada, where federal law is drafted in English and French only, these requirements are not very strict. Some differences in wording and sentence structure are allowed,[6] if 'both versions convey the same idea'.[7] It is important to draft legislation with respect to the spirit of the two official languages. In the EU, the legal acts of which are drawn up in twenty-four languages, such freedom could cause difficulties in rendering the same message in all language versions, interpretation doubts and problems in referring to parts of a legal act. EU law is drafted with respect to the multilingual nature of EU law, which means that terms, expressions and phrases that are 'too specific to the author's own language or legal system' should be avoided.[8] In particular, terms that have no equivalent in other EU languages should not be used.[9] Moreover, the number of sentences in an article should be the same in all language versions.[10] However, with regard to terminology, the same concept might be expressed by terms consisting of a different number of words.[11]

Despite the number of languages in which laws are drafted, the core of Canadian and EU legislative multilingualism is the equal authenticity (authority) of all official language versions of a legal act. Versions are not authentic during their drafting; they become equally authentic after enactment of the legal act. However, drafters are aware that all versions will gain equal status regardless of how they have been drawn up (as originals or as translations). Equal authenticity means that all language versions should be taken into consideration when the legal act is interpreted and that, if divergence exists between versions, none of the versions can prevail and none of them can be ignored when the meaning of a legal act is decided. For drafters, equal authenticity after enactment means that all versions must convey the same message.

Full equivalence between language versions seems to be more feasible to achieve during Canadian federal drafting than during the EU legislative process due to three circumstances: the number of drafted language versions, the drafting methods applied and the legislative processes. Obviously, it is easier to achieve equivalence in two

6 See Šarčević (1997: 190), who gives the example of different structures of language versions in Section 10(3) of the Marine Transportation Security Act (S.C. 1994, c. 40), which includes paragraphing in the English version but not in the French version.

7 McKeil Marine Inc. v. Canada, 2012 FCA 93, para. 13.

8 See guideline 5 of the *Joint Practical Guide of the European Parliament, the Council and the Commission for Persons Involved in the Drafting of Legislation within the Community Institutions.*

9 Guideline 5.3.1 of the *Joint Practical Guide.*

10 Information obtained during an interview with translators in the European Commission in December 2015.

11 Compare, for example, the English term *respondent party* with its French equivalent *défendeur* or the Polish equivalent *strona, przeciwko której wniesiono skargę* in Regulation (EU) No 524/2013 of the European Parliament and of the Council of 21 May 2013 on online dispute resolution for consumer disputes and amending Regulation (EC) No 2006/2004 and Directive 2009/22/EC (Regulation on consumer ODR), OJ of EU, 18.06.2013, L 165/1. See also the example analysed by Engberg (2015a: 172).

language versions than in twenty-four. The number of languages also influences the drafting methods that can be applied. Co-drafting of Canadian federal bills in two languages involves two co-drafters preparing, respectively, an English version and a French version. Each of them is responsible for writing the entire text in one language. During the drafting process, versions are constantly and systematically compared and modified to express the same meaning. Moreover, they are revised by jurilinguists and experts in legal language. EU legal acts are drafted in one language (usually in English)[12] and then translated into twenty-three other languages. Language versions are revised by lawyers and lawyer-linguists. The latter are responsible for scrutinizing whether versions convey the same message. However, the revision is usually limited to comparing the translated text only to a base text (a source text).

The EU legislative procedure does not facilitate drafting semantically corresponding language versions mainly because of political negotiations and the number of institutions involved in creating a legal instrument. In the EU, legislative drafting is dispersed among several institutions, each of which has its own translation services that might be located in different places.[13] In contrast, in Canada at the federal level, legislative drafting is centralized in the Department of Justice. Lionel A. Levert (2011: 29–30), the former Chief Legislative Counsel of Canada, emphasizes that drafters are in constant contact with legislative editors, linguists and law experts (especially with lawyers working for the sponsoring ministry). Moreover, during co-drafting, the representatives of the ministry that proposes a new bill or amendments to binding laws sit in front of the co-drafters, who, while drafting, are able to confirm their understanding of the author's intent. EU translators may pose questions to the authors of a legislative proposal, although they are not in direct and constant contact.

Furthermore, in Canada, a bill proposed by the ministry and co-drafted in English and French in the Department of Justice is then debated in the Parliament and, if passed, it is approved by royal assent. Hence, a bill prepared by the ministry is reviewed only by one institution. In the case of the EU, usually three institutions that represent different interests participate in the legislative process. The European Commission, which protects the interests of the EU, prepares legislative proposals. The Council of the EU and the European Parliament, which guard, respectively, the interests of Member States and of EU citizens, discuss and amend the Commission's proposal. To enact an EU legal act, consensus between the institutions must be achieved. It is particularly challenging to find legislative solutions that satisfy representatives of all Member States. The results of tough negotiations are reflected in the language of a legal act that is often intentionally vague. Hence, EU translators must work with

12 Previously, texts were drafted mainly in French. As late as the late 1990s, 40.5 per cent of texts were drafted in French, whereas 47 per cent were drafted in English. English became the main drafting language in 2004 (62 per cent), after the accession of ten Member States. The data refer to the number of pages, including the legal texts, translated by the Directorate-General for Translation (Translation and Multilingualism 2012: 7).

13 For instance, translators working for the Directorate-General for Translation, which translates texts for the European Commission, are based in Brussels and Luxembourg; see 'Organization chart' available at http://ec.europa.eu/dgs/translation/whoweare/organisation_chart_en.pdf (accessed 1 September 2016).

a text of many authors, who provide it with carefully chosen wording and toughly negotiated meaning.

Legislative multilingualism and legislative processes are not the only sources of challenges for Canadian and EU drafters. Both Canadian and EU laws are applied within territories where other laws shaping a different legal order are already binding. This legislation is enacted, respectively, by provincial legislatures and EU Member States' legislative bodies. The following section explains how this influences the work of drafters of EU legislation and Canadian federal laws.

3 Canadian bijuralism versus the autonomy of EU law

While referring to Canadian law, Courrier (2007) stated that 'federal law is not an island unto itself.' The same can be said about the law of the EU. While Canadian federal law depends on provincial law, EU law is supplemented by the national law of Member States. The character of relations between federal and provincial laws, and between supranational and national laws, influences terminological choices and legislative drafting methods.

Canadian federal law is applied within a civil law tradition in Quebec and within a common law tradition in other provinces. When federal law refers to concepts that belong to the domain of property and civil rights that are exclusively assigned to provinces,[14] drafters of federal legislation must transpose legal terminology not only in two languages but also in two legal traditions (Brown-John and Pawley 2004: 10). Therefore, Canadian federal law is described as *bijural*. If one accepts the definition of bijuralism as the co-existence of common law and civil law or, more broadly, as 'the coexistence of two legal systems or subsystems within a broader legal order' (Breton and Trebilcock 2006: 1), the EU could be considered bijural, since the EU Member States include civil law countries, common law countries and mixed jurisdiction (or bijural countries). This approach is accepted by the authors of *Bijuralism: An Economic Approach* (ibid.: 11, 17).

However, EU law is not required to consider the differences between its Member States' legal systems or to reflect common law and civil law to adjust the legal language for addressees from common law and civil law traditions. Therefore, in this chapter, EU law is not recognized as bijural law. Nevertheless, the EU respects the diversity of its Member States, including their diverse legal systems and cultures, which are to be 'united in diversity'. In certain areas, the EU institutions indicate only those objectives that are to be achieved in Member States. The method employed to meet the objectives is chosen by each Member State. Hence, objectives established by EU institutions are fulfilled by national legislation, in which EU legal concepts and sometimes EU legal terminology are introduced into the legal order of Member States. Although legal scholars emphasize the autonomy of EU law, they also take into consideration a network of reciprocal connections between EU law and the national laws of Member States (Jaroszyński 2011: 64).

[14] Section 92(13) of the Constitution Act, 1867, 30–1 Vict., c. 3 (UK).

The two concepts of bijuralism and autonomy describe, respectively, the relations between Canadian federal law and the law of the provinces and those between EU law and the law of the Member States. The differences between the requirements of terminological choices in EU and Canadian legislative drafting result mainly from the differences between the abovementioned relations.

Autonomy means that EU law is independent from the national law of the Member States. Consequently, new concepts specific to EU law can be developed. Not many originally new legal concepts have been introduced to EU law (Šarčević 2015: 186). Numerous EU legal concepts take their roots from the law of Member States. Regardless of whether the source of a legal concept is an original idea or inspired by the national law of a Member State, as soon as it is introduced to EU law, it becomes an EU autonomous concept. In contrast, because of bijuralism, Canadian federal law must take into account the co-existence of civil law and common law. Consequently, the federal law must be drafted so it is applicable in a civil law province and in common law provinces alike. The relation between federal and provincial law can take one of two forms: *complementarity*, which is a rule; or *dissociation*, which is an exception. The former means that provincial law completes or complements federal law. In this situation, federal law is based on provincial legal concepts; hence, it depends on provincial law. The latter means that federal law is separated from provincial law and, as a result, federal law can create a new norm dissociated from provincial legal concepts and rules (Cuerrier 2007: 58). The practice of dissociation is comparable with the autonomy of EU law.

The reasons for considering bijuralism and autonomy when drafting legislation and interpreting law differ in the Canadian and the EU contexts, and this influences terminological decisions. The preservation of the autonomy of EU law is necessary to guarantee a uniform interpretation and application of EU law in all Member States. Consequently, national courts in Member States are forbidden from searching for the meaning of EU legal norms within national law to give to EU legal terminology meaning specific to national legal systems. Such a practice would jeopardize the harmonization process. In contrast, the recognition of bijuralism in Canada aims at respecting equally two legal systems, that is, common law and civil law. The *Policy on Legislative Bijuralism*[15] indicates that this policy 'aims at providing Canadians with federal legislative texts that will reflect, in each linguistic version, the legal system in use in (the) province'. Moreover, the objective of the *Policy for Applying the Civil Code of Quebec to Federal Government Activities*, adopted by the Law and Policy Committee on 7 June 1993,[16] is to ensure that 'the specificity of Quebec civil law within federal law' is taken into account. Hence, federal law must reflect the specificity of common law and civil law, not to merge them into one legal norm (Wellington 2001: 1). Since 2001, this objective has been confirmed in the preamble of *Federal Law – Civil Law Harmonization Act, No. 1*,[17] which states that 'the objective of the Government of

[15] Available at http://justice.gc.ca/eng/csj-sjc/harmonization/bijurilex/policy-politique.html (accessed 1 September 2016).

[16] Available at http://justice.gc.ca/eng/csj-sjc/harmonization/bijurilex/polici-politi.html (accessed 1 September 2016).

[17] S.C. 2001, c. 4.

Canada is to facilitate access to federal legislation that takes into account the common law and civil law traditions, in its English and French versions.'

Thus, the recognition of legal autonomy and of bijuralism serves to harmonize law both in the EU and in Canada. However, the direction of the harmonization process is different in the EU and Canadian settings. While in the EU, national law should be harmonized with EU law, in Canada, federal law is to be harmonized with common law and civil law in the area of property and civil rights.

The features of Canadian bijuralism and the autonomy of EU law explained here influence the rules according to which laws are drafted and interpreted. Since courts are authoritative interpreters of legal terms and legal norms, lawmakers must be aware of the rules that judges apply in order to make proper terminological choices when drafting a new piece of legislation. It is therefore relevant to compare the rules applied to interpret Canadian and EU laws. Interestingly, in general, in various legal systems, common interpretation rules are applied, although some differences might appear (Morawski 2006: 5). Interpretation rules have usually been developed by legal doctrine and judicial practice and are rarely regulated in legal acts (Morawski 2006: 5–6). However, there are some exceptions. In Canada, for example, the Interpretation Act[18] provides the rules according to which laws must be interpreted. In 2001, two sections that refer to bijuralism were added to the Interpretation Act.[19] Section 8.1 provides that 'both the common law and the civil law are equally authoritative and recognized sources of the law of property and civil rights in Canada'. Section 8.2 confirms that the provincial law of property and civil rights complements federal law (the principle of complementarity of provincial law to federal law)[20] and that, unless otherwise provided by law, federal legal acts in this area can be applied differently in the Province of Quebec and in other provinces if their provisions contain 'civil law and common law terminology, or terminology that has a different meaning in the civil law and the common law'. Accordingly, bijuralism entails the principle of complementarity instead of the principle of uniformity.[21] In the EU, an autonomous and uniform interpretation throughout all Member States is a common rule developed in the case-law of the Court of Justice of the European Union (CJEU).[22] Only if the terms of the provision of EU law expressly refer to the law of a Member State, it is possible to depart from the uniform interpretation.

Hence, differences between the interpretation rules in Canada and the EU confirm that the requirements of drafting Canadian bijural and EU autonomous terminology are not the same. In Canada, it is necessary to search for terms applicable in the two legal traditions, whereas in the EU, terms that allow a concept to be understood uniformly in all Member States must be chosen in all official languages. The following section explains in more detail which terminological requirements and methods can assure bijuralism and the autonomy of law.

[18] RSC 1985, c I–21.

[19] The Interpretation Act was amended by the Federal Law-Civil Law Harmonization Act, No 1, SC 2001, c 4.

[20] See para. 19 of Cartier v. Videotron GP, 2012 CIRB 658.

[21] See para. 19, Cartier v. Videotron GP, 2012 CIRB 658 and para. 11, French v. Canada, 2016 FCA 64.

[22] See, for instance, para. 21, Case C-494/14, Judgment of the Court of 15 October 2015 European Union v. Axa Belgium SA and the case-law cited.

4 Terminological requirements necessary to guarantee bijuralism and autonomy of law

The Canadian legislative services branch must draft bijural legislative texts (Canadian Department of Justice 1995), whereas EU institutions are obliged to draft autonomous legal texts. The terminological requirements necessary to guarantee bijuralism and the autonomy of law are not the same. Canadian drafters are generally recommended to use 'terminology and wording that are respectful of the concepts, notions and institutions proper to the legal system (civil law or common law)' of the province or territory (ibid.: 22). In contrast, EU drafters are required to avoid any terms or wordings that are specific to the law of any Member State or at least to use them with care.

In order to compare drafting and terminological requirements and techniques applied by EU and Canadian drafters, it is necessary to distinguish two terminological approaches. First, as a rule, EU drafters are required to express in all language versions a legal concept that is understood and applied uniformly. This would be an exception compared to Canadian federal law that refers to property and civil rights. Secondly, drafters must express a legal concept so that it can gain different meaning depending on the legal system (of Canadian province or of EU Member State) in which a legal provision is applied. In this case, the Canadian provincial law or the national law of the Member State supplements federal or supranational law. If Canadian federal law refers to concepts related to property or civil rights, the second terminological approach is the rule. In EU law, this approach will be chosen only if an EU legal act makes 'express reference to the law of the Member States for the purpose of determining its meaning and scope'.[23] However, sometimes, it is difficult to determine which terminological approach to choose and which meaning (uniform or specific to provincial law or Member State's national law) to give to the concept. The dilemma is faced not only by legislative drafters but also by addressees of legal norms and courts interpreting legal provisions (see Bastarache 2012: 170).

In the case of EU law, an indication of terminological choices might appear in the legal act. In their recitals, legislative instruments may specify that certain concepts should be understood for the purposes of the instrument as an autonomous concept.[24] This information is addressed to courts that must interpret the legal provisions and suggests that interpreters should not look for the meaning of the concept within national law but should instead search for a uniform meaning applicable in all Member States.

[23] See, for instance, Case C-494/14, para. 21, Judgment of the Court (Fifth Chamber) of 15 October 2015 European Union v. Axa Belgium SA.

[24] See Recital 11 of Regulation (EC) No 864/2007 of the European Parliament and of the Council of 11 July 2007 on the law applicable to non-contractual obligations (Rome II), OJ L 199/40, 31.07.2007, which provides that 'for the purposes of this Regulation, non-contractual obligation should be understood as an autonomous concept'; or Recital 13 of Directive (EU) 2016/680 of the European Parliament and of the Council of 27 April 2016 on the protection of natural persons with regard to the processing of personal data by competent authorities for the purposes of the prevention, investigation, detection or prosecution of criminal offences or the execution of criminal penalties, and on the free movement of such data, and repealing Council Framework Decision 2008/977/JHA, OJ L 119, 4.05.2016, stating: 'A criminal offence within the meaning of this Directive should be an autonomous concept of Union law as interpreted by the Court of Justice of the European Union.'

The indication of the autonomous character of the concept is also important for EU translators. To convey the concept in all official languages, they should find a term that is not recognized as a legal term having a specific legal meaning in the national law of Member States. However, since interpreters are explicitly informed about the autonomous nature of the concept in the recitals, even if drafters choose a term specific to national law, courts will give an EU meaning to this term.

EU legal acts might also explicitly refer to the national law of Member States. For instance, Article 2(2) of Council Directive 80/987/EEC of 20 October 1980 on the approximation of the laws of the Member States relating to the protection of employees in the event of the insolvency of their employer[25] provides that 'this Directive is without prejudice to national law as regards the definition of the terms "employee", "employer", "pay", "right conferring immediate entitlement" and "right conferring prospective entitlement."' Hence, the national law of Member States must specify and define these terms.[26]

Generally, however, there is no indication of whether a concept is autonomous or should be defined by national law. It might not be easy to evaluate the nature of the concept. Therefore, many preliminary rulings issued by the CJEU deal with whether the concept is an autonomous concept of EU law.[27] EU translators, however, cannot ask the CJEU the questions referred for a preliminary ruling. They can ask the author of the text whether a concept should have a uniform or a national meaning. When choosing the term, translators can also consult national experts (Šarčević 2015: 203). While translators usually look for a term not specific to national law, national experts tend to recommend national legal terms.[28]

Unlike in Canada, where the bijural nature of federal law is confirmed in legal statutes,[29] in the EU, the autonomy of EU (formerly European Community [EC]) law has been developed in the case-law of the CJEU (formerly European Court of Justice [ECJ]). As early as 1964, the Court recognized EC law as autonomous in the case of Costa v. E.N.E.L.[30] The autonomous character of EU (EC) terminology has been emphasized by the ECJ in the judgment in the CILFIT case,[31] in which the Court stated: 'It must also be borne in mind, even where the different language versions are entirely

[25] OJ L 283, 28.10.1980.

[26] See para. 27 of Case C-442/00, Judgment of the Court (Sixth Chamber) of 12 December 2002, Ángel Rodríguez Caballero v. Fondo de Garantía Salarial (Fogasa).

[27] To mention just a few, see Case C-494/14, Judgment of the Court (Fifth Chamber) of 15 October 2015, European Union v. Axa Belgium SA, not yet published (concept of a 'third party'); Case C-201/13, Judgment of the Court (Grand Chamber), 3 September 2014, Johan Deckmyn and Vrijheidsfonds VZW v. Helena Vandersteen and Others, not yet published (concept of 'parody'); Case C-34/10, Judgment of the Court (Grand Chamber) of 18 October 2011, Oliver Brüstle v. Greenpeace eV, European Court Reports 2011 I-09821 (concept of 'human embryo').

[28] Information obtained during interviews with terminologists and translators in the European Commission.

[29] See Preamble of the Federal Law-Civil Law Harmonization Act, No. 1 (S.C. 2001, c. 4) and Sections 8.1 and 8.2 added to the Interpretation Act in 2001 by the aforementioned Harmonization Act. Although the Acts do not apply the term *bijuralism*, they recognize common law and civil law as equally authoritative (Section 8.1) and underline the need to take into account both traditions when federal law is drafted (Preamble).

[30] Case 6-64, Judgment of the Court of 15 July 1964, Flaminio Costa v. E.N.E.L., ECR 00585 (English special edition 1964).

[31] Para. 19, Case 283/81, Judgment of the Court of 6 October 1982, Srl CILFIT and Lanificio di Gavardo SpA v. Ministry of Health, ECR 03415.

in accord with one another, that Community law uses terminology which is peculiar to it. Furthermore, it must be emphasized that legal concepts do not necessarily have the same meaning in Community law and in the law of the various Member States.' Hence, although not through legislation, the autonomy of EU law was established at the beginning of the development of Community law. In Canada, bijuralism was recognized by the Department of Justice much later, in 1995, in a standing policy on legislative bijuralism, and it was introduced into legislation in 2001[32] as a remedy for unijuralism or semi-bijuralism, that is, when federal law applies only common law terminology and concepts or when the English version is common law specific and the French version is civil law specific. The late introduction of bijuralism required changes in already binding laws and the development of new drafting methods. Unlike the EU, Canadian methods of drafting bijural legislation are described in detail. For this reason, they will be the starting point for the comparison of Canadian and EU drafting practices that lead, respectively, to bijural and autonomous laws.

Three legislative techniques are applied to draft bijural legislation in Canada: the use of neutral terminology, the use of definitions and the use of doubles, also called *doublets*. The double is very specific to Canadian federal drafting and cannot be applied to draft EU law. The double expresses the legal rule in different terms that correspond to common law and civil law in both language versions and makes this rule applicable in common law and civil law provinces (Wellington 2001). This technique fulfils the principle of complementarity, which is not known to EU law.

The definition and use of neutral terms are techniques known to EU drafters. However, they are not used exactly in the same way as in Canada. Wellington (2001) explains that, in the context of bijuralism, the definition gives to 'a term a meaning specific to both the civil law and the common law'. Hence, the defined concept can be understood differently in Quebec than it is in other Canadian provinces. To rephrase this statement in the context of EU autonomous law, a definition gives to a term meaning specific to the EU law. Accordingly, a term refers to one concept that has the same meaning in all Member States.

In EU drafting, only drafters of a basic (source) text can apply this technique. In a legal act, translators cannot explain how they understand the terms that they use. Conversely, both drafters and translators of a legal act can use neutral terms. A neutral term, which is referred to in Canada as a *generic* or a *general* term, does not have a meaning in a specific legal system. The search for such a term can be similar in Canada and in the EU. However, the reasons for and the results of using neutral terminology for Canadian bijural and EU autonomous drafting differ. A neutral term is applied as a bijural drafting technique to encompass a few concepts understood in a specific way in each province. Therefore, both the term with no legal meaning and the term that refers to concepts existing in civil and common law traditions can be used. Neutral terminology is employed by EU drafters to guarantee that a term will be given the same meaning in all Member States. Therefore, as part of this technique, only neutral terms that do not already have legal meaning and do not refer to legal concepts or institutions in Member States are applicable in EU legal acts.

[32] See note 29 *supra*.

5 Conclusions

The difficulty encountered in drafting bijural law in Canada (when federal law refers to property and civil rights) and autonomous law in the EU is essentially the same: how to recognize whether the meaning of a concept is designated by federal law or EU law, or by provincial law or national law of EU Member States, respectively. In the first situation, a concept has the same uniform meaning in all provinces or all EU Member States. In the second situation, the concept might have a different meaning depending upon where it is applied. Correctly distinguishing between the two situations is a prerequisite to making proper terminological choices. When the concept has a uniform meaning, there is one legal concept under one term. When the concept should have a provincial or national meaning, one term will actually encompass various concepts. In the case of Canadian federal law on property and civil rights, usually the term should have a specific meaning in Quebec and in other common law provinces, whereas EU legal terms as a rule have a uniform meaning in all Member States. Despite these rules, it is not always easy for drafters and interpreters to evaluate which meaning should be associated with the term. The power over meaning actually belongs to the courts,[33] which ultimately decide how terms and legal provisions must be understood.

Both Canadian federal law and EU supranational law are applied within already existing legal systems of provinces and Member States. However, since the relations between supranational and national law, and between federal and provincial law, are governed by different rules and principles, the drafting techniques applied in Canada cannot be directly followed for EU drafting purposes. Definitions with neutralizing effect and the use of neutral terminology are applicable in both Canada and the EU but only to give the same meaning to a legal concept, regardless of the legal system in which the relevant legal instrument is applied.

[33] The final adjudicators in the EU and Canada are, respectively, the CJEU and the Supreme Court of Canada.

8

Legal-Linguistic Profiling as Translation Aid: The Example of an EU Agency

Colin Robertson

1 Introduction

This chapter introduces the concept of legal-linguistic profiling of organizations as an aid to translation, and it offers an example of how to apply it to an organization that operates in a complex legal, linguistic and technical environment. For this, a European Union (EU) agency has been selected, namely the European Aviation Safety Agency (EASA).[1] It is one of many EU agencies called on to perform technical and legal tasks in a multilingual environment that embraces many cultures, languages and legal systems. In such an environment, translation and terminology play an important role, and equivalences across languages of term and text take on particular significance.

The purpose of legal-linguistic profiling is to provide a method for analysing multilingual and multicultural legal environments in which a text to be translated forms part. It comes within the scope of Legal Translation Studies (Prieto Ramos 2014b), as it assists in the identification of the range of genres and types of legal text, and their functions, created by an organization. It provides information about the legal texts creating the organization and the intertextual relations that the texts produced by the organization and those creating it have in the wider legal environment. For a multilingual organization, that may imply different sets of legal environments, as well as a variety of operational languages, which in turn motivates the demand for translation. It thus serves as a form of overarching 'bird's-eye view' of the operational legal-linguistic, but also technical, environment in which the organization's legal texts function, which can assist inter alia with terminology decisions and legal translation methodology (e.g. Gémar 1979, Šarčević 1997, Cao 2007, Bocquet 2008; on the parameters of legal translation decision-making, see Prieto Ramos 2014c). The text in hand may thereby be 'situated' legally, linguistically, culturally and semiotically within a wider 'sea' of texts, 'vertically' within a given language in relation to past texts, 'horizontally' across languages and inter-legally across different impacting legal

[1] https://www.easa.europa.eu/ (accessed 23 September 2016).

systems and legal orders (i.e. national, international and supranational legal orders) where terms may have subtly different nuances.

While it assists in the determination of the legal function and genre of a text in hand (Kurzon 1997), legal-linguistic profiling also helps to reveal the range of users of the text and the variety of possible legal environments in which it may fall to be interpreted and which has potential implications for the meanings attributed. This in turn has implications for translation strategies (see e.g. Šarčević 2000b). The principal focus, however, is initially not at the level of the text but rather at the level of the organization, though it is both created by texts and creates texts and takes its existence from a wider environment of law that is also essentially linguistic and textual. These aspects, too, form part of legal-linguistic profiling. For the individual language professional, the purpose is nonetheless to provide a practical aid for drafting, translation and interpretation. In the case of EASA, there is the additional factor that each of us, as users of commercial airline services, has a direct and personal interest in its activities as they are devoted to our safety. In this way, the connection between legal translation and everyday life is manifest: legal translation may appear abstract, but it is rooted in everyday reality.

This chapter is divided into four sections: First, some background information is given to introduce a range of ideas lying behind the concept of legal-linguistic profiling. Second, the concept of legal-linguistic profiling of organizations is introduced in the form of headings as a framework for enquiry set out in the Appendix. The approach draws on, and extends, ideas presented in *Multilingual Law, a Framework for Analysis and Understanding* (Robertson 2016). The third section applies profiling to an organization to explore how to use the concept in practice. EASA is selected, as it provided the venue in which the ideas were developed. The profiling approach is used to explore legal and linguistic dimensions of the Agency. It enables a broad overview and from there one could go on to make a more extended survey of individual Agency texts, in particular to reveal the range of domains, legal environments, genres, discourse features, specialized language (LSP) and specialist terminology. EASA is one of many EU agencies that work in a complex multilingual multicultural environment, and the concept of legal-linguistic profiling can be applied in principle to any organization. Profiling serves to reveal the role of translation, if any, and it can clarify features of the translation environment and ranges of terminology involved. Profiling is of most benefit where the operational legal, linguistic and cultural environments in which the organization operates are the most complex, which is a further reason for selecting EASA as model.

2 Background

Every organization uses language and produces documents. Each organization is created by legal documents that define its identity, status, purpose, tasks and type. These documents are constructed in accordance with the rules and methods of the legal system and the particular rules of law that apply to the organization. They are in the language(s) authorized by the legal system. When making a legal-linguistic analysis, it helps to start with a broad level of information – to obtain a 'bird's-eye view' of the arrangements. Then one can explore details within the picture thus sketched out. This is the framework concept in a nutshell.

The purpose of legal-linguistic profiling is to explore the language features of organizations that work in a legal environment and make legal texts. Knowledge of law and legal thinking and methods is essential, as is knowledge of language and languages, as well as translation and terminology methods. Profiling makes use of this knowledge and organizes it in particular ways through a set of headings that cover legal, linguistic, translation and terminology issues. It takes into account the contents in terms of the words and sentences of texts, but it also takes into account the methods and procedures by which the texts are produced, translated, interpreted and used, as these all play a role in influencing the meanings that are created and acted upon in practice.

From a legal point of view, it is necessary to be aware that there are different types of law, generally referred to as *legal order* and *legal system*. The law of the EU is seen as creating its own body of law, specific to itself, as a legal order. The treaties founding the EU, notably the Treaty on European Union (TEU) and the Treaty on the Functioning of the European Union (TFEU), were created by the Member States according to the practice of international law, a separate legal order. The purpose of EU legal texts is to have effects in the national domestic legal systems internal to the Member States. National law is a third legal order. However, EU law and international law have, or can have, impacts on the national legal systems of countries that are not EU Member States. Each legal order or system is complex and creates an environment in which both legal and linguistic meanings are constructed. The systems have impacts on each other; sometimes they make contradictory rules on the same matter, sometimes they say nothing on a matter and sometimes they use the same words and terms but give them different meanings. This is the legal-linguistic environment in which EU bodies such as EASA tend to find themselves operating. The purpose of profiling is to map out the influences for the purposes of assisting drafters and translators to thread a path for each text, but equally it can be a tool for general legal-linguistic analysis.

A key issue is to identify the linguistic regime of the legal system that applies to the organization – whether it recognizes a single official language or a multiplicity of them. This information reveals the nature of the need for translation. An organization in a single-language national legal system does not have a translation need. If it operates in a bilingual or multilingual legal system, it probably does. Either it arranges for translation as part of its activities or it contracts translation out to another body. A third scenario is where users of the texts arrange for themselves the translation of texts they need. Profiling helps to clarify these issues.

With multilingualism and translation come issues of terminology and equivalences in meanings between different language versions of the same text. That takes one into the study of individual texts and their terminology and the linguistic features of each of them. Profiling extends to these issues too, but they are not addressed here for reasons of space. Suffice to say that each text can be analysed for the domains to which each word or term might fit, whether that be a particular specialized technical field, a branch of law, general language and so on.

We can summarize the foregoing by suggesting that when considering an organization from a legal-linguistic point of view, one is interested in several levels of contextual information: first, the legal environment in which the organization is embedded; second, its linguistic environment; and third, its tasks and specialized domains of activity. There may be an allocation of roles and responsibilities within the organization, and it then becomes necessary to examine individual subdivisions and organs in order to identify the types of text and terminology that each generates. That entails entering inside the organization structure. It is more difficult to undertake as insider information becomes a factor, but it also forms part of legal-linguistic profiling.

Lawyers draw a distinction between the substantive content of legal rules and the methods by which the texts containing rules are produced. When examining documents for their language, it is generally the words on the page that are studied, but the processes by which a text has been produced also have impacts on the final result. This is the procedural dimension, and lawyers refer to *procedural* law. Examples are court procedures, legislative procedures or negotiating procedures to create contracts. In each case, the procedural dimension involves a series of steps from a start to a finish, from conception to finished product. In a multilingual environment, with a need for multiple language versions, the role of translation forms a part of the procedure and can itself be seen in terms of a series of steps or a procedure leading to an end result. Legal-linguistic profiling embraces procedural aspects by asking about the methods and processes by which the texts are drafted, translated and interpreted. It seeks to clarify the forces at work in each process and their linguistic implications.

Making a legal-linguistic profile accordingly yields both legal and linguistic information about an organization. It helps to clarify the function of terminology used. That, in turn, assists with the translation process and the continual search for quality. But how does one set about making a legal-linguistic profile in practice? What exactly does one look for? How does one organize information? How does one use and apply it? We turn now to outline the concept, and we will then explore how it may be applied to EASA.

3 Legal-linguistic profiling

The concept of legal-linguistic profiling proposed here comprises a series of headings, which are set out in the Appendix. The aim is to assist drafters, translators, readers and users of legal texts with respect to the use of specialist terminology. The main headings are as follows: (a) the organization and legal aspects of its texts; (b) the languages of the organization and its documents; (c) specialist terminology domains and particular terminology; and (d) drafting, translation and interpretation methods. Under each heading, there is a range of subheadings that address individual issues. They can be extended as wished. The profiling aims, among other things, to clarify the following: implications for meanings of words and terms arising from the impact of different legal systems and legal orders on an organization's texts; the range of viewpoints that may be brought to bear in reading and interpreting its legal texts; differences between languages and language versions of texts; whether texts are drafted, translated or interpreted by native or non-native speakers and the potential existence of 'calques' where foreign language forms are implicitly followed (Crystal 2010: 340); multilingual interpretation methods; and terms shared across legal systems but with different technical meanings, such as *person* or *domicile*.

Applying these ideas to an organization and its texts leads to thinking about, first, its legal and linguistic regime; second, its activities, tasks and texts; third, the organs that make legal texts; fourth, text structure, format and guidance; fifth, forces 'pushing' at the drafting of source-language texts and translations; sixth, tensions 'pulling' at the interpretation of source-language texts and translations; seventh, the existence of interactions (or conflicts) between legal systems and legal orders (e.g. between national systems, international law, EU supranational law), which can be seen in terms of 'matrices' and which may impact on the drafting, translation, revision, interpretation and application of the texts; and eighth, the impact on individual terms and terminology of the foregoing. The enquiry can be extended as far as one wishes or has need. The purpose is to make a rapid outline to assist in determining how to 'position' individual legal texts and terms within cultural legal and linguistic contexts in order to clarify subtle aspects of meaning and intention and thereby enhance multilingual term equivalence, drafting, translation and interpretation with an eye to quality. We can take each of the heads in the Appendix and explore them for individual elements.

3.1 The organization and legal aspects of its texts

Under this heading, we study general aspects relating to the organization so as to obtain a broad overview of its function and place within the general scheme of things. Attention is placed, in particular, on the following: the organization's title, foundation documents, legal status, objectives, and organs and bodies that produce documents. The focus is on legal aspects that address the wider system of which the texts that found, establish and construct the organization form part (the external dimension), as well as the legal documents and contexts that flow from the foundation texts that create and structure the organization's working environment (the internal dimensions). The idea here is that each organization creates its own specialized culture through law, language and terminology. Within that, there are also subcultures to explore using discourse analysis methods (Paltridge 2006). Having thus formed a broad overview of the legal dimension, one turns to consider more specifically linguistic considerations.

3.2 The languages of the organization and its documents

Under this heading, we study the linguistic regime of the organization and its documents. Of particular interest are the authorized language versions of the foundation texts and the linguistic regime that applies to each category, or genre, of text produced, for it is possible for different rules to apply according to the category of a text, and a distinction is to be drawn between official languages and internal working languages of an organization. From there, one shifts attention to the language of each type of document produced by the internal organs of the organization. Lastly, there are the users of the texts and the linguistic and cultural contexts in which they operate, which may have impacts on how the users read and interpret the texts. Multilingual drafters and translators of international texts need to pay attention to possible misinterpretations, which can arise, for example, where a reader associates particular words and terms with a national law meaning rather than an intended international one.

3.3 Specialist terminology domains and particular terminology

Under this heading, one thinks about matters such as the range of specialist terminology domains covered, sources of guidance on terminology in the different languages, the possibility of overlaps and divergences in the meanings of terms used by different bodies and relationships between the activities of the organization compared with those of other entities working in the same field. Having analysed the wider dimensions under the aforementioned headings means one comes to this heading with prior background information. The task is thus facilitated when addressing individual terms, and one is aware, for example, how a term may shift meaning according to whether it appears in a text governed by national law, international law or EU supranational law.[2] Such considerations lead to thinking about how to 'position' texts within matrices of law and languages through the selection of terminology, which is a task for drafters, translators and revisers.

3.4 Drafting, translation and interpretation methods

Like the previous headings, this heading covers a wealth of issues. First, there is drafting, which embraces matters such as the styles, precedents and methods for constructing written documents in source language and, where applicable, in translations. Second, drafting in a multilingual context implies a range of options in respect of translation that may vary between translating a final text, translating draft source texts and finalizing them all together or drafting all language versions in parallel at the same time and harmonizing them through a revision process (see also Robertson 2016: 164–8). By asking questions, the translation environment is made clearer. Third, there is the whole question of the interpretation of texts, which covers the methods used by readers in particular courts in order to establish the meaning of words and sentences and give them legal and practical effects. In this connection, we have regard to legal interpretation by lawyers, in particular courts and judges, and the legal literature on interpretation that is typically linked to a particular legal system (e.g. on Scots law, Walker 2001: 412–49; on EU law, Lenaerts and Gutiérrez-Fons 2013). We also have regard to interpretation by linguists (e.g. Mattila 2013).

One can extend the scope and detail of the questions, just as one can use them for purposes other than translation, such as to analyse the discourse style of an organization and thereby reveal its underlying preoccupations and interests. However, we will now turn to think about practical application. We will take EASA as our model and, using published information drawn from the EASA website, we will apply the profiling concept to it.

[2] This shift of meaning is commonplace in the implementation of EU directives in national law. If a term in the EU text is retained for use in a national implementing law, the operational context shifts from EU to national. Inserting definitions is a technique that can reduce uncertainties.

4 Application to EASA

For the purpose of illustrating the application of legal-linguistic profiling, we could have taken any organization. We could have taken a monolingual national body, but that would typically have excluded translation. International bodies work in a multilingual environment where there is generally a need for translation. In the case of an EU body, this need is explicit and formalized through texts and established procedures. The ready availability of information on EU activities facilitates study from a language point of view. EU agencies are less well known than the main institutions. They have an advantage for study in that they are each focused on a specific range of tasks within a particular context. EASA provides a model that permits one to explore the matrix of legal-linguistic and terminological issues that typically arise in the EU organizational environment. Documents must be produced in different languages to deal with complex and technical matters, using words and terms that can be understood, interpreted and acted on correctly by very many persons coming with a diversity of cultures and languages. EASA works in the field of civil aviation safety, and, as air passengers, we all have a direct interest in its work. We will explore the legal-linguistic side of the organization focusing on the principal headings in the Appendix.

4.1 The organization and legal aspects of its texts

The title of the organization is the European Aviation Safety Agency (EASA), as established in Regulation (EC) No 216/2008,[3] the foundation text. We see in its title the letters '(EC)', and that tells us that it is an EU text; we need to know the meaning of the letters and that previously the EU was referred to as the 'European Community' (EC). We identify the authors: European Parliament and Council of the EU. We are accordingly in the EU supranational legal-linguistic environment. Terms and concepts are those of EU law and language.

We study Regulation (EC) No 216/2008 for the information it provides.[4] The title informs us that it applies to civil aviation, establishes EASA and repeals earlier legislation. We note the structure of the act, its chapters, sections, articles and technical annexes. The forty numbered recitals commencing with 'Whereas' provide background information and introduce the articles that contain the rules of law or normative provisions. We note four chapters and over seventy articles.[5] Chapter III deals with EASA (Articles 17 to 64). Article 17 establishes the agency and states its duties: to undertake tasks and formulate opinions on matters covered by Article 1(1) (aeronautical products, aircraft

[3] Regulation (EC) No 216/2008 of the European Parliament and of the Council of 20 February 2008 on common rules in the field of civil aviation and establishing a European Aviation Safety Agency, and repealing Council Directive 91/670/EEC, Regulation (EC) No 1592/2002 and Directive 2004/36/EC. Available online: http://eur-lex.europa.eu/legal-content/EN/TXT/?uri=celex%3A32008R0216 (accessed 23 September 2016).

[4] It does not mention the location of its headquarters, however, which are in Cologne. It also has offices in Beijing, Brussels, Montreal and Washington.

[5] Legal technique is to insert new articles with numbers such as '8a' when amending so as not to disturb the system of references already in operation for unchanged articles. So although the last article is '70', there are in fact more.

operating personnel, aerodromes, aerodrome equipment, air traffic management and air navigation services [ATM/ANS] and personnel and organizations involved with them). A second duty is to assist the Commission in preparing measures to implement the Regulation. Third, EASA takes measures authorized by the Regulation or other EU legislation. Fourth, it conducts inspections and investigations. Fifth, it carries out on behalf of Member States functions and tasks ascribed to them by applicable international conventions, in particular the Chicago Convention (Article 17(1) and (2)(a) to (e)). From Article 28(1), we learn that the agency is 'a body of the Community', which means it is now an EU body. It can act on behalf of Member States, which are national-law entities, in respect of international conventions, in particular the Chicago Convention, defined in Article 3(b) as the Convention on International Civil Aviation and its Annexes, signed in Chicago on 7 December 1944. From this information, we understand that the Agency operates in several different legal environments: EU as it is an EU agency; international, as it has a role in connection with the Chicago Convention; and national, as the day-to-day operations of civil aviation take place within the jurisdiction of individual countries. There are potential implications for terminology should terms be differently used between these legal environments.

As regards organizational structure, we see the Agency as legal person (Article 28) and note the internal organs: management board (Articles 33–37), executive director (Article 38–39), one or more boards of appeal (Articles 41–43) and the staff (Article 29). The organs make texts, and for each of them we may expect a particular structure, style and content adapted to the author and to the tasks in hand. In the case of the Staff, the EU Staff Regulations apply (Article 29).[6] The Agency is responsible for the duties in Article 17(2) mentioned above. Article 18 specifies a range of Agency measures, which means texts that (a) issue opinions addressed to the Commission; (b) issue recommendations addressed to the Commission on Article 14, which provides flexibility for Member States to react immediately to a safety problem; (c) issue certification specifications and guidance material; (d) take decisions in relation to airworthiness and environmental certification, pilot certification, air operation certification, ATM/ANS, air traffic-controller certification, third-country operators, inspections of Member States and investigation of undertakings; and (d) issue reports following standardization inspections.

The management board appoints the executive director and the directors, adopts the Agency's annual general report, adopts the Agency's annual programme of work, adopts guidelines for the allocation of certification tasks to national aviation authorities and qualified entities and carries out other tasks, as set out in Article 33 of the Regulation. One of these is to 'decide on the linguistic arrangements for the Agency' (Article 33(2)(k)). The executive director approves agency measures, decides on inspections and investigations, allocates certification tasks to national aviation authorities or qualified entities and carries out other duties (Article 38(3)). A board of appeal decides on appeals against decisions of the agency (Article 40). The duties of the Agency and its organs imply the creation of texts. Provision is made for actions before

6 Staff Regulations of Officials of the European Communities and Conditions of Employment of Other Servants of the European Communities. Available online: http://ec.europa.eu/civil_service/docs/toc100_en.pdf (accessed 23 September 2016).

the Court of Justice of the European Union (Article 50), so that the case-law of the EU Court of Justice concerning EASA also forms part of the legal-linguistic picture.

4.2 The languages of the organization and its documents

Having formed a view on the legal features of the organization, we turn to the linguistic dimension. A first question is to identify the linguistic regime that applies to EASA and its texts. This is a legal question as it is governed by rules, but it is also linguistic, as it is implemented through practice. Regulation (EC) No 216/2008 exists in twenty-four language versions in accordance with EU rules set down in Council Regulation No 1 determining the languages to be used by the European Economic Community. Regulation (EC) No 216/2008 does not itself lay down rules on languages for the Agency. That might suggest that the general EU rules on languages should apply, but Article 33(2)(k) of the regulation states that the management board is to 'decide on the linguistic arrangements for the Agency'. So we look for a management board decision. That takes us into the question of publication: Is there a published decision on the matter? The Regulation contains a provision on publication of documents in Article 32 that is relevant to the question of linguistic regime, insofar as it lists the documents that must be produced in the EU official languages: safety reviews aimed to inform the public of the general safety level, opinions addressed to the Commission, annual general reports and programmes of work. For those documents, translation into the EU languages is required. The same article states that 'The translation services required for the functioning of the Agency shall be provided by the Translation Centre for Bodies of the European Union' (Article 32(2)). What about other Agency documents? The emphasis on publishing a short list of key documents in the EU languages implies, *a contrario*, that different rules on languages may apply to other documents, and we note in passing that the Agency website is in English.

4.3 Specialist terminology domains and particular terminology

The language of Regulation (EC) No 216/2008 is highly technical, with terms such as *ATM/ANS*, *Chicago Convention*, *certification*, *complex motor-powered aircraft*, *aerodrome*, *airworthiness*, *type-certificate*, *pilot*, *air operation*, *product integrity* and *cyclic loading*. These terms are connected to civil aviation. However, *Chicago Convention* also connects to an international agreement and therefore to international law. In the Regulation, there are also terms that link to administration (*management board*, *appoint*, *guidelines*, *procedures*, *disciplinary authority*) and terms that link to law (*regulation*, *treaty*, *shall*, *appeal*, *Court of Justice*), which can be subcategorized into substantive law terms and procedural law terms. There are also terms relating to safety, environment, legislative technique (*repeal*, *amend*), criminal law (*penalties*) and general language. Institutional online resources are available to deal with these terms, including Interactive Terminology for Europe (IATE), specialized glossaries[7]

[7] For an online list of civil aviation glossaries, see http://inboxtranslation.com/resources/glossaries/aviation/ (accessed 23 September 2016).

and EUR-Lex (for comparisons between language versions), as well as information on terms provided by EASA.[8]

If we study individual texts for their range of terms and tag them according to domain, as well as to the location where one might expect them to be read, interpreted and acted on, we come to realize the pressure that is on certain terms. This arises because readers are located in many places. It arises because readers have different languages and cultures and view the world in different ways. It arises because the texts are being read from the viewpoint of different legal systems. For example, a dispute involving interpretation of terms may arise in a court of any EU Member State, a non-EU State, an international tribunal or the EU Court of Justice. In each case, there will be a surrounding context particular to the court and the legal system within which it functions. The terms being created need to be adapted to such possibilities if they are to retain singularity in meaning. One is aware of possible divergences in the use of terms between different bodies: EASA, EU national aviation authorities, third countries and international aviation bodies such as the International Civil Aviation Organization (ICAO). One of the roles of EASA, as an EU agency, is to enhance standardization in the use of terms. This arises from its role in harmonizing rules internationally under Article 27 of Regulation (EC) No 216/2008.

Readers and users of EASA texts may come from any of the legal contexts and national States identified earlier. If they do not understand English or, for documents listed in Article 32, one of the EU languages, then translation is required for their benefit. Which languages? We need to think about who the potential users of the texts are, as they are the persons who will infer meanings into the words and act on their understandings of those meanings. From this perspective, users of EASA texts would seem to include, first, the EU institutions and bodies, notably the European Commission but, by extension, other EU institutions; second, persons in national civil aviation institutions of Member States of the EU and of the European Economic Area (EEA); third, users in international aviation organizations; fourth, users in third-country non-EU/EEA states; and fifth, individuals such as pilots, flight crew, experts, technicians, trainers and medical staff. We learn all this from Regulation (EC) No 216/2008, supplemented by information on the official website.

4.4 Drafting, translation and interpretation methods

The underlying concept behind this heading is that of communication: a person creates a text through language and another decodes and interprets it – two sides. Who constructs meaning? In a multilingual environment, the translator is inserted as being first a 'receiver' of a source text and second an 'utterer' of a target text. Who drafts, in which language(s) and according to which conventions? These are some initial questions. It is understood that EASA texts are drafted by technical experts in English. Being an EU agency, one expects drafting by persons of different nationalities,

[8] For example, the Annexes to the draft Commission Regulation on 'Air Operations – OPS', which contains lists of terms with definitions, available online at: https://www.easa.europa.eu/system/files/dfu/Annexes%20to%20Regulation.pdf (accessed 23 September 2016).

which implies non-mother-tongue drafting and the desirability of linguistic revision, as well as the usual legal checking of documents. Non-mother-tongue drafting raises the possibility of calques, where the English text takes on the form of another language (Crystal 2010: 340). We expect drafting guidance, but it is internal to the Agency.

EASA does not have a translation department. Article 32(2) of Regulation (EC) No 216/2008 provides for translation to be undertaken by the EU Translation Centre based in Luxembourg. We might expect EASA to produce a completed text in the source language and seek translation of the finished text into other languages, since the clients of the Translation Centre pay for each translation and use a dedicated online tool for that purpose.[9] To proceed further, we would need to study the activities and methods of the Translation Centre and its working relationship with EASA. Similarly, we could study the translations that have been made. As regards interpretation, this takes us to the users. Invariably, these are specialist in view of the field. Expert knowledge is required in order to draft, translate, interpret and apply EASA texts. With respect to its legal texts, one can observe that different specializations come into contact: first, specialist legal knowledge on the construction of legal texts and the meanings applied to them; second, specialist knowledge of the field or discipline in question (here different fields within civil aviation, safety, environment, etc.); and third, general knowledge about use of the language in question. Where a text is a legal text, there is a characteristic that it is interpreted and applied by courts. By virtue of being in a legal text, terms take on a character of being legal – since their meanings are determined by lawyers according to legal methods. That means precise meanings of specialized agency texts may be located in court decisions, such as those of the EU Court of Justice.[10] This may pose difficulties for non-legal specialists, though terminology databases may take account of the interpretations. In this respect, the existence of a matrix of different legal orders and systems affected by a text takes on significance, since interpretation by courts may be by EU Courts using EU methods, national courts using national methods or international courts using international methods. The only way to handle such diversity is through efficient coordination, terminology control and the creation of widely available terminology guidance that is regularly updated. To that end, computer technology may be developed further to check for use of particular terms and the equivalences adopted for other languages. This forms part of the legal-linguistic revision of draft texts undertaken by specialist lawyer-linguists at some EU institutions (Šarčević and Robertson 2013: 181–202).

5 Conclusion

The foregoing is a brief presentation of the concept of the legal-linguistic profiling of an organization. The method does not provide individual answers directly but serves to reveal factors that have an influence on the organization and its texts and to clarify

9 For online information about the Translation Centre, see https://europa.eu/european-union/about-eu/agencies/cdt_en (accessed 23 September 2016).

10 For online information on cases before the Court of Justice involving civil aviation, see http://www.aviationlaw.eu/european-law/european-law-cases (accessed 23 September 2016).

the role or function of particular terms. These factors come into play in the contexts of drafting, translating and interpreting. The profiling set out in the Appendix can be adapted and extended at will. It is simply a list of topics that can serve as questions. They can, for example, be extended by asking what, who, where, when, why, how?

Applying legal-linguistic profiling to EASA, we have uncovered some of the cultural contexts in which the Agency works, drawing on prior knowledge of EU law and language. We have identified that the Agency is part of the EU legal order but has links outside it. We have identified that it works primarily in English and that some of its texts must be translated into EU languages. Its translation needs are serviced by the Translation Centre. We have not analysed individual texts beyond the founding Regulation; that would be a next step. A full study would entail examining a corpus of texts for use of terms and contextual domains, as well as ways in which language has been used. Texts are specialist and use specialist language (LSP) which can be analysed in each language, such as English (ESP) (Gotti 2003). Each aspect of the text has its special considerations and applicable rules and guidance, whether they relate, first, to drafting with standardized format, standardized language and technical terminology; second, to translation with close observance to source format and equivalences in meaning; or third, to interpretation and the search to give meaning to the texts within real-life operational situations for the purpose of actions.

Thus, we can imagine a form of hierarchy of levels that reach down to the most subtle nuances in term and meaning. It is a process of reflection that comes prior to the act of translating a text. It provides information to assist the translator in choosing terminology and in devising translation strategies. As such, it can be seen as preceding the act of translation but also as being a dimension in legal-linguistic revision of draft texts, where the reviser is aware of the complexities and reviews the draft text in the light of them for the purpose of legal-linguistic alignment with the source text while having regard to the other language versions. Thus, in conclusion, legal-linguistic profiling can be seen as simply another tool for contextualizing institutional translation and for ultimately enhancing its quality.

Appendix: Legal-linguistic profiling of an organization

(A) **The organization and legal aspects of its texts**

- (i) title
- (ii) foundation documents
- (iii) legal status
- (iv) objectives
- (v) organs and bodies that produce documents
- (vi) legal aspects:
  - (a) system of which founding texts form part (external)
  - (b) legal context created by founding texts (internal)
  - (c) sub-contexts created by documents in different areas
- (vii) types of documents produced (genres)

(B) **The languages of the organization and its documents**
- (i) linguistic regime of the organization and its documents:
  - (a) authentic languages of the foundation texts
  - (b) linguistic regime (primary, secondary texts or practice):
    - - its official languages
    - - its working languages
  - (c) languages of each type of document of each organ
- (ii) users of the texts and their linguistic/cultural context(s)

(C) **Specialist terminology domains and particular terminology**
- (i) specialist terminology domains
- (ii) sources of guidance on terminology in relevant languages
- (iii) possible overlaps of terms by different bodies
- (iv) relationship between activities of the organization and different legal orders, 'positioning' its texts

(D) **Drafting, translation and interpretation methods**
- (i) drafting:
  - (a) styles, precedents and methods for source and target languages where translation included
  - (b) how all language versions are produced, whether through translation or co-drafting
- (ii) translation: methods of making texts in all required languages
- (iii) interpretation: methods of interpretation of the texts and whether or not undertaken through courts

9

Translating Hybrid Legal Texts for Science and Technology Institutions: The Case of CERN

Mathilde Fontanet

1 Introduction

Few texts can be considered totally homogeneous as to their genre, style and subject matter. Some texts even deal with different fields or have an explicitly mixed nature. This chapter will focus on documents that have both a technical and a legal dimension, in order to discuss how these two facets come together on the textual level and what impact their dual identity has on the translator's task. I will analyse a parallel corpus of hybrid texts published by CERN (the European Organization for Nuclear Research),[1] and will raise the following questions: What are the discursive manifestations of both the legal and technical dimensions of the text? Is there a conflict between these two aspects? Are there interferences on the microtextual level that arise from the hybrid nature of the text? And are the two components still distinguishable or does the hybrid nature of the text (both in the original and in the translation) lead to a new specialized discourse?

The first section will provide some taxonomic considerations and clarify the notion of language for specific purposes (LSP). The second section will deal with technical and legal discourses. The third section will focus on a corpus of hybrid texts from CERN (mostly English originals and their translations) with a view to observing how their technical and legal dimensions cohabit.

[1] CERN is an international organization, established in 1954, based near Geneva, on the Franco-Swiss border. Its mission is fundamental research in particle physics, and it was the birthplace of the World Wide Web. It has 22 Member States. India, Japan, Russia, the United States, UNESCO, the European Commission and JINR have observer status, and many countries from around the globe are involved in its scientific programmes.

2 Specialized languages

Over the past few decades, there has been considerable discussion of the notion of *language for special purposes*, sometimes referred to as *language for specific purposes* (LSP), *specialized language* or *special language.*

2.1 Definition

UNESCO's *Guidelines for Terminology Policies* suggest that specialized languages are the 'major means of domain (i.e. subject-field or professional) communication; representation of specialized ... knowledge; and access to specialized ... information' (2005: 1). They come into existence because 'the various domain communities, which are engaged in a subject-field or other kind of expertise, ... generally agree on their own linguistic conventions, which do not necessarily conform fully with GPL [general-purpose language] conventions' (ibid.).

According to the ISO 1087 standard, the term *special language* refers to a 'language used in a subject-field and characterized by the use of specific linguistic means of expression'. It is noted that 'the specific linguistic means of expression always include subject-specific terminology and phraseology and also may cover stylistic or syntactic features' (ISO 1087–1:2000).

Lerat (1995: 20) defines a specialized language (SPL) as 'a natural language considered as a vector of specialized knowledge' and stresses that it 'cannot be reduced to a set of terms: it uses specialized denominations (terms), including non-linguistic symbols, in utterances involving the common resources of a given language. It can thus be defined as the use of a natural language in order to account technically for specialized knowledge' (ibid.: 21; my translation).

He notes that the characteristic features of SPLs are 'composite morphology ... including both general and specific vocabulary', 'syntax comparable with that of reference languages, but with stylistic preferences and professional phraseologies', adding that 'they impose a non-ethnocentric conception of semantics, due to the potential universality of scientific and technical notions' (ibid.: 29; my translation).

However, when one looks at LSP, it should be pointed out that authors do not agree as to its definition characteristics. As summarized by Edo Marzá, some authors 'consider specialised languages to be codes that can be completely differentiated from general or non-specialised language', whereas others 'believe that the only difference between specialised languages and general language lies in the specialised lexicon used by the former', and yet others 'believe that specialised language is a functional register that constitutes a subgroup within the general code of language' (2009: 34–35).

According to Gémar (1991: 276), legal discourse is based on legal terms (nomenclature), which must be used with their traditional field cooccurrents (sub-technical vocabulary) and embedded in general language so as to produce correct syntactic sentences. The absence of consensus about the definition of LSP may be associated with the diversity of approaches taken by different authors. Gambier (1995: 44) points out that LSPs are sometimes defined on the basis of their user and sometimes on the basis of their content or reference knowledge. He emphasizes that each one is characteristically *plural*, as it is stratified from scholarly language to the jargon of the field (ibid.: 46).

Overall, most authors agree that the main constituents of specialized languages are terms, sub-technical vocabulary and phraseology. These constituents will be characterized below and integrated in the corpus analysis as important features of LSPs.

2.2 Characteristics of LSPs

(a) Terminology

On the basis of the first definition of terminology given by Pavel and Nolet, *terms* may be defined as 'the set of special words belonging to a science, an art, an author, or a social entity' (2001: xvii). Kocourek gives a more restricted definition: 'a term is a defined lexical unit (a defined word-lexeme or a defined lexical phrase). It is, in other words, a subset of occurrences (of a lexical unit) that corresponds to a specialized discourse. A term is constituted by a definition in specialized discourse' (2001: 345).

(b) Sub-technical vocabulary

Baker points out that 'understanding specialised texts is not simply a matter of understanding or acquiring the relevant terminology' (Baker 1988: 91) and stresses the usefulness of the notion of sub-technical vocabulary, even though she considers that '"sub-technical" as a category has proved to be elusive and confusing ..., the reason being that the term has neither been clearly nor consistently defined in the literature' (ibid.). It is also helpful to remember Vangehuchten's description of sub-technical vocabulary: 'Technical terms seem to have a "predilection" for combining themselves with certain general words to the detriment of their synonyms' (2007: 91). This, of course, is not the rigorous type of definition that Baker calls for, but it clearly indicates that there is a degree of predictability to be borne in mind, that is, that we will find a combination of technical terms and general words.

In the field of law, Marín and Rea explain that 'the so-called *sub-technical* terms ..., according to various authors ..., either denote a legal concept in both general and specialized usage (words such as "judge"; "solicitor"; "guilty"; "court"), or activate a specialized meaning in the legal field, being frequently used as general words in everyday language ("trial"; "conviction"; "sentence"; "relief")' (2014: 61).

It is helpful to link the same notion to that of phraseology. Gledhill points out that 'broadly speaking, phraseology involves the study of formulaic sequences of words, including idiomatic phrases and proverbial expressions, which stand in contrast to other more prosaic constructions in the language in that they have a highly conventionalised form and frame of reference' (1997: 1).

He considers that 'extended lexical patterns are often unique to a particular register or genre' (ibid.: 2) and that 'the identification of such patterns should be a fundamental step in the systematic analysis of ESP [English for Specific Purposes] texts' (ibid.: 2). He emphasizes 'the role of phraseology in the discourse community, its role in the textual development of ideas and its possible "genetic" function in the evolution of scientific discourse' (ibid.: 1). He considers that phraseology is as useful in the acquisition of specialized languages as rhetoric and terminology.

Sub-technical vocabulary is not technical in itself, but supports the terms and structures the text – a linguistic reality that Darbelnet (1979: 26) describes as '*vocabulaire de soutien du droit*' and '*vocabulaire para-technique*', while Gémar suggests using '*vocabulaire quasi juridique*' (1991: 281) in legal contexts.

(c) Meta-discourse

One aspect of language that has recently aroused considerable interest is *meta-discourse*, or 'discourse about discourse'. Crismore et al. define meta-discourse as 'linguistic material in texts, written or spoken, which does not add anything to the propositional content but that is intended to help the listener or reader organize, interpret and evaluate the information given' (1993: 40). In a more recent publication, Hyland claims that 'The ability of writers to use meta-discourse effectively, to control the level of personality in their texts by offering a credible representation of themselves and their ideas, is coming to be seen as a defining feature of successful writing' (Hyland 2005: ix). He provides an inter-personal model of meta-discourse, which contains both interactive and interactional factors.[2] The interactive factors include transitions (e.g. 'in addition'), frame markers (e.g. 'finally'), endophoric markers (e.g. 'noted above'), evidentials (e.g. 'according to *X*') and code glosses (e.g. 'namely'), while interactional factors include hedges (e.g. 'perhaps'), boosters (e.g. 'in fact'), attitude markers (e.g. 'unfortunately'), self-mentions (e.g. 'I') and engagement markers (e.g. 'note') (ibid.: 49).

3 Technical and legal discourse

This section presents an overview of general features of legal and technical LSPs, considering that there are in fact many different types of legal texts and technical texts. The features of the three specific genres included in the corpus will be discussed in Sections 4 and 5.

3.1 Legal LSP

Many scholars have addressed the question of legal LSP. According to Cornu, discourse can be characterized as legal if it establishes law in a direct manner or, more generally, if it contributes to the execution of law (2005a: 14). As put by Susan Šarčević, drawing on Gémar's work (1995), 'Gémar identifies six subdivisions of the language of the law: the language of the legislator, judges, the administration, commerce, private law, and scholarly writings (doctrine) (1995-II: 116–22). Not only are there subdivisions of the language of the law, but as Gémar points out, each legal system has its own language of the law; hence, it is more precise to speak of languages of the law' (Šarčević 1997: 9).

In his discussion on legal text typologies, Prieto Ramos (2014b: 263) stresses that the latter comprise many genres and sub-genres. According to him, the fact that law

2 Many of these factors are considered as phraseological elements by other authors. See, for example, the very interesting typology suggested by Biel (2014b: 177–82).

deals with all aspects of life explains the frequent hybrid character of legal texts, and the common denominator of legal texts is 'the link between legal theme and/or function and linguistic features'. He establishes that

1. Legal texts constitute or apply instruments governing public or private legal relations ... or give formal expression to specialized knowledge on legal aspects of such instruments and relations.
2. These functions follow certain linguistic patterns that are characteristic of varieties of legal language in different discursive situations, allowing for the identification of legal text types (according to text producers and purposes), as well as legal genres (according to more specific textual functions and conventions).
3. Legal texts can also contain a great amount of specialized language from non-legal fields covered by law, while legal scholarly writings comprise a wide range of subcategories of general genres such as journal articles and textbooks (ibid.: 264–5).

Sylvie Monjean-Decaudin (2013) adopts a translational perspective and points out that an important feature of the legal text is its degree of juridicity (or '*degré de juridicité*'), which relies on two parameters: (1) the scope of legal knowledge required to understand and translate the legal text or concept, and (2) the legal effect its translation will have.

Even if legal LSP covers a vast scope and varies enormously by genre and context, it has often been associated with the characteristics of 'legalese' in different languages. In the case of English, Ingels (2006: 58–63), for example, refers to the following features, most of which are found in the texts of my corpus: archaic terms (*hereafter, hereby*); obsolete words (*aforesaid, foregoing*); Latin phrases (*inter alia, supra*); doublets and triplets (*attached and annexed, deem and consider*); triplets (*cancel, annul and set aside*); wordy phrases (*visible to the eye, for the purpose of*); formal words (*detain, peruse*); and grammatical structures (obsolete formalisms such as *be it enacted by*, passive voice, long complex sentences, nominalization, impersonal style, namely the avoidance of reference to first and second person, and *shall*).

It is interesting to note that Cornu (2005b: 271–85) lists very similar features for French legal language and adds the use of the timeless present tense and indefinite words such as *chacun, chaque, nul, on, quiconque, tel* and *autrui*. Sourioux and Lerat had also pointed to the importance of the timeless present[3] (1975: 61) and bring out the tendency to reproduce established formulations (ibid.: 69).

It is worth underlining that certain features of legalese do not necessarily apply to all legal genres, which require more specific attention by legal system and language.

3.2 Technical LSP

I deal with *technical texts* in the narrow sense of the term: texts whose subject matter concerns the use of applied sciences or the practical, mechanical or industrial arts, in accordance with the following meaning of the word *technical*, as defined in the *Shorter*

[3] 'Le présent juridique est grammaticalement un cas particulier du présent 'intemporel', celui des vérités générales, des défintions et des maximes'.

Oxford English Dictionary (vol. II, p. 2140): 'of or pertaining to the mechanical arts and applied sciences generally'.

Once again, many scholars have addressed this question. Sharma (2004) discusses various features of technical style, which he also refers to as 'impersonal style'. He mentions the unmarked present, the agentless passive, functional use of the pronouns *we* and *you* and technical vocabulary (2004: 75).

Koulaidis et al. (2001: 8), referring to Halliday and Martin (1996: 8), list among the specialized characteristics of the techno-scientific linguistic code 'the use of specialized terminology and notation' (terms, symbols or equations), 'the use of nominalisation', (which 'enhances the compressive expression of complex information, allows the smooth development of the arguments and allows the formation of new conceptual entities'), 'syntactic complexity' (which 'is achieved through the use of hypotaxis (subordination) as the dominant syntactical structure instead of clauses being placed side-by-side in a paratactic way (coordination)') and 'the use of passive voice' ('language used in science describes and interprets the world, projecting the objective character of scientific knowledge').

Bédard (1986) has described French technical LSP, pointing to its grammatical and lexical freedom ('*infractions aux règles formelles*' and '*impropriétés de vocabulaire*'; ibid.: 160–1), as well as the following features: impersonal turns, the passive voice, nominalization, complexity and analytical vocabulary (ibid.: 165).

From a stylistic point of view, technical writing is characterized by semantic precision, neutrality of tone and absence of formal effects. Besides, it can be noted that technical texts, through their reference to factual concepts, differ from legal discourse, which contains more abstract-oriented concepts. Indeed, Barbara Folkart (1984: 230) considers that 'transparency – i.e. immediacy of access to the referent – is the only feature of the source text *qua* text that need be preserved in [technical] translation'.

4 Corpus analysis

4.1 The corpus

The analysis focuses on three parallel corpora of hybrid legal-technical texts (cf. Table 9.1), all from CERN. This international organization publishes many texts, not only on its scientific and technical activities but also on administrative, legal and economic matters related to its mission. It is therefore not surprising to find texts that belong to a legal genre but also deal with technical aspects. The three sub-corpora include three legal genres: international agreements, rules and contract adjudication proposals.

In this context, both originals and translations deal with a single legal international order and the same extra-linguistic reality. Almost all the English texts were drafted directly in English at CERN with the help of technical specialists and legal experts and according to well-defined standards, before being approved by the relevant committees. All the translations were produced by translators from CERN's Translation and Minutes Service, and were revised and validated by legal and technical experts. All the

Table 9.1 Corpus composition

Type of document	Number of documents	Number of words (English version)	Number of words (French version)
Cooperation agreements	15	25,332	28,017
Safety rules	14	15,498	17,465
Contract adjudication	20	19,624	22,945

documents were considered sensitive and were therefore carefully drafted and revised. The three sub-corpora of representative hybrid texts include

- Fifteen cooperation agreements (three of which were drafted in French and translated into English);
- Fourteen safety documents (two of which were drafted in French and translated into English);
- Twenty contract adjudication proposals (all drafted in English).

All these documents, issued between 2013 and 2016, are drafted according to a predefined format and contain standard paragraphs or phrases, many of which were approved after long discussions within a drafting committee that included technical and legal experts. The translators are involved in the discussion of the French version, so both original and translated versions meet CERN requirements and can be considered as illustrative of CERN's textual genres and translation practice.

(a) Cooperation or membership agreements

CERN's Legal Service regularly drafts protocols which will be signed both by CERN and other institutions or governments in order to enforce cooperation agreements and grant observer or associate member status. For example, Ukraine became an associate Member State of CERN in 2016, the European Space Agency signed a cooperation agreement in 2014 and CERN signed an International Cooperation Agreement with the Government of the Republic of Latvia in 2016. Most of these documents are not confidential and can be found on the webpage of CERN's Council.[4] The documents are submitted to the delegates of Member States sitting on the CERN Council and typically consist of a few pages outlining the scientific and economic situation of the country or institution concerned, followed by the agreement itself, which must be approved by the Council before it is signed by the parties. Fifteen such documents were included in the corpus.

(b) Safety rules

As indicated on the site of CERN's Occupational Health and Safety and Environmental Protection Unit,[5] 'Safety Regulations translate CERN's Safety policy into rules applicable to various activity fields of the Organization, for the purposes

[4] http://indico.cern.ch/category/59/.
[5] https://espace.cern.ch/safety-rules-regulations/en/rules/Pages/default.aspx.

of occupational health and safety, environmental protection, safety of equipment and installations, and operational Safety.' CERN safety rules aim to ensure a high level of safety commensurate with relevant safety practice in Europe, take into account the intergovernmental status of the Organization and are applicable to all those who work on the CERN site. I analysed fourteen such documents that are in force, both in English and in the French translation. They can all be downloaded from the relevant website.[6]

(c) Contract adjudication proposals

Four times a year, in accordance with CERN's Procurement Rules, which stipulate that the Finance Committee's approval is sought for any new contract exceeding CHF 750,000, CERN's Finance Committee must approve the adjudication of some fifteen to twenty contracts concerning equipment and services necessary for its activities. These documents are confidential and are only aimed at the Member State delegates sitting on the Finance Committee. Twenty such documents were included in the corpus.

4.2 Methodology

With the exception of automatic word counts carried out with AntConc 3.2.4,[7] the analysis was done manually. All the terms, sub-technical words and meta-discourse elements pertaining to the two domains were marked in each text of the three sub-corpora. Their respective localization and density in the texts were then established in order to determine

- the numbers and ratios of legal/technical terms in the various texts, paragraphs and sentences;
- the numbers and ratios of legal/technical sub-technical elements in the various texts, paragraphs and sentences;
- the fluctuation of their respective densities throughout the document.

5 Results

When a text deals with different domains, it is interesting to observe what impact its content hybridity has on its form. There are two different possible situations: one domain may prevail (there is a predominant 'host LSP' setting the frame and governing the form) or both domains may cohabit (either by combining or by alternating their features), in which case we may find their respective characteristics in full or attenuated. Moreover, the interaction between LSPs may be homogeneous or may fluctuate within the text. In the next sections, different quantitative data and examples are provided to illustrate this interaction in the three sub-corpora analysed.

6 https://espace.cern.ch/safety-rules-regulations/en/rules/byType/.

7 The freeware corpus analysis toolkit for concordancing and text analysis can be downloaded from http://www.antlab.sci.waseda.ac.jp/software.html.

5.1 Agreements

These documents are drafted in a standard format. The introductory part has a predefined structure, and the convention clauses that follow also contain standard paragraphs; these are only slightly modified to account for the parties' specificities. In this group of texts, technical or scientific content is generally limited to a few paragraphs.

The introductory part, which deals with economic indicators and the status of higher education and scientific research in the country, is of an economic or technical nature. It has no legal effect and is written in standard, formal English or French (with expressions such as 'falls under the responsibility of'/'*relève de la responsabilité de*'). Terminology is limited to basic economic terms in the relevant paragraphs ('nominal GDP'/'*PIB nominal*', 'annual growth rate'/'*taux de croissance annuel*'), names of scientific institutions and scientific terms related to the expected technical contributions or research fields. This part represents between 9 and 14 per cent of the document (based on the number of words).

The convention part is fully standardized. It contains formulaic expressions such as 'Considering'/'*Considérant*' or 'Have agreed as follows'/'*Sont convenus de ce qui suit*'; and the various sections have established titles, such as 'Scope'/'*Champ d'application*', 'Non-military purposes'/'*Fins non militaires*' or 'Disputes'/'*Différends*'. A few paragraphs may purely refer to scientific or technical elements. They are generally very dense in terms, listing fields of cooperation or experiments, and are set out in an annex to a section on technology matters.

There is a predefined structure typical of legal agreements, including characteristic legal meta-discourse, and the content of all the paragraphs is predominantly legal, which is reflected by both terminology and sub-technical vocabulary (e.g. 'hereunder'/'*le présent accord*', 'hereinafter referred to as'/'*ci-après dénommé*' or 'shall'/ use of the timeless French present tense).

In this type of document, both LSPs cohabit at some distance without intermingling. In the non-legal introductory part, there is hardly any trace of anything of a legal nature, whereas in the highly legal-oriented agreement, which has an important legal effect, the few technical paragraphs are very dense, well circumscribed and appear isolated from the rest of the text, as in the following example: 'Members of the Institute of Solid State Physics of the University of Latvia contributed to the Crystal Clear Project with a study of BGO and PbWO4 scintillators.'/'*Des membres de l'Institut de physique de l'état solide de l'Université de Lettonie ont participé au projet Crystal Clear par une étude sur les scintillateurs en germanate de bismuth (BGO) et en tungstate de plomb ($PbWO_4$).*'

In the convention part, the legal paragraphs accounts for 43–82 per cent of the text, whereas the technical/scientific paragraphs fluctuate between 18 and 57 per cent. The latter can, however, reach 100 per cent in the annex. In this type of document, the technical sub-technical/term ratio is generally lower than in the other sub-corpora: it fluctuates from 9 to 45 per cent in technical paragraphs. On the contrary, in the legal-oriented paragraphs, the legal sub-technical/term ratio is higher than in the other sub-corpora. It fluctuates between 49 and 82 per cent (in number of words). This may be due to the fact that technical passages are often almost a mere enumeration of terms, whereas the legal ones are more elaborate. The target reader probably explains these differences. The introductory part is basically aimed at Member State delegates, the agreement clauses must meet the requirements of legal experts and the annex is aimed at scientific or technical staff from both parties.

5.2 Safety rules

These documents conform to a well-established structure and always contain the following sections: 'Legal basis'/'*Base juridique*', 'Purpose and scope'/'*Objectif et champ d'application*', 'Definitions'/'*Définitions*' (a detailed glossary of between five and fifteen terms), 'CERN Safety Rules and Laws'/'*Règles de Sécurité du CERN et droit en vigueur*' (a section listing all applicable regulations) and 'final provisions'/'*dispositions finales*'. Other sections are almost purely technical.

Most of the sections are, nonetheless, of a technical nature and can have a high density of technical terms and sub-technical vocabulary. The strictly technical part fluctuates between 20 and 57 per cent of the total, the list of applicable regulations (both legal and technical) between 2 and 16 per cent, and the strictly legal part between 5 and 22 per cent.

The correlation between legal terms and sub-technical legal vocabulary, on the one hand, and between technical terms and sub-technical vocabulary, on the other, is very high. The more elaborate a sentence, the greater the proportion of sub-technical vocabulary (the sub-technical/term ratio fluctuates from about 10 per cent in lists of terms to almost 60 per cent in passages that are more formally written). In the legal-oriented paragraphs, the sub-technical/term ratio never falls below 25 per cent and can reach 75 per cent. In the purely technical passages, the register tends to be higher (through the choice of more formal alternatives) than in most non-hybrid technical texts issued by CERN, such as instructions for use or maintenance procedure manuals.

5.3 Contract adjudication proposals

These documents are drafted according to a very rigid format, with standard or very repetitive paragraphs on the legal aspects. However, very complex and specific information is given in a few technical paragraphs, and a few paragraphs are of a really hybrid nature.

Rather dense technical sentences such as the following can be found: 'The technologies involved in the construction of the LAr containers must meet stringent requirements with respect to LAr temperature stability at the 1 K level and must ensure an unprecedented level of purity of the cryogenic liquid'/'*Les technologies utilisées pour la construction des conteneurs d'argon liquide doivent satisfaire à des exigences très strictes, la température de l'argon liquide devant être stabilisée à 1 K, et assurer un niveau de pureté sans précédent du liquide cryogénique.*' The translator, while being very precise, chose the somewhat formal expressions '*satisfaire à*' and '*sans précédent*'.

Here is a hybrid passage: 'This service contract is intended to cover all CERN optical-fibre cabling installation work, including fibre connectivity, tests, the removal and modification of existing installations and the supply of all new systems including ducts, microducts, optical-fibre cables, patch cords and optical-fibre termination equipment.' This passage was translated as follows:

> *Le présent contrat de service est destiné à couvrir tous les travaux d'installation de câblage par fibres optiques au CERN, y compris la connectivité par fibres optiques, les tests associés, le retrait et la modification des installations existantes, ainsi que la fourniture de tous les nouveaux systèmes, qui comprennent les conduits, les microconduits, les câbles à fibres optiques, les cordons de raccordement optique et les équipements de terminaison de fibres optiques.*

The translator chose to use rather formal language, with the expressions '*Le présent contrat est destiné à*' (instead of '*ce contrat*'), '*ainsi que*' (instead of '*et*') and '*qui comprennent*' (instead of '*comprenant*'). Sub-technical vocabulary ('*cover*'/'*couvrir*', '*work*'/'*travaux*', '*removal and modification*'/'*le retrait et la modification*') are used alongside specialized terms.

In such texts, the legal discourse is slightly less elaborate and the technical discourse slightly more formal than in purely legal or technical texts, respectively, but sub-technical vocabulary always accompanies the relevant terminology. It is striking that even in paragraphs with purely technical content, some traces of legal meta-discourse appear.

Figure 9.1 shows the analysis of a randomly chosen set of seven sentences from a contract adjudication proposal, where the use of technical and legal words (both terms and sub-technical) clearly fluctuates; Figure 9.2 illustrates the

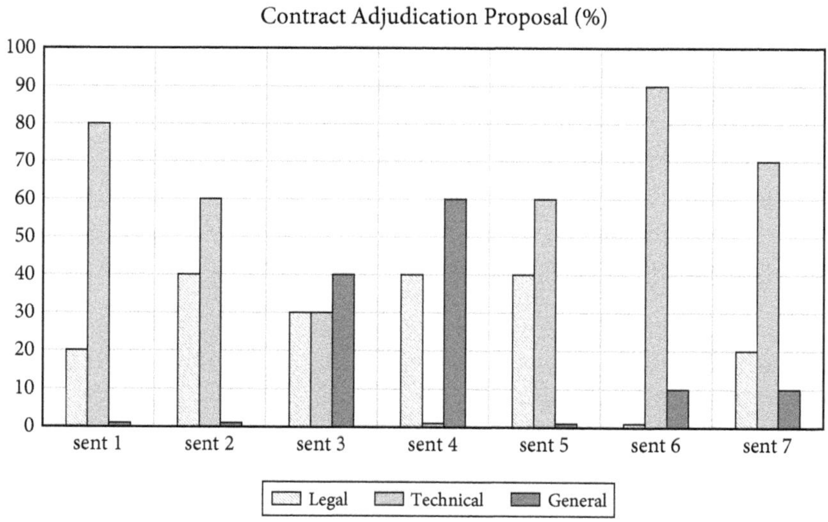

Figure 9.1 Example of analysis of a contract adjudication proposal: rate (in per cent) of types of words by sentence.

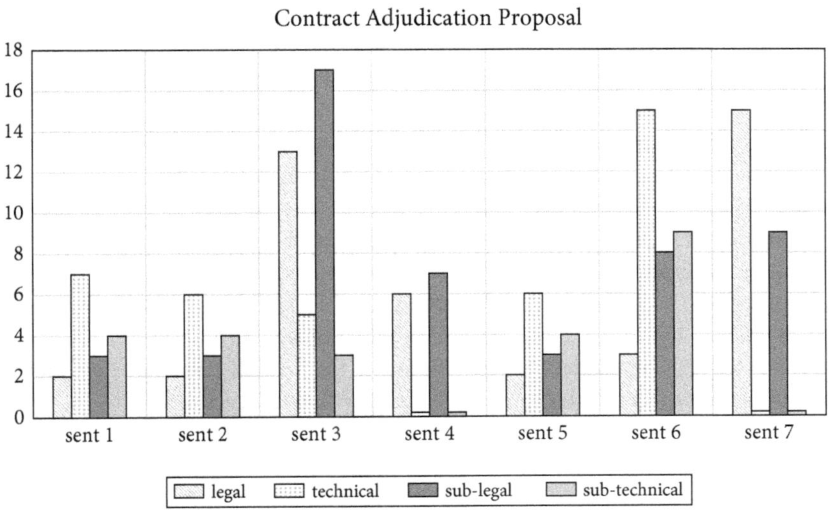

Figure 9.2 Example of analysis of a contract adjudication proposal: number of types of words by sentence.

interdependence of terminology and sub-technical vocabulary in the same sample adjudication proposal.

6 Conclusions

The results of the corpus analysis confirm that technical and legal LSPs cohabit in the documents considered. Generally, legal and technical discursive features are clustered by paragraphs or sentences. The density of terms and sub-technical vocabulary is consistent: they belong together and clearly show which part is technical and which part needs to be read from the legal perspective. Interestingly, meta-discourse establishes a link between the two LSPs and acts as a fine-tuning mechanism. All the documents belong to legal genres and have a legal effect, and, as such, it is understandable that they follow macrotextual legal conventions. At microtextual level, when the legal aspect of a document is clearly more relevant, the technical language takes on a more archaic or elegant form. When the two LSPs are present, a clear trend can be seen: the legal LSP functions with a relatively low register, whereas the technical LSP uses a relatively high register. They thus combine together in harmonious fashion. When there is a balance between the two discourse types, the technical passages tend to be written using a higher register than is usually the case for technical texts. However, these formal effects in no way have a negative incidence on the clarity of the text.

Both LSPs studied here are relatively rich; as pointed out by Gambier (1995), they can exploit several different registers. The more hybrid passages clearly show a good fit between content and style. When technical matters are discussed, the sub-technical vocabulary becomes more technical, only to take on a more legal character in other passages dealing more with regulatory or administrative matters. In other words, while the density of terms belonging to each of the LSPs varies according to the needs of the texts, when certain sections of the texts have a marked technical or legal character, they use the appropriate LSP. Intermediate passages are written in relatively neutral language. From the reader's point of view, there are no problems of interference or ambiguity, as both the context and the sub-technical vocabulary point to the predominant LSP. Thus, for instance, when polysemic terms are used, there is no doubt as to which field they belong to.

What are the implications for the translation? Translators should ensure that there is absolute consistency between sub-technical vocabulary and terminology. They must also observe the other discursive conventions established in the relevant domains as they interact in the institutional setting. As this chapter illustrates, when translating legal texts to support international cooperation in the fields of science and technology, translators can expect a high degree of hybridity within legal genres.

Part Three

Translation and Multilingual Case-Law

10

The Impact of Multilingualism on the Judgments of the EU Court of Justice

Susan Wright[1]

1 Introduction

In a Community/Union of multiple States without a common language, where the EU Court's judgments are a binding source of law that must receive uniform application throughout the Member States, the fundamental principles of *access to the courts* and *access to the law* make some measure of multilingualism inevitable at the Court. The objective of the multilingual system is to enable the *understanding, participation in, resolution,* and *publication of proceedings* brought before the Court, whatever the national language(s) of the Member States from which the parties come or in which the law is to be applied.

The purpose of this chapter is to present the multilingual system within which the EU judiciary operates and the effect the system has on the judgments of the Court.[2] I will thus set out the *legal framework* and *management of multilingualism* at the Court (with primary reference to [written] translation rather than [oral] interpreting) and the consequent *influences on (the text of) the judgments* produced in French and their twenty-two other language versions. I will not analyse the substance of the case-law on multilingualism.[3]

2 Legal framework of multilingualism at the EU Court of Justice

The composition of the two EU Courts is necessarily *multinational*. The Court of Justice consists of 'one judge from each Member State' and eleven Advocates General,

[1] All views expressed are personal. The chapter is based on my paper presented to the EU and competition law subject section meeting at the 2016 Society of Legal Scholars Annual Conference. It draws in part on my earlier article published by Oxford University Press (Wright 2016).

[2] Unless otherwise specified, references are to the two remaining EU Courts which make up the institution.

[3] See generally van der Jeught (2015).

six from the 'large' Member States and five more appointed on a rotation basis. The General Court is to 'include at least one judge per Member State': there is provision for forty-seven judges as from 1 September 2016 and for two judges per Member State as from 1 September 2019.[4] Until 31 August 2016, when it was dissolved, the Civil Service Tribunal was composed of seven judges drawn from any of the Member States.

Against this multinational and therefore *multilingual* backdrop, the Court is subject to *mandatory language arrangements* that reflect the Member States' choice to respect linguistic diversity within the EU. The key provisions on these arrangements are to be found in the Treaties, the Protocol on the Statute of the Court ('the Statute'), Council Regulation No. 1 of 15 April 1958 ('Regulation No. 1'),[5] and the Rules of Procedure of the Court of Justice ('CJ Rules of Procedure') and of the General Court ('GC Rules of Procedure').[6]

Each founding Treaty, as amended and supplemented, states the languages in which the texts are 'authentic'. These 'Treaty languages' are currently listed in Article 55(1) TEU. Article 20(2)(d) TFEU (Treaty on the Functioning of the EU) then provides that citizens of the Union have the right to 'address' – potentially not in writing – the EU institutions in any of those Treaty languages and to obtain a reply in the same language, while Article 24 TFEU makes similar provision for 'written' communication in the same languages.

Article 342 TFEU provides that the rules governing the 'languages of the institutions' of the Union are, without prejudice to the provisions contained in the Statute, to be determined by the Council, acting *unanimously* by means of regulations. In its turn, the Statute provides in Article 64 – which may not be amended by the ordinary legislative procedure – that 'the rules governing the language arrangements applicable at the Court' are to be laid down by a regulation of the Council acting *unanimously*. Such a regulation has never been adopted, and so it is the arrangements under the Rules of Procedure that continue to apply.

Regulation No. 1 determines 'the languages to be used' by the European Community/Union pursuant to the precursor of Article 342 TFEU and therefore had to be adopted by a *unanimous* vote in Council. It first lists the 'official languages' and 'working languages' of the institutions, without giving the meaning of those terms or explaining the difference between them. It then states that 'regulations and other documents of general application' must be drafted, and the Official Journal of the EU published, in those official languages. As regards written communication, the institutions are required to reply to Member States and persons 'subject to the jurisdiction of a Member State' in the official language chosen by the sender, although

[4] See respectively Article 19(2) TEU (Treaty on European Union), Council Decision 2013/336/EU of 25 June 2013 increasing the number of Advocates General of the Court of Justice of the European Union [2013] OJ L179/92, and Article 48 of Protocol (No. 3) on the Statute of the Court of Justice of the European Union (consolidated version [2016] OJ C202/210).

[5] Version consolidated in 2013 http://eur-lex.europa.eu/legal-content/EN/TXT/PDF/?uri=CELEX:01958R0001-20130701&qid=1474979796554&from=en.

[6] Consolidated versions of 19 July 2016 (http://curia.europa.eu/jcms/upload/docs/application/pdf/2012-10/rp_en.pdf) and of 1 September 2016 (http://curia.europa.eu/jcms/upload/docs/application/pdf/2016-08/rp_en.pdf), respectively.

spontaneous communications from the institutions will be sent in the language of the State in question. Special provision is made for the Court to lay down in its rules of procedure the languages to be used in its proceedings, and indeed all the institutions 'may stipulate in their rules of procedure which of the languages are to be used in specific cases'. It should be noted that partial derogations from the requirements of Regulation No. 1 applied in respect of Maltese until 2007 and continue to apply to Irish.[7]

The language arrangements specific to the Court can be found in Chapter 8 of Title I of the CJ Rules of Procedure (and in Title II of the GC Rules of Procedure). In accordance with the Statute, these provisions may only be amended or repealed with the *unanimous* consent of the Council. They refer to the 'language of a case', and how such a language is to be determined and used in any given proceedings, the use of 'official languages' before the Court, the 'languages of the publications of the Court', and the languages in which the Court's texts are 'authentic'. They also provide for a 'language service' to be set up by the Court, and for translations into the language of the case in particular. Beyond Chapter 8 it is Article 98 of the Rules which provides for the translation of requests for a preliminary ruling.

Soft law published in the Official Journal, in the form of recommendations, directions or non-legislative rules, also addresses the questions of language and translation at the Court. The Court of Justice 'Recommendations to national courts and tribunals in relation to the initiation of preliminary ruling proceedings' ('CJ Recommendations to national courts') replace the previous 'information note'; the Court of Justice 'Practice directions to parties concerning cases brought before the Court' ('CJ Practice directions') are intended to make the Rules of Procedure easier to understand; and the General Court 'Practice rules for the implementation of the Rules of Procedure of the General Court' are designed to explain, detail and supplement certain provisions of those rules.[8]

In accordance with the mandatory language arrangements outlined, which have evolved with each successive enlargement of the European Community/Union while continuing to reflect the Member States' unanimous desire to maintain multilingualism, the *status and numbers of languages and language combinations* used at the Court are complex. Table 10.1 details developments over the last six decades, and the terminology used should be understood as follows:

- The *Treaty languages* (originally four and currently twenty-four) are those in which the Treaties are authentic. At the Court, these are official source texts. At the same time, in contexts other than proceedings, citizens are entitled to communicate with the Court in any of those languages.

[7] The Maltese derogation was introduced by Council Regulation (EC) No. 930/2004 of 1 May 2004 [2004] OJ L169/1 and brought to an end by Council Regulation (EC) No. 1738/2006 of 23 November 2006 [2006] OJ L329/1. The Irish derogation was introduced by Council Regulation (EC) No. 920/2005 of 13 June 2005 [2005] OJ L156/3, extended by two subsequent regulations, and should cease to apply as from 1 January 2022. It relieves the institutions from the obligation to draft or translate *all* acts (including Court judgments) in Irish and to publish them all in that language (in the Official Journal).

[8] Respectively [2016] OJ C439/1, [2014] OJ L31/1, [2015] OJ L152/1 (consolidated version of 2016 http://curia.europa.eu/jcms/upload/docs/application/pdf/2016-08/dpe_vc_en.pdf).

Table 10.1 The status and numbers of languages used in the EU Courts

	Member States	Treaty languages	Official languages	Languages of the case	ECR languages	Language combinations
Original Communities	6	4	4	4	4	12
1/1/1973 **UK, Ireland, Denmark**	9	7 (including Irish)	**6** (excluding Irish)	7 (including Irish)	**6** (excluding Irish)	42
1/1/1981 **Greece**	10	8	7	8	7	56
1/1/1986 **Spain, Portugal**	12	10	9	10	9	90
1/1/1995 **Austria, Finland, Sweden**	15	12	11	12	11	132
1/5/2004 **+ EUR-10**	25	21	20	21	**19** (excluding Maltese)	420
1/1/2007 ***Irish derogation***	=	=	**21** (including Irish)	=	=	=
1/1/2007 **Romania, Bulgaria**	27	23	23	23	21	506
1/5/2007 ***End of Maltese derogation***	=	=	=	=	**22** (including Maltese)	=
1/1/2012 ***Continuation of Irish derogation***	=	=	=	=	=	=
1/7/2013 **Croatia**	**28**	**24**	**24**	**24**	**23**	**552 (24x23)**
1/1/2017 ***Continuation of Irish derogation***	=	=	=	=	=	=
1/1/2022 ***End of Irish derogation?***	=	=	=	=	***24*** *(including Irish)*	=
BREXIT?	*27*	*24?*	*24?*	*24?*	*24?*	*552?*

- The *official languages* (originally four and currently twenty-four) are those in which EU legislation is authentic, providing official source texts for the Court and its services. They are also the languages to be used for all Court texts to be published in the Official Journal and for 'publications' of the Court. In contexts other than proceedings, the Court is required to communicate with Member States, and indeed citizens, in the official languages of their choice. In proceedings before the Court, the Member States enjoy certain privileges in their use of official languages: in direct actions against a Member State, it is the official language of that State which becomes the language of the case; in preliminary ruling proceedings, the language of the case is the language of the referring court or tribunal; and irrespective of the language of a case, a Member State is entitled to use its official language when submitting observations in preliminary ruling proceedings and intervening in other cases. In addition, each Member State receives a translation into its official language of the requests for a preliminary ruling served on it.
- *Languages of the case* (*langues de procédure*) (originally four and currently twenty-four) are those in which actions may be brought before the Court. The language of the case must, as a general rule, be used in written and oral pleadings, and proceedings must be made available, and the text of the judgment is authentic, in that language. From the moment of accession, a case may be brought in the recognized language(s) of a new Member State.
- *Languages of the ECR* (originally four and currently twenty-three) are those into which the Court's case-law is translated for the purpose of 'publication' in the general European Court Reports.
- *Language combinations* (originally twelve and currently 552) are those that result from the Court's translation and interpreting obligations in respect of all twenty-four EU languages.

3 Management of multilingualism at the EU Court of Justice

It is evident from Table 10.1 that the 2004 enlargement raised the number of language combinations from 132 to 420 overnight, posing a major challenge for the management of multilingualism at the Court. *Within the framework prescribed* by the Member States, the Court is responsible for complying with and implementing the legislative regime laid down, while fulfilling its mission as the EU judicial body. It must apply the mandatory provisions, exercise its power to interpret those provisions, take internal measures of organization not requiring changes to the mandatory regime and initiate amendment of the original provisions, where appropriate. The challenge is to ensure that supply meets demand, when demands on (the language services of) the Court are largely beyond its control.

From the language point of view, the *stages of proceedings* before the Court unfold as follows (also see Wright 2016: 161):

- *Actions are brought* in any of the EU official languages.
- *Requests for a preliminary ruling* are translated into French for the case-file and the official languages for service on the Member States in particular.

- *Notices for the Official Journal* on the application initiating proceedings or the request for a preliminary ruling are drafted in the language of the case and translated into and published in all official languages (except Irish during the derogation).
- *Pleadings* are lodged in the language of the case, as a general rule.
- Pleadings from a Member State may be lodged in the State's EU official language.
- Pleadings lodged in a language other than French are translated into French for the case-file.[9]
- Pleadings legitimately lodged in a language other than the language of the case are translated into that language for the parties.
- Any *written questions* from the Court to the parties are drafted in French and translated into the language of the case.
- The *preliminary report* is written in French by the Judge-Rapporteur for the general meeting of the Court.
- Any *Report for the Hearing* is prepared in French by the Judge-Rapporteur for the Bench and is translated into the language of the case for the parties.
- Any *hearing* takes place in the language of the case and other necessary official languages, with interpretation from and into the official languages as required.
- Any *Advocate General's Opinion* is drafted in his or her chosen official language and made available for the day of its delivery, both in French for the Court and in the language of the case for the parties (translated if necessary).
- *Deliberation* among the Judges takes place in French, in closed session without interpretation.
- The *judgment* is drafted in French by the Judge-Rapporteur, translated into the language of the case to be delivered, signed as the 'authentic' version in that language, served on the parties and made public.
- Judgments and Opinions are also translated as soon as possible (usually by the day of delivery) into all the other ECR languages for 'publication'.
- *Notices for the Official Journal* on judgments and orders closing proceedings are drafted in French, and translated into and published in all official languages (except Irish during the derogation).

The *resulting model* of case management can be seen as an *hour-glass*, as Sir David Edward reportedly called it (Brady 2014: 35) and as illustrated in Figure 10.1. All official languages can feature at the beginning and the end of the process, but a very limited number are used along the way in any given case, as a result of two *key factors*. First, the Court's case-file has always been compiled in the one common *language of deliberation*, which has by convention been French since the Court was established; and second, the Court communicates with the parties in the *language of the case*. The operation of such a rationalized model is clearly dependent upon extensive translation and interpreting, and the Court has its own translation service established under the CJ Rules of Procedure, as well as its own interpreting service.

[9] The EU institutions are required to produce their own French language version pursuant to Article 57(3) of the CJ Rules of Procedure.

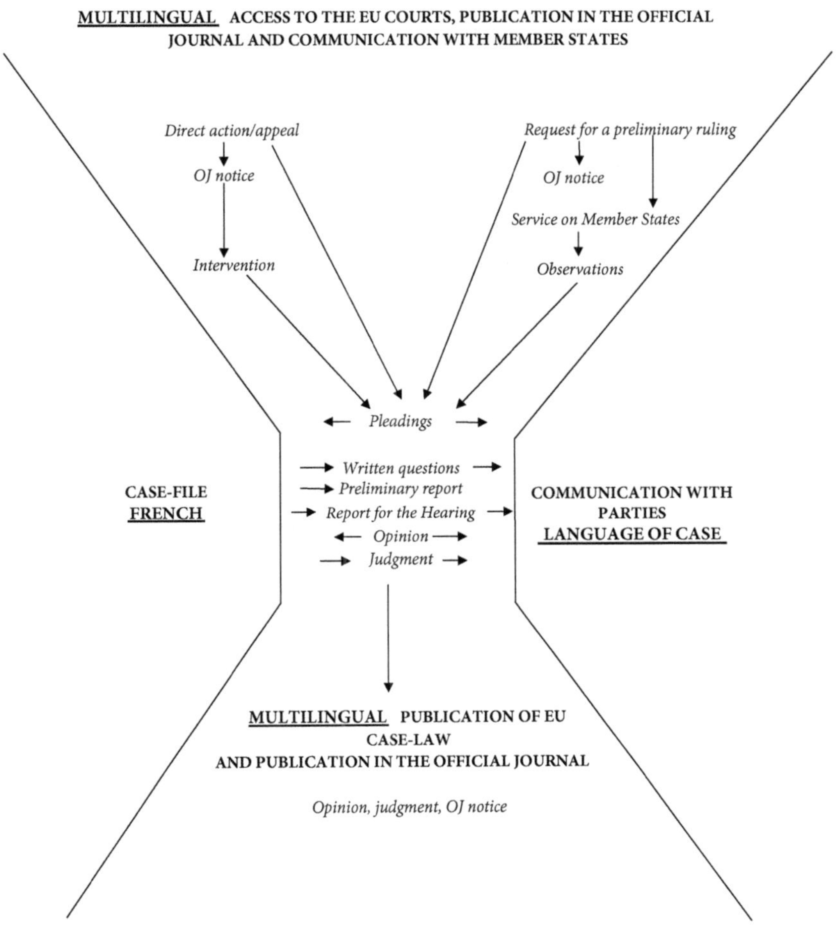

Figure 10.1 The hour-glass model of multilingual management in the EU Courts.

As the caseload of the Court has grown, resulting in an increasing workload for the translation service,[10] a number of *economy measures* have been taken that *support the multilingual system* outlined, many precipitated by the 2004 enlargement. Some are merely internal measures of organization within the Court, but others constitute changes to the mandatory language arrangements which the Court could only initiate, in the interest of effectively fulfilling its judicial mission. On the one hand, a significant number of measures rationalize procedure and thereby *limit the demand on the language service*. On the other hand, it is important to understand the inherent design features of the system, which exist to *maintain the quality of supply in terms of language*.

[10] Over one million pages per year (Court of Justice of the European Union 2016: 18).

First, the *quantity of pages* to be translated is restricted. As a direct result of the hour-glass model, pleadings and Reports for the Hearing[11] are not translated into languages other than French and the language of the case. Under the amended Statute and CJ Rules of Procedure, longer requests for a preliminary ruling may be summarized before they are translated, written pleadings may be limited to a single round (without reply or rejoinder), the length of pleadings may be restricted, hearings may be arranged in a smaller percentage of cases, and Opinions are delivered in a smaller percentage of cases. In addition, of the Court's own volition, Reports for the Hearing and Opinions are shorter than they were, and the Court practises selective 'publication' (and therefore translation) of judgments and orders and also publication by extracts.

Second, the *breadth/diversity of demand* is restricted. Although it is necessary for direct translation into French (the language of deliberation) to be available in any case from any of the twenty-three other official languages, the translation service otherwise practises a 'mixed' system. This means that direct translation between source and target languages will be undertaken wherever possible, but that translation via *predetermined 'pivot' languages* has been available since 2004, particularly for requests for a preliminary ruling and notices for the Official Journal.[12] Similarly, the Advocates General now draft the majority of their Opinions either in French or the pivot languages, thereby reducing the need for comprehensive language cover in all the translation units. The *hour-glass model* of case management is thus also applied to translation management.

Third, the Court seeks to bring about through soft law the *rationalization or simplification of documents lodged* at the Court, and makes express reference to the needs of the translation service in this connection. Point 14 of the CJ Recommendations to national courts states that, 'owing to the … need to translate it into all the official languages of the European Union, the request for a preliminary ruling should therefore be drafted simply, clearly and precisely by the referring court or tribunal, avoiding superfluous detail.' And the CJ Practice directions address 'The form and structure of procedural documents' (points 34–9), stating that 'the written pleadings or observations must therefore be drafted in clear, concise language, without use of technical terms specific to a national legal system. Repetition must be avoided and short sentences must, as far as possible, be used in preference to long and complex sentences which include parenthetical and subordinate clauses.' The parties are also asked to produce accurate citations and references and are reminded that annexes to pleadings are not, as a general rule, translated.

As far as maintaining the *quality of supply* is concerned, the system addresses on the one hand the question of producing judgments in French. It should be noted that draft judgments are reviewed both by *Francophone* 'readers of judgments' (*lecteurs d'arrêts*) and by Francophone proofreaders. In addition, the Judges' ability to acquire proficiency in 'the working language of the European courts' is now taken into

[11] One of the 'unavoidable sacrifices' made in 1994, as explained by Edward (1995: 547).

[12] For example, when a reference is made by a Lithuanian court, the request for a preliminary ruling will first be translated from Lithuanian into an English pivot version, which then becomes a source text for all the other language versions required (though not the French). The pivot languages are currently English, German, Italian and Spanish.

account by the advisory panel (on appointment) provided for by Article 255 TFEU (2013: 19). On the other hand, as regards the other language versions of judgments, the organization of the translation service is key. First, it is staffed by *lawyer-linguists drawn from all the Member States*, who are lawyers qualified in both law and languages. Second, the service includes a *translation unit for each ECR language*, with a team of lawyer-linguists translating into that target language, which is their first language and the language of their legal studies. Third, every aspect of *translation management* – including recruitment, training, working methods and freelance resources – is subject to ongoing review, with provision for multilingual legal terminology databases, centralized and semi-automated identification of sources and references and coordinated quality control mechanisms.

4 Impact on EU Court judgments of the Court's multilingual regime

The unique multilingual regime described clearly influences the EU Court's judgments. This impact will be considered under four headings.

First, what is the impact of the multilingual regime on the text of judgments produced in French (also see Wright 2016: 158; Künnecke 2013: 252–3; McAuliffe 2012: 203–6)?

- The judgments are *drafted in French* irrespective of the language of the case or the first language of the Judge-Rapporteur, his or her fellow Judges on the Bench and their staff.
- The judgments are *built on translations*, specifically of written pleadings, since, while the case-files include any French originals, they contain above all translations produced by the Francophone lawyers of the Court's translation service. As a result, the French terminology and language of judgments depend greatly on the input of the translation service, where terms must be found, or coined, to convey the meaning of national concepts, procedures, institutions and offices that are unknown to the French legal lexicon.[13]
- The judgments are *deliberated on in French* irrespective of the language of the case or the first language of the Judge-Rapporteur and his or her fellow Judges on the Bench.
- The judgments are *produced by a team* – a series of contributors – and thus it is difficult to identify any individual style.
- Judgments may be the *product of a majority view*,[14] without any provision for a dissenting opinion (such public dissent being almost unknown in the supreme

[13] Technical terminology can also pose a challenge: see the complex English jargon encountered in Case T-201/04 *Microsoft* v. *Commission* EU:T:2007:289.

[14] This was expressly stated in Article 25(5) of the original version of the CJ Rules of Procedure [1953] OJ of 7 March 1953, p. 37 (available in the four original EC languages).

courts of the original Member States [Raffaelli 2012])[15]. The single text is thus the product of debate and may represent a compromise, both legally and linguistically.

- The resulting French is *Court French*. The Francophone readers of judgments and proofreaders ensure the use of correct legal French, which is also consistent with the language and conventions of the Court's case-law (Pescatore 2007).
- The *style* of the Court's judgments *was developed in the 1950s* by lawyers belonging to the civilian tradition. As a result, we can see the influence of the style (traditionally) used in the highest French courts: there is a predetermined structure or template; each judgment originally consisted of one single sentence; they are full of set formulae with fixed meanings, including building blocks made up of entire paragraphs; they were originally gnomic and impenetrable for the novice; and explanation was available to all in the Report for the Hearing and the Advocate General's Opinion.
- The Court's *style has evolved*. Judgments of the General Court, subject to appeal, are fact bound, longer, with ample reproduction of pleadings; since Reports for the Hearing are no longer made available in all languages (and no longer exist in the Court of Justice) and Opinions are not delivered in all cases, judgments need to be more self-explanatory and freestanding; the availability of a larger corpus of European law means that many questions have already been considered and the corresponding terms and formulae invented; and the availability in digital form of full-text versions of pleadings, case-law and legislation means that more building blocks are readily to hand.
- *Quality assurance and risk management* are vital to the successful production of judgments in French in a multilingual court. Francophone lawyer-linguists, readers of judgments and proofreaders all play a role in ensuring the quality of the French language used in judgments. The translation service is alert to the risk that a judgment may be based on a false premise if procedural documents are not faithfully rendered in French for the case-file: systems to minimize such mistranslation include the review of French translations of requests for a preliminary ruling by lawyer-linguists whose first language is that in which the reference was made by the national court.
- *The very fact that the judgment will be translated* has an influence on the way it is produced. Since judgments are, as a general rule, translated in-house prior to delivery, there are frequent contacts between the translation service and the Judges' chambers and between individual translators and draftsmen. The resulting input and influence on the original text will relate to choice of terms (e.g. where a single term in French has two or more correct translations in a target language), clarity of formulation (where unintentional ambiguity has been discovered at the point of translation) and avoidance of language-specific reasoning (e.g. the legislation at issue does not have precisely the same meaning in all its language versions). Perhaps counter-intuitively, translation is in fact a safety net (cf. McAuliffe 2016: 13, on the perceived absence of lawyer-linguists' influence).

[15] For assessments from former EU Judges, see Azizi (2011) and Edward (1995: 555–8), who explains the process of deliberation, and addresses the impact of 'collegiality' on the judgment produced as well as the pros and cons of dissenting opinions.

Second, what is the impact of the multilingual regime on the text of judgments in language versions other than French (also see Wright 2016: 159, 162; Künnecke 2013: 251–2; McAuliffe 2012: 209–14)?

- These twenty-two language versions are all *translations* of complex legal texts. Just as when the pleadings were translated into French, terms need to be found, or coined, in the legal lexicon of the target language. Each translation must faithfully reflect the original in terms of accuracy, rigour, precision, clarity and consistency.
- The *authentic* version of every judgment is a translation (unless the language of the case is French). Any (legally significant) change to that version after delivery of the judgment requires a formal corrigendum by the Court, since it is the translation into the language of the case that will have been signed by the Bench and served on the parties.
- The lawyer-linguist is *not drafting ex novo*, even if he or she is translating into the language of the case and/or his or her text is likely to be the language version which is most read. As a natural result, there is potential for unintentional departure from modern (legal) usage in the target language. There is also a more or less discernible terminological/linguistic shift within (preliminary ruling) judgments, from the unavoidable (national) reality of facts, pleadings and legislation towards the Court's analysis and findings.
- The texts are translations *from French*. The nature of the challenge varies according to the language combination, Italian and Spanish being much closer to French than are Lithuanian, Hungarian or Estonian, for example. There will be much less figurative language than in UK or Irish judgments; there will be less 'elegant variation' (at least in English) than in the French original; and there is potential for linguistic interference from the original French (e.g. false friends, unnatural sentence length, misuse of tenses, overuse of commas).
- The original language version and official EU translations of many *source documents must be respected*, and direct quotations reproduced faithfully, in the relevant language versions of judgments. The principal sources in question are EU legislation and case-law in all EU languages, decisions at issue adopted by the Commission and EUIPO[16] in the languages available, national legislation and case-law in the original language and pleadings in their original language.
- Some of the source documents were produced in the language of the case or another official language by *a draftsperson not writing in his or her first language*. As a result, there may be an obvious contrast within a single judgment between, on the one hand, quotations taken from references made by national courts and observations submitted by national authorities and, on the other, quotations from certain EU legislation, EU authority decisions and observations, and pleadings.
- The language of translated judgments must be recognizable, understandable and acceptable, principally for those who have the target language as their first language. However, certain of the EU official *languages are not specific to a single*

[16] European Union Intellectual Property Office, known as the Office for Harmonization in the Internal Market (OHIM) until 23 March 2016.

legal system – German is shared by Austria, Belgium, Germany and Luxembourg; French by Belgium, France and Luxembourg; Dutch by Belgium and the Netherlands; Swedish by Finland and Sweden; English by Ireland, Malta and the UK; and Greek by Cyprus and Greece – meaning that highly system-specific terms need to be used judiciously, if not avoided.[17]

- *Quality assurance and risk management* are essential to the success of the Court's translation service. Its mission includes maximizing correspondence between language versions; ensuring that translations convey the Court's message; avoiding plausible errors in translation that will be invisible to the non-Francophone public; avoiding unintended (terminological) inconsistency (not present in the French original) with consistent case-law, which may be wrongly interpreted as a subtle change in the Court's position; and avoiding the pitfall of 'Euro language' in the absence of an EU law concept with an autonomous meaning. In addition to the general quality measures described above, translations of judgments, particularly those into the language of the case, are often reviewed by the relevant judge.

Third, what is the impact of the multilingual regime on the availability of judgments in individual cases?

Where the judgment is to be published in all languages, all language versions will, as a general rule, be produced for the day of delivery. If the judgment is to be published in all languages, but the urgency of proceedings is deemed to outweigh the interest in simultaneous access to all language versions,[18] it is possible that only translation into the language of the case will be required prior to delivery. If the language of the case is French, the judgment is sometimes delivered (particularly by the General Court) prior to its translation into any other language. If the judgment is not to be published in all languages, only translation into the language of the case is required (prior to delivery).

In all of these cases, in preliminary ruling proceedings, the request for a preliminary ruling will in any event have had to be translated into (French and) the other official languages. Similarly, in all proceedings, any pleadings must have been translated if necessary into French and the language of the case, any Report for the Hearing must have been translated into the language of the case (unless it is French) and any Opinion must have been translated if necessary into French and the language of the case (and will probably already have been translated into the other languages of publication).

Fourth, what is the impact of the multilingual regime on the availability of the case-law in general?

Between delivery of the first Court of Justice judgment in 1954 and the first enlargement of the European Communities in 1973, the Court's case-law was consistently published in all the languages of the ECR. That case-law is thus fully available in the four original official languages.

Prior to each enlargement of the Communities/Union, a decision had to be taken on how much of the *pre-accession case-law* should be translated into the official

[17] E.g. *Saisie-arrêt* might usefully be translated as order for attachment rather than garnishee order.

[18] E.g. in urgent preliminary ruling proceedings under Article 107 et seq. of the CJ Rules of Procedure.

languages about to be added to the list. For every new language, it is a selection of that 'historic' case-law which has been made available by the Court in the new language versions, sometimes in full and sometimes in summary form. In respect of the twelve ECR languages added as a result of the 2004, 2007 and 2013 accessions, details of the selection are given in an explanatory note available on the Curia website.[19]

Until 1994, *staff case judgments* were all translated and published in the same way as general case-law. After that date, the Reports of Staff Cases (published until 1 September 2016) included the full text of General Court (formerly Court of First Instance) staff case judgments and judgments of the Civil Service Tribunal[20] (between 2005 and 2016) in the relevant language of the case, together with a summary of each judgment in all the languages of publication.[21] In a limited number of cases each year, these judgments are translated in full into all the languages of publication for the general ECR.

Until 2004, when the number of Member States increased from fifteen to twenty-five and the number of official languages went from eleven to twenty, there was no selective reporting of new general case-law – all such judgments were translated in full and published in all ECR languages. Since 2004, however, a new distinction has been introduced (beyond that relating to EU staff cases) between 'publication' in the general ECR (now digital, but always multilingual) and 'dissemination'. The Court's '*Case-law publication criteria*' are available on the Curia website.[22] They have applied to the Court of Justice since 1 May 2004 and to the General Court since September 2005, and they are subject to the interpretation of the Court formation responsible for the judgment in question. Further to these criteria, in respect of the most recent case-law:

- All judgments are still accessible in full in French, whether published in the ECR or disseminated on Curia.
- All judgments are still accessible in full in the relevant language of the case, whether published in the ECR or disseminated on Curia.
- Many judgments are published in full in the ECR (in all the languages of publication).[23]
- Certain judgments of the General Court are published by extracts in the ECR (in all the languages of publication).
- 'Unpublished' judgments are referenced in the ECR (in all the languages of publication).

19 http://curia.europa.eu/jcms/jcms/Jo2_14955/en/.

20 Also published in full in French.

21 Another of the 'unavoidable sacrifices' referred to by Edward (1995: 547).

22 http://curia.europa.eu/jcms/jcms/P_106308/en/ (accessed 6 January 2017) where references to official languages should be read subject to the derogations.

23 As a general rule, the Court of Justice does *not* publish 'judgments delivered, in cases other than requests for preliminary rulings, by Chambers sitting with three Judges, judgments delivered, in cases other than requests for preliminary rulings, by Chambers sitting with five Judges ruling without an Advocate General's Opinion, orders'. As a general rule, the General Court *does* publish 'judgments of the Grand Chamber [and] judgments of Chambers sitting with five Judges' and '[t]he formation of the Court concerned will decide on the publication of judgments of Chambers sitting with three Judges on a case by case basis.'

5 Concluding remarks

On the basis of the explanations set out above, of the multilingual system within which the EU judiciary operates, the *influence of multilingualism on EU Court judgments* can be summarized in four statements. The judgments are produced in 'Court French', based on translations, with the assistance of Francophone lawyers. The other language versions of judgments, including many of the authentic versions, are produced by a specialized translation service staffed by lawyers from all the Member State legal systems. The duration of proceedings may be affected by the number of translations required to permit the prescribed multilingual access to a multilingual court. And access to the full text of all case-law is no longer ensured in all official languages.

In order to place these findings in *context*, it is interesting to assess whether the underlying, or *overall purpose of multilingualism at the Court*, as initially defined, is being served.

First, multilingual *access to the courts* is maintained, thanks to the system of languages of the case. Cases may be, and are, brought in any of the official languages, and there is provision for procedural documents to be successfully lodged in all of them. The caseload of the Court demonstrates the success in uptake across the official languages.

Second, the provision of translation and interpreting *into* any official language makes it possible for the parties to *understand the proceedings* in the chosen language of the case, at both the written and oral stages. Translation of requests for a preliminary ruling into the official languages makes it possible for all Member States to understand the questions referred and to decide whether to submit observations.

Third, the provision of translation and interpreting *from* any official language makes *participation in proceedings* possible at both the written and oral stages. The parties may express themselves in the chosen language of the case, in particular, and Member States may intervene in their chosen official language.

Fourth, the *resolution of proceedings* is supported at every stage. The provision of translation from any official language into French, according to the hour-glass model, makes it possible for the Members to understand the full case-file. The provision of interpreting from and into the official languages chosen by the Members makes it possible for them to take full advantage of the hearing. The provision of translation from any official language gives the Advocates General the freedom to adopt their preferred language of self-expression in their Opinions. The existence of a common language makes it possible for the Judges from all Member States to deliberate together without interpreters and to reach agreement on the draft judgment.

Fifth, the approach to the *publication of proceedings* has evolved. Notices are published in all languages of the Official Journal on the introduction of originating applications, requests for a preliminary ruling and appeals, and on orders and judgments bringing proceedings to a close. Reports for the Hearing are no longer published at all. Opinions are published in all languages of the ECR. Judgments (and orders) in full text are disseminated in French and the language of the case but subject to selective multilingual publication. Information on unpublished decisions is published in all languages of the ECR.

Lastly, there is comprehensive *access to the case-law* in French and complete access in the respective languages of the case. There is multilingual access to preliminary rulings and other important decisions.

This assessment raises a number of questions on *striking the balance between competing objectives*, particularly in the light of changing circumstances. It is clear that there is still the will to protect the national languages of the Member States,[24] to defend the use of EU official languages,[25] to ensure that they are all treated equally as languages of proceedings before the EU Courts and to protect the fully multinational nature of the Court's composition.[26] However, over the five-year period leading up to 2017, an interinstitutional agreement required the EU institutions, including the Court, to reduce their staff numbers (Court of Justice of the European Union 2016: 6). This has made for some difficult choices in the face of a growing caseload which the Court cannot itself control. In a continuing effort to ensure that supply keeps pace with the demands inherent in a multilingual system, the Court's translation service benefits directly from the Court's policy on selective publication and publication by extracts (whose full potential has not yet been realized), the system of translation via pivot languages and an ever more extensive use of information technology (ibid.: 20–1). It must be recognized, however, that under the current hour-glass model described, it will be necessary to create a new Irish-language translation unit when the Irish derogation comes to an end and case-law must be translated into Irish. An analogous need would arise in respect of any other new official language.[27]

As regards the use of the English language at EU level in the event that the United Kingdom ceases to be an EU Member State, several obvious factors should be borne in mind. First, the question of whether the UK is a Member State is distinct from the question of whether English is an EU language in any of the senses explained above. Second, any change to the status of English as a Treaty language, an official language (of communication between citizens and EU institutions), a language of proceedings before the EU Courts[28] and a language of publication for legislation and case-law would require unanimous agreement between the Member States in the Council. Third, English is one of the official languages at national level in both Ireland and Malta, recognized in their constitutions. Finally, as every lawyer knows, it is political reality that sets the limits to all legal analysis and commentary (European Commission Representation in Ireland 2016).

24 See the terms of the preamble to the latest regulation on phasing out the Irish derogation, Council Regulation (EU, Euratom) 2015/2264 of 3 December 2015 [2015] OJ L332/1, legislation requiring unanimity in the Council.

25 See the judgment in Joined Cases T-353/14 and T-17/15 *Italy* v. *Commission* EU:T:2016:495 rejecting restrictive language requirements in EU staff competitions.

26 The latest reform of the EU Court system sees the dissolution of the Civil Service Tribunal, where the Member States were not all represented, and the advent of two Judges per Member State in the enlarged General Court. See the Court documents on 'Reform of the EU's Court system' at http://curia.europa.eu/jcms/jcms/P_64268/en/.

27 http://ec.europa.eu/enlargement/countries/check-current-status/index_en.htm on the state of enlargement negotiations.

28 Some 40 per cent of cases before the General Court are brought in English, many by persons not connected with the United Kingdom, who are represented in English. Using the case-law search form available on Curia, a search on 6 January 2017 for 'cases pending' before the General Court gave 606 with English as the 'language of the case' out of a total of 1,496.

11

A Corpus Investigation of Translation-Generated Diversity in EU Case-Law

Aleksandar Trklja

1 Introduction

European integration remains one of the fundamental aims of the European Union (EU), and that aim has been largely achieved through the development of an EU legal order (Harmsen and McAuliffe 2014). Harmonization and uniformity of the law of the EU are key features necessary in order to achieve that integration aim. Indeed, they form a theme explicitly or implicitly expressed in various key EU texts and cases of the Court of Justice of the European Union (CJEU).[1] Although harmonization and uniformity do not have exactly the same meaning, they share a common goal. They serve to prevent divergence that could 'jeopardise the very unity of the EU legal system and detract from the fundamental requirement of legal certainty' (Case 314/85 – *Foto-Frost* [1987] ECR 4199, para. 15; Case C-27/95 – *Bakers of Nailsea* [1997] ECR I-1847, para. 20; and Case C-461/03 – *Gaston Schul Douane-expediteur* [2005] ECR I-0000, para. 21). Due to the principle of language equality laid down in the Council Regulation 1958/1/EEC, EU law does not exist in only one linguistic version. According to this principle, all 'State languages' of Member States serve as official languages of the EU institutions (Milian i Massana 2002). Although EU law exists in different linguistic versions because of the 'metaprinciple' of uniformity (Paunio 2013), it is considered that all these linguistic versions have the same meaning. In other words, regardless of the number of languages in which EU law exists, its content is always the same.

It is this assumption that is the main concern of the present chapter. The problematic aspects of this assumption have been addressed by various legal scholars (e.g. McAuliffe 2013b; Paunio 2013), but apart from several exceptions (e.g. Kjær 2004; Šarčević 2015), it has not received sufficient attention in linguistics and translation studies. In order to consider implications of the assumption, I will begin by presenting an extreme scenario of requirements for absolute uniformity. I will then address this abstract presumption

[1] See, for example, the Treaty of Rome and the Treaty on European Union for Harmonization and the Treaty on the Functioning of the European Union (TFEU); see also the CJEU case *Srl CILFIT and Lanificio di Gavardo SpA v. Ministry of Health* [1982] ECR 3415 for uniformity.

in the light of linguistic findings obtained through a quantitative analysis of relations between translation correspondences. I will argue that these findings pose challenges to the notion of uniformity.

The chapter will focus in particular on the case-law produced by the CJEU. The Court's task includes making sure that EU law is interpreted and uniformly applied in the same way across EU Member States. The judgments of the CJEU serve, therefore, as appropriate material to investigate the linguistic basis of the notion of uniformity.

I will first describe the role of translation at the CJEU (Section 2) and then summarize general assumptions on which the uniformity hypothesis is based (Section 3). In Sections 4 and 5, I will demonstrate, through theory-derived and empirically induced arguments, why the assumption has no basis in linguistics. In the final section, I will discuss the implications of these results.

2 Translation-based communication at the CJEU

The CJEU is the highest judicial authority of the EU, and as such, it is responsible for ensuring that 'in the application of the [EU] Treaties, the law is observed'.[2] In reality, this means that the CJEU hears and rules on cases of breach of EU law (direct actions) and delivers binding judgments regarding questions of interpretation of EU law under the procedure for references for preliminary rulings set out in Article 267 TFEU (indirect actions). Under the Article 267 TFEU procedure, a national court submits questions on the interpretation of EU law arising in a national dispute before it, together with other relevant documentation on the case and national legal system in question, to the CJEU. Direct actions involve proceedings taken directly before the Court for alleged breaches of EU law by Member States or EU institutions. Each type of procedure involves the submission of various documents and interventions by relevant and interested parties, as well as internal processes of deliberating and drafting judgments. All of these individual processes of submitting, hearing, ruling on cases and drafting and delivering judgments are forms of communication.

Four types of language regimes shape the communication at the Court: (i) the regime of authentic version of judgments, (ii) the regime of working language, (ii) the regime of official languages and (iv) the regime of pivot translation. The first language regime means that there is only one authentic version of a procedure of a case; according to Article 41 of the CJEU's Rules of Procedure of 2012, the text 'of documents drawn up in the language of the case or, where applicable, in another language authorised pursuant to Articles 37 or 38 of these Rules shall be authentic'. This can be any of the official languages of the EU (currently twenty-four). The second language regime defines the working language of the Court as French. It means that submissions are translated into French and that the final version of judgments of the CJEU is also produced in this language and then, following the third-language regime, it is translated into twenty-two of the remaining twenty-three EU official languages.[3] Finally, since it is

2 Article 19 TFEU, OJ C 83 30/03/2010.

3 Irish is excluded because CJEU case-law is not currently translated into Irish. For more details on the Court's multilingualism, see also Chapter 10.

impossible to find lawyer-linguists for all language pairs (552), the system of five pivot languages is created (the fourth language regime). There are five pivot languages: French, English, German, Spanish and Italian. Each of these languages is paired with one or more 'smaller' languages. Within this language regime, certain documents are translated first into 'pivot languages' and then from pivot languages into the other EU official languages.

This brief description suffices to show that the communication at the CJEU and between the Court and national courts takes place on many occasions through translation and can be regarded as translation-mediated communication. Because of such a strong involvement of translation, it can be argued that CJEU case-law is created through translation (McAuliffe 2012).

3 Semantic requirements of CJEU judgments

The notion of uniformity was described in the introduction in general terms. In this section, I will explicate the semantic requirements that should be met if the notion is to be true. These requirements can be seen as assumptions on which this notion is based, and they will be theoretically and empirically investigated in Sections 4 and 5, respectively.

- Requirement of single meaning per use: The concept of uniformity is based, on the idea that it is possible to precisely determine the meaning of linguistic units for each particular use.[4] It is assumed here that linguistic units have fixed meanings or sets of meanings that can easily be observed. In addition, uniformity requires that there is one single meaning per use and that linguistic units are always used in the same way.
- One-to-one relation requirement: The notion of uniformity requires that these fixed and easily distinguishable meanings of linguistic units can neutrally be transmitted across languages. In other words, different linguistic forms in different languages will have no impact on the content of a message being transmitted. It follows, then, that it is not only the case that linguistic units have fixed meanings but also that *these* meanings can be conveyed across languages. In other words, there is a one-to-one relation between linguistic units from different languages because this meaning is always the same, although different languages have different representations of a meaning,
- Symmetry requirement: It follows that since meaning can be conveyed, the direction of meaning transmission has no impact on the meaning itself. In other words, if a linguistic unit *A* can be translated as *B*, then *B* can also be translated as *A*.
- Transitivity requirement: If meaning is a universal category and different languages are only different forms, actual language pairs have no impact on meaning. In other words, it is of no significance whether linguistic units are translated from, say,

[4] I use the terms *linguistic units*, *expressions* and *lexical items* instead of *words* to refer to both individual words and multi-word units.

French into English or from French into Finnish. Besides, the number of languages plays no role in translation. It follows that if a lexical item is translated from French into English and then the English item is translated into German, it can be expected that the French and German items will have the same meaning.

4 Theoretical consideration

In this section, I will provide arguments as to why the first and second requirements discussed in the previous section cannot be supported by linguistic research.

Natural language is a system in which individual semantic concepts are not mapped to singular linguistic signs. Instead, linguistic expressions are typically associated with more than one meaning, and there is no one-to-one correspondence between meaning and form. 'Although there are natural languages in which every word has one and only one form, it is almost certainly the case that there are no natural languages, and never have been, in which every word has one and only one meaning' (Lyons 1995: 26). If it were not the case, each time a new meaning is created, speakers would need to coin a new expression, which would create redundancy in the linguistic system. The study of polysemy is as old as the field of lexicography itself (Hartmann 1986), and the polysemic nature of lexical items has been thoroughly documented in dictionaries and other reference works. Polysemy emerges from language use. Through language use, linguistic expressions acquire new or lose existing meanings or senses. Besides, lexical items inherit semantic potentialities from previous usages (Lotman 2009), and any of these potentialities can be actualized through new usages[5].

An exhaustive and universally agreed record of all existing meanings is impossible to determine. Even in lexicography, which provides the most systematic documentation of semantics of lexical items, there are no universal taxonomies, criteria or features that one could use to achieve this. For example, Merriam-Webster dictionary (online) describes the meaning of the verb *exclude* in terms of two general senses and two sub-senses placed within the first one. Macmillan dictionary (online) lists three senses, with the second sense being divided into two sub-senses. Collins Cobuild (online) offers an explanation with two general senses divided into four and two sub-senses, respectively. Finally, Wordnet (online) lists only two general senses. In addition to these differences, the descriptions of senses are immeasurable and they are only approximate.

The argument that meaning has a given and fixed value reflects a rather simplistic and misguided view. Meaning is actually 'jointly constructed by the participants in communication' (Scollon et al. 2011: 11) through joint intentionality (Tomasello 2014). It is negotiated between language users through a meaning-making activity (Halliday 1978; Thibault 2004), which is an ongoing cognitive process. Participants

5 The actual realization of these potentialities depends on other factors such as the frequency of specific senses, situations in which the language is used or speakers. These factors cannot be discussed here because of space restrictions.

engage in communication situations equipped with their linguistic competence. Linguistic competence of adult language users can be regarded as a structured inventory of linguistic constructions (Tomasello 2009). The inventory is created through the experience of language use. The basic principle here is that '[t]okens of linguistic experience are categorized and matched with similar tokens of experience which have previously been stored as exemplars' (Bybee 2010: 19). These exemplars are established in memory. Semantically similar exemplars group together and create exemplar clusters. The reuses of existing exemplars strengthen their status within respective clusters. Those items that are more frequently re-used will be easier to access and process. They will also be morphologically stable and, as a result, they will be selected as ready-made chunks. Formally, these chunks can be fixed or semi-fixed expressions. Finally, clusters should not been seen as firmly established entities. The constellation of exemplars within clusters may change through language use, and new exemplars under specific circumstances can either enter or leave existing sets.

Recent studies (Barlow 2013; Dabrowska 2012) demonstrate that there are significant individual differences in linguistic competence between mature language users. These findings correspond to the view that individual speakers always speak in idiolects and that they have some sort of individual grammars (Muwfene 2001). The structure of the linguistic inventory of speakers depends on the type of language that has been imposed on them during their lifetime. Since there will be no two individuals that are exposed to exactly the same speech events, it is also not possible to find identical inventories of constructions shared between them. However, this does not mean that language users live in private languages understood in Wittgenstein's sense (Mulhall 2008). Because languages exist only through collaboration (Tomasello 2009), those idiolects come in contact and language users create jointly shared meanings.

From the above discussion, it follows that communication in natural language is possible even though the requirement of a single meaning per use cannot be met and clear sense disambiguation is not always possible. The notions introduced above can also account for translation-mediated communication. Since the differences between individuals that learn and use the same language are undeniable, it would be unreasonable to expect that there are no such differences between participants involved in translation-mediated communication. In analogy to what has been said above, we can safely assume that there will be no two individuals that will be exposed to a second language in identical circumstances. Thus, in translation-mediated communication, we can distinguish between two kinds of differences: those related to monolingual and those related to multilingual language competence. Multilingual competence consists of an inventory of constructions mapped across languages. Such constructions can be regarded linguistically as translation units and cognitively as exemplars that constitute clusters. The exemplars emerge through language users' attempts to match linguistic expressions across languages. The clusters of translation units have the same nature regarding stability and constellation as the clusters from the monolingual system. The main difference between communication in one language and translation-mediated communication is that in the latter case, participants are involved not only in selecting among exemplars from clusters but also in matching between those that belong to different languages. It is due to these two layers (selection and matching) that translation-mediated communication has the potential to induce more semantic diversity than monolingual communication.

These features of translation-mediated communication and of multilingual language users clearly demonstrate the unreliability of the thesis that there are universal semantic units that can be systematically found across languages and that the only differences between languages concern linguistic forms (one-to-one relation requirement).

5 Empirical consideration

In the present section, empirical evidence will be provided as to why the third and fourth requirements of the notion of uniformity cannot be justified. The findings derive from an analysis of the relation between translation correspondences in judgments produced by the CJEU.[6] I will first briefly introduce the data and methodology used in the study and will then discuss relations between correspondences in terms of the Court's ideal of uniformity.

5.1 Method and data

Data used in the present analysis contain all CJEU judgments published in French, English and German until 2011. A parallel corpus was created by aligning these judgments at the sentence level. This made it possible to identify systematically corresponding lexical items across three languages. The identification of corresponding linguistic units was carried out by means of ParaConc tools (Barlow 1995). First, all the sentences in a target language that contain a lexical item that corresponds to the same search term from a source language were identified. Second, a comprehensive list of corresponding items is obtained through a collocation analysis of results. This analysis was carried out by means of WordSmith tools (Scott 2008) and Shell scripts designed specifically for the purposes of this study. This procedure made it possible to investigate the ideal of linguistic uniformity by operationalizing the usage-based theory of meaning discussed in the previous section in the study of translation correspondences.

There are two reasons why the present study focuses on multi-word units instead on individual words. First, as already discussed in Section 4, individual words are usually semantically ambiguous. This ambiguity can be reduced[7] when words are studied in context, which is why multi-word units are in general less polysemous than individual words. Second, recurrent multi-word units are conventionalized semantic units that can be regarded as clusters of exemplars. As such, they serve as building blocks of knowledge of EU case-law. As will be seen, these multi-word units are not fixed expressions but lexico-grammatical constructions with constant and replaceable elements. They are associated with specific meanings.

[6] The results presented here come from the ERC-funded research project *Law and Language at the CJEU*.

[7] Semantic ambiguity cannot be entirely eliminated in this way; here, I disagree with Teubert (2004), who argues that 'extended units of meaning' are always monosemous.

5.2 Analysis of corresponding constructions

The initial construction selected for the present analysis is <exclure DET application PP_{GEN}>, which serves as an extended unit of meaning (Sinclair 1996) in the present corpus. All other constructions included in the analysis are also extended units of meaning, and they are represented in terms constants and variables. Constant elements are presented as lemmata and variables are given in terms of grammatical categories. For example, <exclure> denotes all word forms of this verb such as *exclue*, *exclus*, *exclurais*. DET refers to determiners, PP_{GEN} to genitive prepositional phrases and NP to noun phrases (see examples below).

Table 11.1 lists English and German constructions that correspond to <exclure DET application PP_{GEN}> identified in the corpus of CJEU judgments.[8] Also included are probability values with which the constructions occur. For example, <exclude DET application of PP_{GEN}> corresponds in 40 per cent of all its occurrences to <exclure DET application PP_{GEN}> in the present corpus. All the translation correspondences can be regarded as exemplars that belong to the same cluster.

The results show that <exclure DET application PP_{GEN}> corresponds to four constructions in English and one in German. According to these results, therefore, the one-to-one relation requirement holds for the French–German language pair but not for the French–English language pair. As it will be seen below, this is only a temporary conclusion about the behaviour of corresponding constructions in CJEU judgments.

At the next stage, we want to investigate whether the symmetry requirement can be supported by data. Following this requirement, it can be expected that the English and German constructions identified above will always correspond only to the original French expression.

The results for the two most frequent English constructions and the German construction are displayed in Tables 11.2 and 11.3, respectively. It can be observed that in both cases, in addition to <exclure DET application PP_{GEN}>, other French constructions occur as well. The additional corresponding items of <exclude DET application PP_{GEN}> in French are <écarter DET applicabilité PP_{GEN}>, <écarter DET

Table 11.1 Constructions in English and German that correspond to <exclure DET application PP_{GEN}>.

<exclure DET application PP_{GEN}>	
<preclude DET application PP_{GEN} > (43%)	<DET Anwendung PP_{GEN} ausschließen> (98%)
<exclude DET application PP_{GEN}> (40%)	
<exclude DET applicability PP_{GEN}> (2%)	
<preclude NP from applying> (2%)	
<rule out DET application PP_{GEN}> (2%)	

8 All the tables contain only the most frequent items and those that correspond at least in 2 per cent of the case to the items from other languages. These items can be regarded as the most typical translation correspondences.

Table 11.2 Constructions in French that correspond to <exclude DET application PP$_{GEN}$> and <preclude DET application PP$_{GEN}$>

<exclude DET application PP$_{GEN}$>		**<preclude DET application of NP>**	
<exclure DET application PP$_{GEN}$>	69%	<s'opposer à DET application PP$_{GEN}$>	59%
<écarter DET application PP$_{GEN}$>	11%	<faire obstacle à DET application PP$_{GEN}$>	15%
<écarter DET applicabilité PP$_{GEN}$>	2%	<exclure DET application PP$_{GEN}$>	7%
<exclure DET applicabilité PP$_{GEN}$>	2%	<écarter DET application PP$_{GEN}$>	3%

Table 11.3 Constructions in French that correspond to <DET Anwendung NP$_{GEN}$ ausschließen>

<DET Anwendung NP$_{GEN}$ausschließen>	
<exclure DET application PP$_{GEN}$>	55%
<s'opposer à DET application PP$_{GEN}$>	9%
<écarter DET application PP$_{GEN}$>	6%
<faire obstacle à DET application PP$_{GEN}$>	5%

application PP$_{GEN}$> and <exclure DET applicabilité PP$_{GEN}$>. The additional French constructions that correspond to <preclude DET application PP$_{GEN}$> are <s'opposer P DET application PP$_{GEN}$> and <faire obstacle P DET application PP$_{GEN}$>. These same additional items correspond to the German construction <DET Anwendung NP$_{GEN}$ ausschließen> as well.

It can also be observed that probability values associated with corresponding relations are not identical for both language directions. Table 11.1 shows that <preclude DET application PP$_{GEN}$> and <exclude DET application PP$_{GEN}$> correspond 43 per cent and 40 per cent of the time to <exclure DET application PP$_{GEN}$>. However, as can be seen in Table 11.2, these values do not correspond to those observed with the same lexical items for the English–French language direction. Although <preclude DET application PP$_{GEN}$> serves as the strongest translation candidate of <exclure DET application PP$_{GEN}$>, the reverse is not the case.

Since the items do not correspond mutually in each case, it follows that there are no strict symmetric relations between corresponding constructions that occur in CJEU judgments. Lexical items from different languages, therefore, only partially correspond to each other and, instead of a one-to-one relation, a some-to-some type of relation can be observed.

Another important point to stress is that when new exemplars are added to the existing cluster in one language, this leads to an increase in the number of exemplars in another language. This is supported by the findings that follow from the next corpus investigation of correspondence relations associated with the French constructions from Tables to . Performing yet another search with these items in the present parallel corpus produces additional constructions in English and German. Some of the frequently occurring items identified are <escape DET application PP_{GEN}>, <oppose DET application PP_{GEN}> and <prevent DET application PP_{GEN}> for English; and <sich DET Anwendung PP_{GEN} zu widersetzen>, <DET Anwendung PP_{GEN} entgegenstehen> or <sich gegen DET Anwendung PP_{GEN} wenden> for German. It clearly follows that the translation process multiplies the number of linguistic units in CJEU judgments. These results suggest that the assumption of the one-to-one relation that appeared to be valid for the French–German language in the above analysis (Table 11.1) should also be rejected.

In order to understand better the partial correspondence relations between constructions from different languages, these relations can be displayed in the form of a matrix. Such a matrix is provided in Figure 11.1.

Due to space restrictions, only relations between French and English constructions are displayed but similar results can be obtained for any language pair. For the sake of clarity, individual constructions and relations have been encoded where *a*-items refer to English, *b*-items to French constructions and *R* to corresponding relations. '0' values designate no correspondence relations, and '1' values indicate that there are such relations. The first matrix shows relations from English to French and the second one for the opposite language direction. Individual constructions are coded in English and French in the following way:

1. a_1 is <exclude DET application PP_{GEN}>, a_2 is <preclude DET application PP_{GEN}>, a_3 is <preclude DET applicability PP_{GEN}>, a_4 is <escape DET application PP_{GEN}>, a_5 is <oppose DET application of PP_{GEN}>, a_6 is <prevent DET application of PP_{GEN}> and a_7 is <rule out DET application of PP_{GEN}>.
2. b_1 is <exclure DET application PP_{GEN}>, b_2 is <exclure DET applicabilité PP_{GEN}>, b_3 is <écarter DET application PP_{GEN}>, b_4 is <écarter DET applicabilité PP_{GEN}>, b_5 is <s'opposer à DET application PP_{GEN}>, b_6 is <faire obstacle à DET application PP_{GEN}> and b_7 is <faire obstacle à DET applicabilité PP_{GEN}>.

First, it can be observed that the number of relations associated with individual items varies. For example, <exclude DET application PP_{GEN}> (coded as a_1) corresponds to four French constructions and is unrelated to three French constructions. On the other hand, <preclude DET application PP_{GEN}> (coded as a_2) corresponds to all but one French constructions and <oppose DET application PP_{GEN}> (coded as a_5) corresponds to only two French constructions. Second, the mutual correspondence relations also show considerable variations. We can see that <exclure DET application PP_{GEN}> (coded

$$
aRb = \begin{array}{c} \\ a_1 \\ a_2 \\ a_3 \\ a_4 \\ a_5 \\ a_6 \\ a_7 \end{array}
\begin{array}{c} \begin{array}{ccccccc} b_1 & b_2 & b_3 & b_4 & b_5 & b_6 & b_7 \end{array} \\
\begin{bmatrix}
1 & 1 & 1 & 1 & 0 & 0 & 0 \\
1 & 1 & 1 & 0 & 1 & 1 & 1 \\
0 & 1 & 0 & 0 & 0 & 1 & 1 \\
0 & 0 & 0 & 0 & 1 & 0 & 0 \\
0 & 0 & 0 & 0 & 1 & 0 & 0 \\
0 & 0 & 1 & 0 & 1 & 1 & 0 \\
1 & 0 & 1 & 0 & 0 & 1 & 0
\end{bmatrix} \end{array}
\qquad
bRa = \begin{array}{c} \\ b_1 \\ b_2 \\ b_3 \\ b_4 \\ b_5 \\ b_6 \\ b_7 \end{array}
\begin{array}{c} \begin{array}{ccccccc} a_1 & a_2 & a_3 & a_4 & a_5 & a_6 & a_7 \end{array} \\
\begin{bmatrix}
1 & 1 & 0 & 0 & 0 & 1 & 1 \\
0 & 1 & 0 & 0 & 0 & 0 & 0 \\
1 & 0 & 0 & 0 & 0 & 0 & 0 \\
0 & 1 & 1 & 0 & 0 & 0 & 0 \\
0 & 1 & 0 & 1 & 1 & 1 & 0 \\
0 & 1 & 0 & 0 & 0 & 1 & 0 \\
0 & 0 & 1 & 0 & 0 & 0 & 0
\end{bmatrix} \end{array}
$$

Figure 11.1 Correspondence relations for the language pair English–French and French–English.

as b_1), <exclure DET applicabilité PP_{GEN}> (coded as b_2), <écarter DET application PP_{GEN}> (coded as (b_3) and <écarter DET applicabilité PP_{GEN}> (coded as b_4) correspond to <exclude DET application PP_{GEN}> (coded as a_1), and that this English construction corresponds only to two French constructions. It follows that bidirectional relations and symmetry do not exist at the general level but only between individual items from corresponding clusters.

Finally, it remains to consider the transitivity requirement, that is, whether corresponding constructions established between one language pair automatically apply to other language pairs. Correspondence relations between the language pairs French–English, English–German and French–German will be examined by looking at the distribution of the constructions identified in the previous analysis. Additional data for the language pairs French–German and English–German are displayed in Tables 11.4 and 11.5.

It can be seen that, for example, two most frequent translation correspondences of <écarter DET application PP_{GEN}> are <preclude DET application PP_{GEN}> and <prevent DET application PP_{GEN}>. The results displayed in Table 11.4 indicate that the same French construction corresponds to the German construction <DET Anwendung NP_{GEN} ausschließen>. According to the requirement of transitivity, we would expect that the same German construction also corresponds to the two English constructions. However, Table 11.5 shows that this is true only for <preclude DET application PP_{GEN}> but not for <prevent DET application PP_{GEN}>, because the latter has no common translation correspondences in German with of <écarter DET application PP_{GEN}>. Similarly, we find no common German translation correspondences between the mutually corresponding <opposer à DET application PP_{GEN}> and <oppose DET application PP_{GEN}>. In fact, instances of transitivity can be observed in our data, but they are almost always associated with different probabilities of correspondence. For example, <DET Anwendung PP_{GEN} ausschließen> corresponds mainly to <exclure DET application PP_{GEN}> (98 per cent of the case, Table 11.4) and only in some cases the shared construction <preclude DET application PP_{GEN}> (32 per cent of the cases, Table 11.5).

It can be concluded that transitivity relations exist only between individual items but not as a general feature for entire clusters. Besides, even when this type of relation does occur, the observed constructions are associated with different distribution probabilities.

Table 11.4 German constructions corresponding to French constructions

<exclure DET application PP_{GEN}>,	**<s'opposer à DET application PP_{GEN}>,**	**<faire obstacle à DET application PP_{GEN}>**	**<écarter DET application PP_{GEN}>**
DET Anwendung PP_{GEN} ausschließen> (98%)	<DET Anwendung PP_{GEN} entgegenstehen> (97%)	<DET Anwendung PP_{GEN} entgegenstehen> (70%)	<DET Anwendung PP_{GEN} ausschließen> (60%)
	<DET Anwendung PP_{GEN} ausschließen> (2%)	<DET Anwendung PP_{GEN} verhindern/behindern> (3%)	<DET Anwendung PP_{GEN} ablehnen> (2%)
			<DET Anwendbarkeit PP_{GEN} ausschließen> (2%)

Table 11.5 German constructions corresponding to English constructions

<preclude DET application PP_{GEN}>	**<oppose DET application PP_{GEN}>**	**<exclude DET application PP_{GEN}>**	**<escape DET application PP_{GEN}>**	**<rule out DET application PP_{GEN}>**	**<prevent DET application PP_{GEN}>**
<DET Anwendung PP_{GEN} entgegenstehen>, (63%)	<sich DET Anwendung PP_{GEN} widersetzen>, (28%)	<DET Anwendung PP_{GEN} ausschließen>, (99%)	<DET <sich DET Anwendung PP_{GEN} widersetzen entgehen lassen>, (12%)	<DET Anwendung PP_{GEN} ausschließen>, (99%)	<DET Anwendung PP_{GEN} entgegenstehen>, (56%)
<DET Anwendung PP_{GEN} ausschließen>, (32%)	DET Anwendung PP_{GEN} widersprechen>, (15%)		<DET Anwendung PP_{GEN} entgegenstehen>, (10%)		<DET Anwendung PP_{GEN} verhindern>, (15%)
	<sich gegen DET Anwendung PP_{GEN} wehren>, (12%)		<DET Anwendung PP_{GEN} entziehen >, (10%)		<DET Anwendung PP_{GEN} ausschließen>, (10%)
	<sich gegen DET Anwendung PP_{GEN} widersetzen> (7%)		<DET Anwendung PP_{GEN} ausschließen>, (10%)		

6 Implications and concluding remarks

The theoretical and empirical evidence presented in this chapter provides arguments from linguistics as to why the notion of uniformity of EU law stands on weak grounds if absolute uniformity requirements are considered. In this section, I will discuss implications of this finding and provide some proposals for future research.

First, it was demonstrated that any communication by means of natural languages necessarily involves indeterminacy because polysemy is an intrinsic feature of any linguistic system. Second, because relations between lexical items from different languages are based on non-symmetric and non-transitive relations, translation-based communication creates lexical diversity. Lexical diversity and partial commensurability between semantics of corresponding lexical items from different languages give rise to indeterminacy of meaning. As demonstrated in McAuliffe and Trklja (2017), translation in EU case-law does create diversity but, due to the specific dynamics of re-use of established exemplars, it also prevents this diversity from devolving into chaos and disintegration. These findings suggest that both the semantic diversity and the intrinsic multilingual nature in EU case-law should be acknowledged.

Paunio (2013) argues that translation and multilingualism cause legal uncertainty in EU case-law. Legal indeterminacy is understood here as not having the same interpretation of the same situation or not having one right answer to a legal question (Raymond 2000). In linguistic terms, divergence in interpretation in EU case-law arises (i) because in all EU official languages there will be semantically related lexical items but, for the majority of terms, this will mean that their meanings are similar but not identical; (ii) because lexical items in all EU official languages usually have more than one meaning; and (iii) because lexical items from different EU languages are never semantically equivalent in mathematical terms. In other words, different linguistic versions of CJEU judgments contain lexical items that judges from national courts might not always understand and interpret in the same way. Sometimes, if linguistic divergence is recognized, it may become part of legal argumentation (Prieto Ramos 2014a, Vismara 2006). It can be concluded that judgments, which should make sure that EU law is uniformly applied across Member States in reality, might be a source of divergence.

Several options are available to address the issue of linguistic diversity in EU case-law. First, the Court could continue with the existing practice, pretending that the idea of uniformity can be linguistically justified. An advantage of this approach is that it has been in use for decades and there are established ways in law to deal with its fictitious status (Paunio 2013). Second, the Court could adopt a word-by-word translation approach, which would involve the process of redefining the meaning of linguistic expressions and detaching them from their previous usages. The problem with this option is that it would create an artificial language. In addition, since EU case-law is created through a dialogue between national courts and the CJEU, new problems would arise in translating terms between EU and non-EU legal sub-languages. Third, the Court could introduce a new language regime that would require the use of one official, working and authentic language at the Court. This option has been repeatedly discussed in the literature in relation to various EU institutions (e.g. Gazzola 2006; Pool 1996) but, because of the basic principles of EU law, it is not very likely that it will ever be accepted by all Member States. Fourth, the Court could acknowledge reality and allow development of legal pluralism. I will provide a few arguments in favour of the last option by relying on the views advocated by White (1989, 1994). Although his discussion is mainly restricted to the monolingual context, his conclusions are also relevant for translation-mediated communication.

White's view on language corresponds to the usage-based theory of meaning discussed in Section 4. According to this view, there is no universal language, and every speaker is 'a maker of a language that is in some respects different from any other' (White 1994: 253). He also argues that in order to be able to communicate with others, we need to learn their languages. Linguistically, it means abandoning the idea of reducing the meaning of several expressions to one fixed meaning. Instead, a new attitude is needed that does not regard uncertainty of meaning and impossibility of reaching an identical reading as a hindrance. 'It is not a defect but a merit of our system that judges are acknowledged to have discretion, that legal questions are as open and difficult, that juries can decide within a wide range' (White 1989: 97). In a pluralist legal system, it is the whole legal community that establishes the meaning of legal texts through coherent readings and exchange of arguments. In the context of EU case-law, this legal community includes not only judges and judges' cabinet members, but also members of the translators' community (although this is not often acknowledged). The difference between a uniformity and pluralistic view can be explained in terms of Gärdenfors's (1993) distinction between two basic power structures that can determine meaning: oligarchic and democratic. In the first case, determination comes from above, from experts; in the second, from above, from the practice of communication.

Translation-mediated communication is a type of intercultural communication (Schäffner 2003), but it is also a form of language contact and the contact of pragmatic and semantic systems (Koole and ten Thije 1994). For a better understanding of these issues in the context of EU case-law, future research should address the issue of similarities and differences between expressions from various linguistic versions of CJEU judgments, and of similarity and dissimilarity of linguistic items from CJEU judgments and national judgments. This research should address cultural, semantic and pragmatic aspects of linguistic expressions.

Finally, if we accept the idea that law is a type of knowledge (Latour 2010), lexical diversity in EU case-law can be regarded as the source of a new kind of legal knowledge. It is through collaboration that new understanding and innovative knowledge is created (Peschl and Fundneider 2014). The pluralist view creates an opportunity for the development of collaborative legal knowledge in EU law. This would mean that the whole community would be engaged in a collective reasoning process and plural intentionality (Pattaro 2007). In fact, this kind of knowledge already exists in the form of semantically similar exemplars stored in the communal memory of all the relevant parties involved in the creation and reception of EU law. The linguistic chunks or exemplars of the type studied in the present chapter are examples of this kind of memory.

Acknowledgements

I wish to thank anonymous reviewers and especially the editor (Fernando Prieto Ramos) and Karen McAuliffe for their constructive and helpful suggestions, which greatly improved the manuscript. The usual disclaimers apply.

12

Specificities of Translation at the European Court of Human Rights: Policy and Practice

James Brannan[1]

1 Language policy: Background and consequences

To quote Dame Rosalyn Higgins, former president of the International Court of Justice (ICJ), 'the past two decades, in particular, have seen the burgeoning of international courts and tribunals equipped to deal with disputes that might arise under the growing reach of international law' (Higgins 2016: 16). Such courts could never have functioned without translators.[2] This chapter will focus on the European Court of Human Rights ('the ECtHR' or 'the Court') in Strasbourg, which has jurisdiction in respect of forty-seven States with their diverse legal systems and languages, and on the staff of its Registry (linguists and lawyers). While a former judge of the Court once remarked 'language issues bedevil all international courts' (Terris et al. 2007: 71), it will be shown how the ECtHR has adapted its relevant policies to ensure efficient internal operation and external dissemination, with the advantages – and occasional difficulties – of having only two official/working languages, English and French.[3]

1.1 Applications

The subject matter of cases before the Court relates to alleged violations of the European Convention on Human Rights ('the Convention'), which dates back to 1950 but is often described as a 'living instrument which must be interpreted in the light of present-day conditions'. Cases start with an application lodged by an individual (or, rarely, a government in inter-State cases) against any of the Member States. The right of petition, as it is known, would be meaningless if the applicant were unable to use his or her own language, hence the lack of any obligation to translate the application itself into an official language of the institution. This has been a crucial democratic principle since

[1] All opinions are personal to the author.
[2] Or of course interpreters, but this contribution concerns only written translation; the Registry does not have a specific interpreting service but calls upon Council of Europe interpreters when needed.
[3] Rule 34 of the Rules of Court.

it was realized in the 1960s that applicants (at the time of the European Commission on Human Rights) who did not speak either English or French were at a disadvantage. The Commission's Rules of Procedure thus authorized the use of other languages in correspondence with applicants (Westerdiek 1998: 365). The Registry lawyers today deal with initial applications in all European languages (their own) without requiring the assistance of a translator.

The instructions for applicants on the Court's website advise as follows: 'If it is easier for you, you may write to the Registry in an official language of one of the States that have ratified the Convention. During the initial stage of the proceedings you may also receive correspondence from the Court in that language.'[4] Applications in non-European or non-official minority languages may nevertheless be dealt with if they can be understood by a member of staff. In any event, from the point where the application is accepted and notice is given to the government, the applicant is expected to use either English or French, unless he or she is specifically given leave to continue using another national language.

1.2 Judgments and decisions

Prior to the reform of 1998, the 'old' Court published all its judgments in both official languages (*en regard* in the printed reports).[5] After some debate about the new language regime,[6] the 1998 Rules of Court established that bilingualism would be an exception, so very few judgments are now available in both languages. The limitation of bilingualism in 1998 could already be explained by budgetary constraints, but there was also a concern about the slowing down of case processing. One argument was that, as judges worked collegially, it was more efficient to focus on a single text. On the other hand, if judgments were delivered in both languages, the upstream *confrontation* of the two language versions would be beneficial. The result is thus a compromise, and only the leading case-law is now translated into the other official language, before or after delivery. The exercise of pre-delivery translation reveals any lack of clarity and ambiguity in the original, and there may be a degree of cross-fertilization between the two versions, while post-delivery translation can have little or no influence on the source text and is arguably less motivating for the translator.

The current situation is that, in those few cases where judgments and decisions[7] are translated, the translation will be produced before delivery in Grand Chamber cases,[8] or otherwise after delivery for the purposes of publication (sometimes in the form of extracts) on the website (HUDOC database) and occasionally also in the printed reports.[9] Other significant case-law will be summarized in separate press releases at

4 http://www.echr.coe.int/Documents/Application_Notes_ENG.pdf (accessed 12 September 2016).

5 Judgments were authoritative in only one language before the mid-1980s.

6 See Malinverni 2000 and Decaux 2000.

7 Decisions concern mainly inadmissibility and striking out; a few are selected for inclusion in the printed reports and are therefore translated.

8 A small proportion of cases involving new and complex issues, either referred to the Grand Chamber at the request of a party after a Chamber judgment or where the Chamber relinquishes jurisdiction.

9 There is still an obligation, under Rules 57 and 76, for decisions and judgments published in the official reports to be bilingual.

the time of delivery and shortly afterwards in case-law information notes, all of which are bilingual.

While the Court is still allowed by Rule 74 § 1 to indicate the 'authentic' text 'where appropriate' in bilingual cases, it has become common practice for Grand Chamber judgments to be given equal authenticity in English and French,[10] thus theoretically placing a heavier burden on the translator. While one version is usually a 'pure' translation (except for the odd sentence inserted in the target-language text during the deliberations, or if the drafting language has switched at any stage), it is not identified as such.[11] The original version can at best be guessed from the country concerned (e.g. a judgment against France or Belgium will probably have been drafted in French). It is only where a judge's separate opinion is translated that the indication 'translation' is added to the heading.

Other international courts have continued to prefer a single authentic text. On the establishment in 1920 of the Permanent Court of International Justice, predecessor of the ICJ, a French delegate[12] called for 'unity of language' (i.e. the use of French) on the ground that multilingual case-law would be problematic in the event of discrepancy; it was ultimately decided that one of the two official languages (French or English) would be authoritative. In the Court of Justice of the European Union (CJEU) the language of the case (one of twenty-four official languages) is authoritative, even though the original draft will have been in French. Judgments of the International Criminal Court are 'done' in both English and French (that court's working languages), with one language text being authoritative; the translation may be completed post-delivery.

The potential discrepancy between language texts in Grand Chamber cases inevitably raises the question of the translator's liability, although certain 'safeguards' reduce the possibility of errors in the final translation. Prior to delivery, the translated text will be re-read by a reviser, by a senior lawyer and by the judges in connection with their second deliberation. Any remaining mistakes may be picked up when the press release is drafted or when the judgment is finalized by a legal assistant. Failing that, since the vast majority of Grand Chamber cases are published in the official series of reports, the proof readers in the Publications division will inevitably make any necessary corrections after delivery (to both the printed and electronic versions). In actual fact, all judgments (originals and translations) carry the disclaimer that they 'may be subject to editorial revision'.[13]

So how do domestic courts deal with the language versions of Strasbourg case-law, and have any discrepancies actually been identified? The multilingual case-law of the CJEU has been the subject of more research in this area (see, in particular, Derlén 2015). The Strasbourg case-law is different in that, while much remains monolingual, its bilingual Grand Chamber judgments are considered to have a single meaning; there is not even an obvious de facto original. Taking the example of the UK Supreme Court,

10 Grand Chamber judgments typically end with 'Done in English and in French ...' (and *vice versa* in the French: 'Fait en français et en anglais ...').

11 However, where a *Chamber* judgment is earmarked for publication in the official report series, it will be translated after delivery, and the original language will be indicated in a footnote to the summary.

12 Léon Bourgeois; Extract from the Procès-Verbal of the tenth session of the Council of the League of Nations, PCIJ Documents 1920.

13 At least until publication in the printed reports, where that is the case. There is also a more formal 'Rectification of Errors' procedure under Rule 81.

it does look at monolingual (French-only) case-law and then uses its own unofficial English translations.[14] When referring to *Maumousseau and Washington v. France* (2007), the Supreme Court used the Court's published translation – although not an authentic text as it was a Chamber case – without considering the French text at all.[15]

However, in analysing the Grand Chamber case of *Salduz v. Turkey* (2008), it did compare the French and English texts, and an unfortunate discrepancy was found.[16] Lord Rodger stated: 'The language [of the English text] might seem to suggest that in *Salduz* the Grand Chamber was innovating and laying down a rule under which restrictions [on legal assistance] for good cause would now be treated differently'. He concluded, however, 'The language of the French text of para 52 is different and gives no support for any such inference.' He thus drew a conclusion from the French, in support of his argument, without considering that the French might have been the translation and that the English was possibly more accurate. There was of course no reason to question the validity of either Grand Chamber text; by contrast, when analysing the CJEU's judgments, domestic courts do often rely on the de facto original, that is, the French, rather than the authoritative 'language of the case' (Derlén 2015: 65–7).

1.3 Dissemination of case-law in non-official languages

To quote Sir Stephen Sedley, 'it seems an elementary principle of justice that those to whom a judgment is addressed should be able to understand it' (Sedley 2011: 571). If linguistic equality were ensured by the ECtHR for the publication of its judgments, as at the CJEU, then about forty languages would have to be catered for; such a policy has never been seriously considered. Over the past few years, however, efforts have been made by the Court to provide, through its HUDOC database, external translations into other languages. In its preliminary opinion for the Brighton Conference,[17] the Court stated that it would 'continue its efforts to ensure better dissemination of the case-law, including in national languages'.

The HUDOC team began by collecting existing translations, some having been commissioned in the past by the Council of Europe and others from third-party collections of case-law, as well as posting links to websites hosting further translations. The translation project 'Bringing Convention standards closer to home' was launched in May 2012, funded by the Human Rights Trust Fund (for three years, later extended to four), with the aim of having key case-law translated into the languages of eleven Member States outside the EU[18] by external translators in the relevant countries. The

14 See *R and Thompson v. Secretary of State for the Home Department* [2010] UKSC 17 – translation of *B.B. v. France* criticized by Lord Rodger – and *Flood v. Times Newspapers Limited* [2012] UKSC 11 – where a certified translation of the judgment in *Polanco Torres and Movilla Polanco v. Spain* had been provided.

15 *E (Children)* [2011] UKSC 27.

16 *Cadder v. Her Majesty's Advocate (Scotland)* [2010] UKSC 43.

17 See the Brighton Declaration of April 2012 (point 9(d)(i)), encouraging the States parties to 'ensure that significant judgments of the Court are translated or summarized into national languages').

18 Albania, Armenia, Azerbaijan, Bosnia and Herzegovina, Georgia, the Republic of Moldova, Montenegro, Serbia, FYROM, Turkey and Ukraine (see Press Release ECHR 288 of 6 July 2012, 'Human Rights Trust Fund enables the European Court of Human Rights to launch case-law translations project').

Registry has also commissioned a significant number of Russian translations of key case-law, legal summaries, factsheets, research reports and case-law guides, and in 2013 it organized translations into Bulgarian, Greek, Hungarian and Spanish. By the end of 2015, over 15,000 case-law translations in some thirty non-official languages had been made available on HUDOC.[19] Some of the translations are thus the result of outsourcing, while others have been completed independently by external bodies, including government ministries and non-governmental organizations (NGOs).

While Registry lawyers from the countries concerned may have a look at an external translator's work when first received, the vast majority of such translations remain unrevised, hence the disclaimer: 'Translations into non-official languages are not made by the Registry of the Court and it does not check their accuracy or linguistic quality. They are published in HUDOC for information purposes only and the Court accepts no responsibility for their quality or content.'[20]

2 Structural features

2.1 Organization of translation activity

The Court had no translators of its own until 1987 (Weston 2010: 77). It gradually built up its English and French divisions with up to eight and nine translators respectively. Out of that number, there have traditionally been two on each side at a higher grade (L4, reviser/team manager). Since 2010, there has been an overall head of the Language Department (L5); prior to that, one of the L4s for each language served as the de facto head of division. The Department additionally provides assistance with drafting in the form of a 'language check', in cases where the drafting lawyer is not a native speaker of the official language in question. In recent years, the number of translators on the English side has been slightly reduced (now six) in order to create more English language-checker posts.[21] That reduction has coincided with a drop in translation volume as a result of a change in the publications policy. With fewer judgments and decisions published in the printed reports,[22] there is somewhat less mandatory post-delivery translation, into French and English. There have been no vacant posts in the English division for over ten years, at the time of writing; until recently, permanent

[19] See http://www.echr.coe.int/Documents/Case_law_info_training_outreach_2015_ENG.pdf (accessed 12 September 2016), pp. 4–6; the Case-law Information and Publications Division is responsible for this activity. The Public Relations Division also produces information materials in a range of languages, including some non-European languages; see http://www.echr.coe.int/Pages/home.aspx?p=languagedocs (accessed 12 September 2016).

[20] A new challenge will arise with the entry into force of Protocol No. 16, which provides for preliminary questions from the highest national courts and an advisory opinion by the Court in response; at the time of writing, it has not yet been decided whether the opinion will be bilingual and/or translated into the domestic court's language, if non-official.

[21] There are currently eight English and four French language checkers. The translators also do some language checking, mainly Grand Chamber drafts and judges' opinions.

[22] In 2011, it was decided that about thirty texts per year, as opposed to 100, would be earmarked for the printed reports; some of those that would formerly have been in print are now translated for HUDOC alone.

contracts were offered to new recruits, resulting in a relatively low turnover. This stability has of course been highly beneficial in terms of institutional memory. The lower-grade translators (L2/3), once they have finished their probationary period, are generally autonomous, and only their translations of Grand Chamber draft judgments are revised.

Unlike the lawyer-linguists at the European Court of Justice (see e.g. Gallo 2006: 182), ECtHR translators do not have to be qualified to practise law. A typical vacancy will merely require some legal knowledge,[23] although a number of the current translators do have legal qualifications. Recruitment is by competitive examination, with an age limit of 55, and candidates must have either English or French as their mother tongue.

The Department includes a small team of secretaries, who help with document management but do not provide a referencing service. Translators thus have to find their own source material when needed.[24] Judgments may notably contain extracts from international instruments that will have to be traced in the other official language.

2.2 Working with judges and drafting lawyers

It is no secret that the Registry's lawyers do most of the drafting of the Court's judgments (see e.g. Kosař 2015: 133), working in English or French (sometimes both) regardless of their mother tongue,[25] in collaboration with the Judge-Rapporteur and, in some cases, a drafting committee of judges. Where a draft is translated prior to delivery, the translator will be able to consult the author and may find some corrections to be made to the source text. As regards judges' separate opinions (concurring or dissenting), unless the judge is a native speaker of an official language, a language check by a translator will usually be required, and sometimes a translation, which will be mandatory not only in Grand Chamber cases but also in Chamber cases where the opinion is not in the same language as the judgment. It is mainly in the context of such opinions that translators work closely with the judges, who always have to approve the final text(s).

As is the case in other international courts, 'language skills have always been considered one of the most important non-binding substantive criteria for Strasbourg judges' (Kosař 2015: 133). While such skills obviously vary, all judges are now required, as a condition of appointment, to be fluent in one of the Court's official languages and to have a passive knowledge of the other[26] (or a commitment to acquire such knowledge), so as to be able to play a full part in the work of the Court. As stated in a 2016 vacancy for the UK judge, they 'may communicate in either official language of

23 The vacancy notice for an English translator in 2000 and 2004 required simply 'knowledge of European legal systems, especially the English and the French'. In 1993, '*good* knowledge' was called for.

24 Assistance can be obtained from the Court's helpful library staff.

25 On recruitment, assistant lawyers (B-grade) are required to have 'very good knowledge of one of the two official languages' and an 'ability to draft legal texts therein clearly and precisely'. A-grade vacancies have the same requirement but additionally require '(good) knowledge' of the other official language.

26 See Guidelines of the Committee of Ministers on the selection of candidates for the post of judge at the European Court of Human Rights, CM(2012)40 final, 29 March 2012.

the Court ... but must be able to understand case documents in both languages'. More drafts are produced in English than in French,[27] because fewer lawyers and judges use the latter actively. Both languages are used in deliberations (with simultaneous interpreting), unlike the situation at the CJEU, where deliberations are held in only one language (French).

After the draft judgment is completed in a Grand Chamber case, the translator attends the deliberations, where it is particularly important for judges to be able to review the validity of both language texts, which are scrutinized in parallel. The translator notes any linguistic comments and responds to questions about his or her translation – a useful exercise that is a specificity of the ECtHR. Such comments often come from judges who are not native speakers of the official language in question, and it may not be obvious at first sight whether the translation is at fault or whether the problem lies in the original text, especially where the judge has only been looking at the translation. Judges may believe that there is a mistake in the translation when it is in fact a drafting issue – that is, any improvement to the English may require amendment of the French or *vice versa*. Moreover, a translation may be valid (even possibly better than the original!) but criticized by a judge for not corresponding closely enough to the source-language wording. Actual mistakes can arise when amendments have not been properly brought to the attention of the translator during the drafting process. Changes may of course be made to the translated version by the judges during the deliberation, subject to confirmation by the translator and back translation into the other official language if necessary.

Translators may thus have a role in the drafting of the original document as well as the translated text (through either a language check or comments on the source text during a translation), depending to some extent on the receptiveness of the drafting lawyer (or Judge-Rapporteur). In some cases, translators may be called upon to give linguistic advice.[28] While relations between translators and lawyers/judges are usually excellent, some drafters are more sensitive about making corrections to the original, especially at a late stage in the proceedings.

2.3 Specificities of procedures and documents

Specific difficulties arise for the translator in Grand Chamber cases, in addition to the problem of meeting deadlines. Such cases often involve new issues and case-law and, therefore, terms that have not previously been considered. Each case is allocated to a single translator, who works on it from beginning to end. The documents to be translated will be more numerous than in Chamber cases. Those that are not confidential will usually be outsourced (regardless of the source language): the referral request (if appropriate) and the parties' observations, including those of the third-party

[27] One report found that 'typically around two-thirds of documents before Chambers were in English only, and one-third in French only' (Steering Committee for Human Rights CDDH-SC(2011)R1, 14 September 2011, pp. 2–3).

[28] Contributing, for example, to a note on terminology in the *Rohlena v. the Czech Republic* judgment (2015), §§ 28–9.

interveners (often NGOs).[29] The confidential documents translated internally (from one official language to the other) include the Judge-Rapporteur's note, a research report and the various press releases (on referral/relinquishment, for the public hearing and on delivery). Then, of course, the draft judgment itself will be the main in-house task, in a number of stages, not forgetting separate opinions at the end of the proceedings.

Judgments (Chamber or Grand Chamber) follow the same pattern, starting with an outline of the procedure, which is based on a template, followed by the 'Facts' part, which is often complicated to translate in terms of culture-bound language and may include lengthy extracts from domestic judgments. There is usually a section headed 'Domestic law and practice', containing passages from national legislation and case-law, sometimes with a similar section on the relevant international or comparative law. The 'Law' part is the focus of the judges' deliberations. It begins with any preliminary objections and summarizes the parties' arguments; then it deals with the alleged violation(s) of the Convention, setting out the general principles before the key paragraphs on their application in the present case (where the language is perhaps freer but more sensitive). The judgment ends with a section on any award of 'just satisfaction' and the operative paragraph(s). The degree of creativity left to the translator will largely depend on the relevant part of the judgment. The most idiomatic language can arguably be used in the translation of separate opinions.

3 Practical issues

3.1 Terminological choices

The choice of terms at the Court has been analysed in more detail elsewhere (see Brannan 2013 and Weston 2005), and only a few general points will be made here. Similar issues will of course be familiar to translators in other organizations, although actual usage will vary; existing international terminology, unless we are referring to a particular instrument, is not always consistent or suitable for our purposes. Some of the Court's terminology is of course based on the Convention, from which it has derived a certain number of autonomous concepts, and other terms have become enshrined in the case-law, as will be shown below.

The Registry does not employ a terminologist and, to date, there is no database; individual translators still use their own lists or published glossaries.[30] However, there has been some effort to organize terminology meetings and to compile notes on usage, principally in the form of a style manual. Teamwork is crucial for consistency, and translators discuss terms more informally on a regular basis.

The Court's translators have the problem not only of ensuring consistency in case-law by using generic or 'supranational' terms, but also of finding translations in the two official languages for the domestic specificities of the State concerned, the range of subject matter being vast. On the one hand, there are certain features of domestic law for which a functional – or otherwise linguistic/formal – equivalent will have to be

[29] One problem with translating parties' observations is that the authors cannot be consulted.

[30] A well-used dictionary is Bridge (1994), of which a revised edition is pending.

found in translation, and on the other, there is a need for harmonization through more generic terminology. It may thus depend on whether the passage translated concerns the specific country (e.g. in the 'Facts' or 'Relevant domestic law' parts of the judgment) or relates to a general principle being expounded by the Court.

Translators are wary of choosing culture-specific terminology (e.g. common law terms in English) where there is an alternative that would be more easily understood by the European reader (or indeed by the judges themselves, when they are not native speakers). For example, in criminal law, *warning* may be better than the UK-specific *caution*, albeit less idiomatic in English – this would neatly correspond to *avertissement* in French rather than the more specific *rappel à la loi*. Similarly, the generic term *minor offences* could be translated into French as *infractions mineures* rather than *contraventions*.[31] The question may also arise whether to continue to use an obsolete term where the legal terminology has evolved. It is better to choose the term that is more meaningful and as close as possible to the concept in the particular jurisdiction; for example, preferring *inculpation* to the more recent (in France) *mise en examen* where the French text concerns a case against Turkey; or, on the other hand, using *claimant* as opposed to the more archaic *plaintiff*, which may not always be clear to non-native speakers. Sometimes the older term may be enshrined in an international instrument.[32] Translators may have their own preferences, inevitably leading to a certain degree of inconsistency over the years.

Another major issue for the Court's translators is how to deal with terms already translated from a 'hidden' third (non-official) language. For example, a case against Romania may be drafted in French, using the drafting lawyer's own translations from Romanian of the facts and domestic law[33] and will then have to be translated into English via the 'relay' of French. The English translator may, if the French is unclear, have to ascertain from the lawyer the precise meaning of the Romanian term. If necessary, on account of cultural specificity combined with the term's importance for the relevant facts, the translator may of course retain the third-language term in brackets after the translation.[34] There may be some disagreement as to the best rendering of the non-official language term (e.g. names of courts and institutions or whether to use *Article* or *section* for legislation) between the native speakers (linguists) and non-native speakers (drafting lawyers from a given country). Discussions on terminology with the Registry's lawyers are thus frequent and sometimes endless!

3.2 The weight of precedent

As reiterated in *Jones and Others v. the United Kingdom* (2014), 'while the Court is not formally bound to follow its previous judgments, it is in the interests of legal certainty,

[31] Such generic terms are also used in the EU's procedural safeguard directives (e.g. Directive 2010/64/EU, Article 1 § 3).

[32] For example, *custody* and *access* in the Hague Convention on international child abduction.

[33] For example, *Creangă v. Romania* (2012) and *Blaj v. Romania* (2014), concerning Romanian criminal procedure.

[34] It is rare, however, for the source-language term to be left untranslated without even an explanation; that is our practice for a limited number of domestic court names (e.g. *tribunal de grande instance*) and procedures (e.g. an *amparo* appeal).

foreseeability and equality before the law that it should not depart, without good reason, from precedents laid down in previous cases.' A logical consequence of this reliance on the Court's own case-law is the need for consistency of language, a principle that can neatly be described as *linguistic precedent* – a term probably coined by former Head of English Martin Weston (1988: 687). It may, of course, be seen by the translator as a constraint to have to use language from previous judgments, however much a translation could otherwise be improved upon. Some rather unidiomatic language can be found in the Convention itself or has become so enshrined in the case-law that it cannot be changed; 'margin of appreciation' (a Gallicism) is just one example of an expression that has taken on a specific meaning.

Translators constantly have to deal with 'hidden' quotes (i.e. not between inverted commas) followed by a string of case-law references that should at least help them find the 'linguistic precedent' relatively quickly (although it is not always obvious which of the cases cited contains the closest wording). The Court thus tends to rely on existing stock phrases and the result is not always as elegant as it should be. There may be a problem of sentence structure (with a potential lack of clarity or redundancy) when short segments are placed together to form a summary of a given case-law principle. A distinction can be made here between bilingual precedent, where there is an existing version in the target language; and monolingual precedent, where the translator has to deal with a principle that has hitherto been rendered only in the source language.

As a bilingual example, a passage to be translated from French in the 2015 case of *Morice v. France* (§§ 132–3) consisted of a number of segments from previous cases. If those segments had been copied from the English case-law word for word, it would have read: 'The special status of lawyers gives them a central position in the administration of justice as intermediaries between the public and the courts. They therefore play a key role in ensuring that the courts, whose role is fundamental in a State based on the rule of law, enjoy public confidence … . That special role of lawyers …' The repetition of 'special' and 'role' here is clearly undesirable, and the passage is generally stilted. While not being able to rewrite it completely, the translator improved it by using synonyms. The amended wording, however, led to a problem in connection with an opinion, where the judge criticized the Court's *dictum*, in this and previous cases, about the 'special status of lawyers'; as the judgment in question now referred to '*specific* status', it had to be indicated in the English version of the opinion that two different adjectives had been used for the same finding.[35]

By 'blindly' copying previous translations, there is also a risk of perpetuating errors that have never been dealt with. One example is the use of the term *due diligence* in a number of cases that can be traced back to a translation of the French *la diligence requise*,[36] referring more to the notion of promptness or expedition in English; *due diligence* is arguably a Gallicism in that context and probably should have been corrected over the years. The translator is of course entitled to improve upon the

[35] Concurring opinion of Judge Kūris (§ 3) in *Morice v. France*; the French translation does not reflect the fact that the adjective *spécifique* had remained unchanged.

[36] *Quinn v. France* (1995), § 48.

existing wording if it is clearly misleading, provided the quotation is not a formal one, although any such corrections should be brought to the attention of the drafting lawyer and kept to a minimum.

A related issue is that of 'back translation', that is, where the translator's source text is already a translation, in a previous case, from the other official language. Disregard of original wording may contribute to the development of varying and misleading formulations, even though the translation may not actually be erroneous.[37] The translator is then faced with a dilemma: 'Do I translate a sentence accurately and idiomatically *ab initio*, or do I strictly adhere to an original version (perhaps drafted many years ago) already in the target language?'

Other examples can be found of purely monolingual precedent, where the translator is confronted with a 'hidden quote' that cannot be traced back to any bilingual case-law, that is, it has only been used hitherto in an untranslated Chamber judgment. This is quite a common occurrence, as drafting lawyers tend to cite cases concerning their own countries (as observed by Kosař 2015: 136) or in their drafting language; therefore, the precedent may exist in only one official language (e.g. Italian lawyers commonly cite French-only judgments concerning Italy).

It is therefore the translator's role to help ensure the linguistic consistency of ECtHR case-law to avoid diverging formulations and varying terms for the same concept in a given language, although existing wording may sometimes have to be reconsidered so that it is appropriate to the context of the case and preferably not stilted or obscure.

4 Concluding remarks

Although the ECtHR supervises the implementation of only one international instrument, the European Convention on Human Rights, translators are nevertheless faced with a considerable variety of subject matter and difficulties, stemming in part from the range of legal systems within the Court's jurisdiction, as a result of which there is a certain amount of 'hidden' translation in source texts already carried out by Registry lawyers from non-official languages. While only a small minority of judgments and decisions are actually available in both official languages, those earmarked for translation (including in summary form) constitute leading case-law, often on particularly sensitive or new issues. The translator has particular responsibility in Grand Chamber cases where both language texts are authentic. The Court's linguists must never forget that their translations will be read and interpreted by domestic courts and lawyers across Europe and may in turn be translated into other languages. Ultimately, the relevant Convention standards will have to be 'translated' into reality in the legal order of each country; the clarity, accuracy and terminological consistency of the official-language case-law are therefore all the more important.

[37] For an example, compare § 79 (last sentence) in *Kamasinski v. Austria* (1989), original English, with § 68 (last sentence) in *Hermi v. Italy* (2006), original French.

13

Comparative Interpretation of Multilingual Law in International Courts: Patterns and Implications for Translation

Fernando Prieto Ramos and Lucie Pacho Aljanati

1 Introduction

In an increasingly globalized and digitalized world, transnational law has achieved new prominence. The need for greater international cooperation has prompted a proliferation of multilingual legal instruments. The analysis of these texts and their genesis calls for interdisciplinary approaches involving both legal and linguistic aspects. Since multilingual legal instruments are predominantly produced through translation, legal translation plays a key role in the development, application and interpretation of international and supranational law. When law is produced in multiple official languages, it is equally authentic in all of them and presumably entails multilingual interpretation, that is, consideration of the different language versions when ruling on a certain provision.

Articles 31 and 32 of the Vienna Convention on the Law of Treaties (1969) (VCLT) set out, respectively, the general rule and the supplementary means of interpretation of international treaties. Article 33 deals with the interpretation of treaties authenticated in two or more languages. The unity of the treaty is 'safeguarded' by both the principle of equal authenticity and 'the presumption that the terms are intended to have the same meaning in each text' (United Nations [UN] 1967b: 225). As also highlighted by the International Law Commission of the United Nations (ILC), 'the existence of more than one authentic text clearly introduces a new element – comparison of the texts – into the interpretation of the treaty' (ibid.). However, as suggested by previous studies (e.g. Bengoetxea 2011; Condon 2010; Kuner 1991), multilingual comparison does not seem to be systematically or consistently carried out by international courts. Some authors (e.g. the latter two) argue that this can lead to the risk of textual divergences and the subsequent perpetuation of disputes.

In practice, the existence of authentic texts in two or more languages can either complicate or facilitate the interpretation of a multilingual instrument. As reported by the ILC to the General Assembly, 'the different genius of the languages, the absence of a complete *consensus ad idem*, or lack of sufficient time to coordinate the texts may result in minor or even major discrepancies in the meaning of the texts' (UN 1967b: 225). At the same time, when the meaning of terms is ambiguous or obscure in one language but it is clear in another, the multilingual character of the legal instruments can facilitate interpretation. Considerable scholarly attention has been devoted to the subject of treaty interpretation in general (e.g. Gardiner 2015; Linderfalk 2007; Pauwelyn and Elsig 2012) and also, to varying degrees, to multilingual interpretation at specific organizations, particularly the European Union (EU) (e.g. Baaij 2012; Derlén 2009; Solan 2009). However, systematic comparison of multilingual interpretation between international courts remains limited.

Against this background, our study first provides an overview of the intrinsic relationship between legal interpretation and translation (Section 2). The legal framework for the interpretation of multilingual international treaties and EU legal instruments will then be examined (Section 3) with a view to exploring the practice of multilingual interpretation in three contexts: the International Court of Justice (ICJ, the main judicial organ of the UN); the World Trade Organization's Appellate Body (AB); and the Court of Justice of the European Union (CJEU). These three multilingual bodies (called 'international courts' for the purposes of this study) were chosen as part of a larger project on institutional legal communication* because: (1) they are representative of adjudicative bodies within the multilateral and the EU legal orders; and (2) despite their differences, they share the principle of equal authenticity, as well as concomitant challenges to ensure legal certainty and uniform interpretation in the application of multilingual legal instruments (e.g. Prieto Ramos 2014a).

More particularly, we delve into the following questions: To what extent are legal provisions compared in different languages in proceedings before the three courts? How often do they resort to Article 33 of the VCLT? Are there any remarkable differences in the patterns of comparative interpretation, particularly between intergovernmental and EU judicial organs? To answer these questions, we will analyse instances of comparison, as well as their initiators and motivation, in all case-law involving multilingual interpretation in each institution until 15 July 2016. Before reaching initial conclusions on the implications of these patterns for institutional language professionals, we expect to establish correlations between the complexity of each language regime, the nature of court proceedings, and the level and features of comparative interpretation at each institution.

2 Legal interpretation and translation

The nature of interpretation can be perceived in a broad or narrow sense. Interpretation *lato sensu* means 'the process of understanding and applying a given text', a piece of legislation (Conway 2012: 13). In this sense, every time we deal with a text to which we attach a meaning (either consciously or unconsciously), we are engaged in an act of interpretation (Linderfalk 2007: 10). Interpretation *stricto sensu* refers to the process

* 'Legal Translation in International Institutional Settings' (LETRINT), supported by the Swiss National Science Foundation through a Consolidator Grant.

of 'understanding and applying the meaning of a text' when that meaning is obscure and requires 'more considerable input from the interpreter than ordinary textual apprehension' (Conway 2012: 13). In *stricto sensu*, it is only when we read a text and the text proves to be unclear that we can consider that we interpret it (Linderfalk 2007: 10).

However, even when the meaning of a legal instrument is clear, it is the result of having determined a certain meaning. 'It may have been a simple task, certainly easier than the case of expounding the meaning of abstruse words' but, in every case, meaning must be assigned to terms (Gardiner 2015: 29) because meaning is dynamic and created in context. 'Legal texts are not immediately palpable but only come to life in acts of interpretation' (Venzke 2014: 1).

As active players in multilingual law production, translators find themselves in the middle of these processes. The relevance of hermeneutics in legal translation has been noted by several authors (see e.g. Piecychna 2013: 145; Prieto Ramos 2011: 208; Šarčević 1994: 304; Stolze 2002). Translators must not only conduct interpretation *lato sensu* to reformulate any text, an activity described as an 'art of interpreting' by Gémar (1995), but they are also exposed to issues of interpretation *stricto sensu*. In dealing with these issues in institutional contexts in particular, they may contribute to clarifying obscure text and to enhancing the quality of a multilingual legal instrument (see strategies to tackle ambiguity in Prieto Ramos 2011). Interpretation issues initially confronted (or overlooked) by translators may lead to semantic divergences between different language versions of a text. These divergences then may become the subject of argumentation in court proceedings.

Considering the risks involved, international organizations can only benefit from measures aimed at the application of predictable principles of interpretation by both legal drafters and legal translators. This entails integrating such principles in legal translation methods (ibid.: 212). Institutional legal translators should be familiar with the general rules of interpretation of the law they translate and also, whenever possible, with any interpretation patterns that may help them detect and solve new interpretation problems, and prevent divergence between language versions. While 'the interpretation of documents is to some extent an art, not an exact science' (UN 1967b: 218), and this could also be said about translation, as pointed out by Shabtai Rosenne, the law can indicate 'the nature of the rules governing the process by which this art is applied in a particular case, the kind of intellectual discipline with which an interpreter must gird himself' (2007: 454). Translators can learn from comparative interpretation of multilingual law by authoritative interpreters in each legal order.

3 Rules of interpretation of multilingual law

3.1 Interpretation of multilingual multilateral treaties

Customary principles of treaty interpretation were codified by the ILC in the VCLT. In principle, they apply to all international courts, 'irrespective of their institutional setup, subject matter, or geographical scope' (Pauwelyn and Elsig 2012: 445). When the ILC completed its first reading of the draft articles on the law of treaties in 1964, its chairman Roberto Ago recalled that 'the reason why the UN had entrusted it with the codification of international law, and in particular the law of treaties, was that the main objective was certainty of the law; and certainty of the law of treaties depended mainly on certainty of the rules of interpretation' (UN 1965: 23).

With regard to the 'General rule of interpretation' (Article 33 of the VCLT), the Commission explained that by referring to 'rule' in the singular, it intended to highlight that 'the process of interpretation is a unity and that the provisions of the article form a single, closely integrated rule' (UN 1967b: 220). The application of the means of interpretation would be a 'single combined operation'. In addition, the Commission acknowledged that the article 'cannot properly be regarded as laying down a legal hierarchy of norms for the interpretation of treaties' (ibid.: 219). The 'elements of interpretation' had to 'be arranged in some order', but 'logical considerations' rather than 'any obligatory legal hierarchy … guided the Commission in arriving at the arrangement proposed in the article' (ibid.: 220). 'The starting point of interpretation' should be 'the meaning of the text.' Then logic implies that first consideration should be given to the 'ordinary meaning' of a treaty's terms, in their specific context and in light of the treaty's 'object and purpose' (ibid.).

If Article 31 is applied and the meaning needs to be ascertained, Article 32 provides that one can resort to 'supplementary means of interpretation, including the preparatory work of the treaty and the circumstances of its conclusion'. Article 32 may also be employed when 'the interpretation according to Article 31: (a) leaves the meaning ambiguous or obscure; or (b) leads to a result which is manifestly absurd or unreasonable'.

Moreover, certain difficulties may arise that are unique to the interpretation of multilingual treaties. Article 33(3) safeguards 'the unity of the treaty' by the presumption that the terms of a treaty are intended to have the same meaning in the authentic text in each language, which results in the right to rely on a single text. In case of doubt, this presumption is refuted and the different authentic texts need to be compared in an effort to find their 'common meaning … before preferring one to another' (ibid.: 225). From the records of their discussions, some members of the ILC thought that the proper approach would be for an interpreter to investigate the treaty in all of its languages before deciding on the meaning. However, this was seen as too demanding, and a proposal requiring language comparison in every case was rejected (UN 1967a: 211).

According to Article 33(4), if the texts are compared and there is a difference in meaning that the application of Articles 31 and 32 does not resolve, 'the meaning which best reconciles the texts, having regard to the object and purpose of the treaty, shall be adopted'. 'Teleological interpretation, therefore, is the final resort in the assignment of meaning to multilingual treaty texts' (Labuschagne 1999: 327). The following graph (Figure 13.1) summarizes the basic principles of interpretation.

With this in mind, as noted by Gardiner (2015), it can be concluded that an interpreter 'may legitimately use a single language for "routine" interpretation', but a cautious interpreter must acknowledge that linguistic divergences may exist, and comparison may actually help to clarify the meaning of a provision without necessarily complicating the process of interpretation (ibid.: 421). In the words of Shabtai Rosenne, 'a good practitioner would almost automatically compare the different language versions before commencing any process of interpretation' (UN 1967a: 209). The question would be to what extent, why and how comparison is conducted in practice in international court proceedings.

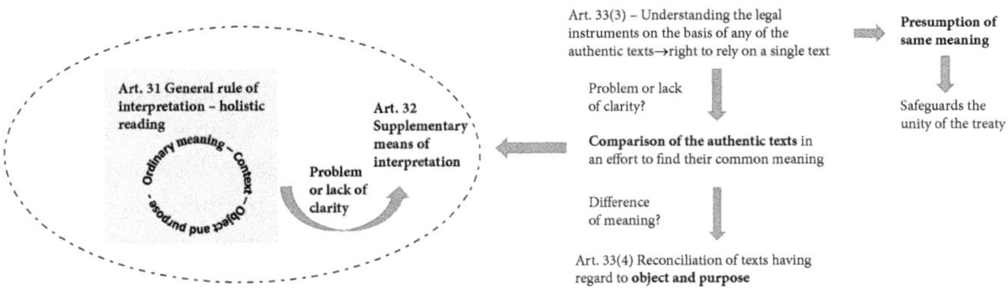

Figure 13.1 Interpretation of multilingual treaties (Art. 31–33 of the VCLT).

Previous studies have highlighted the flexible and non-exhaustive nature of the VCLT principles as guidance for treaty interpretation, as well as the resulting divergence in the application of interpretative methods by different international adjudicators (Pauwelyn and Elsig 2012; Weiler 2010). The ICJ and the AB have traditionally applied a more text-oriented approach (see e.g. Abi-Saab 2010; Torres-Bernárdez 1998; Van Damme 2009), while the CJEU's hermeneutic practice has been predominantly teleological (see Section 3.2) and 'activist' or 'gap-filling', which contributes to the CJEU 'gradually coming closer to being a domestic rather than a truly international tribunal' (Pauwelyn and Elsig 2012: 458).

The AB is regarded as particularly formalistic and systematic in its analysis of 'the ordinary meaning' of the terms of the World Trade Organization (WTO) covered agreements, often using contextualized dictionary definitions as the starting point of interpretation (see Van Damme 2009). Article 3.2 of the WTO's *Understanding on Rules and Procedures Governing the Settlement of Disputes* (*Dispute Settlement Understanding* or DSU) states that the WTO's dispute settlement mechanism serves 'to clarify the existing provisions of those agreements in accordance with customary rules of interpretation of public international law', and the AB has invoked Articles 31 to 33 of the VCLT as having attained the status of customary international law.[1] Its reports do not establish binding precedents and its interpretations are only applicable to the relevant dispute, but, in practice, they are relied upon in subsequent disputes. According to Article IX:2 of the WTO Agreement, the Ministerial Conference and the General Council of the WTO have the 'exclusive authority to adopt interpretations' that are binding on all WTO Members (although this authority has rarely been exercised).

3.2 Interpretation of multilingual EU law

As an autonomous legal order of international law (see *Van Gend & Loos* and *Costa v. ENEL* cases),[2] EU multilingual law interpretation deserves specific attention. Since EU law contains no explicit interpretation rules (see e.g. Itzcovich 2009), in principle, the CJEU has the discretion to apply the methods of interpretation that it deems appropriate.

1 See e.g. reports in *US — Gasoline*, WT/DS2/AB/R, pp. 16–17; *Japan — Alcoholic Beverages II*, WT/DS8/AB/R, WT/DS10/AB/R, WT/DS11/AB/R, p. 104; *US — Softwood Lumber IV*, WT/DS257/AB/R, para. 59).

2 Case 26/62, *Van Gend en Loos v. Administratie der Belastungen*, EU:C:1963:1; and Case 6/64, *Flaminio Costa v. ENEL*, EU:C:1964:66.

However, international agreements to which the EU is a party, as well as EU secondary legislation implementing international obligations, must be interpreted by the EU in the light of international law. The CJEU has held that 'even though the Vienna Convention does not bind either the Community or all its Member States, a series of provisions in that convention reflect the rules of customary international law which, as such, are binding upon the Community institutions and form part of the Community legal order' (Case C-386/08, *Firma Brita GmbH v. Hauptzollamt Hamburg-Hafen*, para. 42).[3]

In his analysis of the CJEU's application of the VCLT, Pieter Jan Kuijper concluded that the Court is 'rather unselfconscious about applying the rules of interpretation of Article 31' and 'never makes clear *why* it feels bound to have recourse to these rules'; for the CJEU, 'they are simply the proper rules to apply when interpreting an international agreement without it being clearly stated that the Community, and therefore its institutions, are bound to apply these rules of interpretation as a matter of customary international law' (Kuijper 1998: 22–3).

As regards the VCLT's rules of interpretation, the same author and other scholars (e.g. Dengler 2010; Šarčević 2013) have highlighted the strong teleological orientation of the Court's interpretative practice. This is often combined with literal and contextual interpretation methods also present in the VCLT but with an overall 'functional perspective' driven by the main objective of 'practical effectiveness of EU law' (see, for example, Rösler 2012: 979).

What about inter interlinguistic comparison as part of legal interpretation? The CJEU's case-law soon moved beyond the subsidiary rule of comparison set out in Article 33(3) of the VCLT, which it vaguely followed when it called for consultation of the different language versions only in 'cases of doubt' in the *Van der Vecht* case of 1967.[4] Since the *Stauder* case of 1969 (i.e. almost six months after conclusion of the VCLT), the CJEU has reiterated that consideration of all language versions is mandatory when interpreting EU law.[5] This was confirmed with regard to national courts' interpretation in the *CILFIT* judgment of 1982, in which the CJEU established that all language versions of EU secondary legislation are equally authentic and have the same weight; 'an interpretation of a provision of Community law thus involves a comparison of the different language versions.'[6]

It is worth noting that the CJEU's case-law has been systematic in referring to the 'language versions' rather than the 'authentic texts' of a legal instrument as in Article 33 of the VCLT. In line with the principle of equal authenticity, the 'vanishing original'

[3] According to Article 81, only States can be parties to the VCLT. Its rules of interpretation, however, have been applied by different bodies (such as the European Court of Human Rights or the European Patent Office's Enlarged Board of Appeal) to cases to which the VCLT does not strictly apply.

[4] 'The need for a uniform interpretation of Community regulations necessitates that this passage should not be considered in isolation, but that in cases of doubt, it should be interpreted and applied in the light of the versions existing in the other three languages' (Case 19/67, *Bestuur der Sociale Verzekeringsbank v. J. H. van der Vecht*, EU:C:1967:49, p. 353).

[5] 'When a single decision is addressed to all the Member States the necessity for uniform application and accordingly for uniform interpretation makes it impossible to consider one version of the text in isolation but requires that it be interpreted on the basis of both the real intention of its author and the aim he seeks to achieve, and in the light in particular of the versions in all four languages' (Case 29/69, *Erich Stauder v. City of Ulm – Sozialamt*, EU:C:1969:57, para. 3).

[6] Case 283/81, *Srl CILFIT and Lanificio di Gavardo SpA v. Ministry of Health*, EU:C: 1982:335, para. 18.

(Dollerup 2004) is not acknowledged in EU texts. In the CILFIT landmark judgment, the CJEU also referred to two important aspects of EU law interpretation: the fact that 'legal concepts do not necessarily have the same meaning in Community law and in the law of the various Member States' (para. 19) and the prominence of teleological interpretation mentioned above: 'every provision of Community law must be placed in its context and interpreted in the light of the provisions of Community law as a whole, regard being had to the objectives thereof and to its state of evolution at the date on which the provision in question is to be applied' (para. 20).

Advocate General Francis Jacobs, at a lecture delivered in 2003, described the CJEU's approach to interpretation as 'consistent over the years'; 'teleological, taking account of the purpose of the legislation'; and 'contextual, taking account of the scheme of the legislation and its place in the framework constituted by the Treaties and European law in general' (European Commission 2003: 1). He referred to the VCLT in connection with two aspects: (1) 'Reflecting the involvement of different States in European law – and Article 31 of the [VCLT] – the ECJ may have regard to the travaux préparatoires, such as the Commission proposal and the explanatory memorandum' (ibid.: 1); (2) 'Because of the multilingual nature of Community law, the ECJ may take an approach inspired by Article 33 of the [VCLT]: if comparison of different language versions reveals differences, the interpretation should be chosen which best reconciles the text and the purpose' (ibid.: 1–2). He added that the approach 'may be compared with, but is not the same as, other bodies confronted with multilingual texts such as the European Court of Human Rights and the World Trade Organization' (ibid.: 2). This practice will be quantified and comparatively analysed in the next section.

4 Patterns of comparison

4.1 Methodology

Corpus analysis was used to compare the level of explicit comparison of language versions at the institutions under review. The corpus is composed of all case-law involving multilingual interpretation from the establishment of each organization until 15 July 2016. The relevant decisions were compiled using search engines of different databases: (1) Westlaw Next (ICJ), (2) WTO Documents Online (AB)[7] and (3) CVRIA (CJEU). These decisions include documents issued under several denominations in both advisory and contentious cases (except for the AB, with no advisory function): ICJ's judgments, orders or advisory opinions; AB's reports; and CJEU's judgments in contentious cases (direct actions) and references for a preliminary ruling (indirect actions). Exhaustive searches were carried out using keywords and keyword phrases, including 'Article 33 of the Vienna Convention' (and variants), 'language version/s',

[7] In order to test the reliability of sources and select the databases, search results were also verified in the ICJ's repository, Cambridge Law Reports/International Law Reports, WorldLII and LexisNexis in the case of the ICJ; and the Dispute Settlement Gateway and the Trade Law Guide in the case of the WTO.

'various languages' and references to the official languages in each organization followed by 'text/s' or 'version/s' (e.g. 'English text', 'French text', 'Spanish version', 'Greek version'). The lists of documents retrieved through the different searches were merged into a single list for each organization, duplicates were removed and instances of explicit comparison were carefully verified in order to establish the final consolidated lists.

As this research deals with publicly accessible ICJ and CJEU documents and AB's dispute settlement reports, our study can only account for instances of comparison that are acknowledged in texts. It cannot determine whether comparative interpretation was actually conducted more frequently than it may have surfaced in the texts. For the purpose of the study, however, it is presumed that explicit references to comparison provide a reliable indicator of the frequency of this practice in each court.

4.2 Frequency of explicit comparison

Given the potentially higher margin of error in detecting instances of comparison (i.e. instances potentially overlooked) in the extensive judicial activity of the CJEU (by far the most productive of the three bodies),[8] a sample period of three years (2013–2016)[9] was used in order to double-check the validity of the overall results for this Court and also to facilitate the subsequent analysis of comparative interpretation as carried out in recent years. The overall results (Table 13.1 and Figures 13.2 and 13.3) confirm that there is no significant difference between the frequency of comparison over the whole period[10] (3.12 per cent of cases) and in the sample period (3.59 per cent of cases). This contrastive exercise also shows that the level of comparison in EU law interpretation in CJEU cases has remained stable (and proportionally low) despite a dramatic increase in the number of both court cases and EU languages of applicable legislation.

During the sample period, the CJEU issued a total of 2,785 judgments. The search using 'language versions' retrieved almost all instances of comparison. After verification of all occurrences of this keyword (104), only four documents were excluded for not including comparison, while the other 100 comprised all the judgments retrieved through searches with other keywords. If extrapolated to the whole period (510 documents retrieved with 'language versions' out of a total of 16,327 judgments), the margin of error in the detection of explicit comparison would be negligible (+/−0.14 per cent). Cases include interpretation or advisory proceedings initiated by national courts (868 references for a preliminary ruling and nine cases of preliminary reference urgent procedure) and 1,908 direct actions (including actions for annulment, actions for damages and actions for failure to fulfil an obligation).

In the case of the ICJ, with the lowest productivity and the second-lowest level of comparison of the three settings, the tool primarily used, WestLaw Next, retrieved

[8] For the purpose of this study, the CJEU sub-corpus includes all judgments issued by the CJEU bodies or courts under its different denominations since the establishment of the Court, in both advisory and adjudicative cases.

[9] The sample period covers three years from 1 July 2013, date of Croatia's accession, until 1 July 2016.

[10] The whole period covers from 1 January 1954 until 15 July 2016.

Table 13.1 Instances of explicit comparison

	Period	**Languages**	**Total no. of cases**	**Average of cases adjudicated per year**	**Cases including instances of comparison between languages**
ICJ	1947–2016	6 UN languages (5 until 1980)	163 137 contentious (84.05%) 26 advisory (15.95%)	2.36	19 (11.66%) 14 contentious (10.22% of subgroup) 5 advisory (19.23% of subgroup)
AB	1995–2016	3 WTO languages	137	6.37	37 (27.01%)
CJEU	1954–2016	24 EU languages (initially 4)	16,327	263.34	510 (3.12%)
CJEU *sample period*	2013–2016	24	2,785 1908 direct actions (68.51%) 877 preliminary rulings (31.49%)	928.33	100 (3.59%) 35 direct actions (1.83% of subgroup) 65 preliminary rulings (7.41% of subgroup)

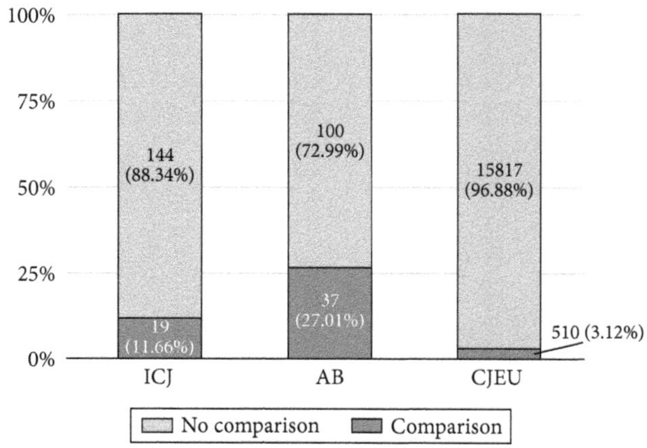

Figure 13.2 Proportion of explicit comparison in entire corpus (all bodies).

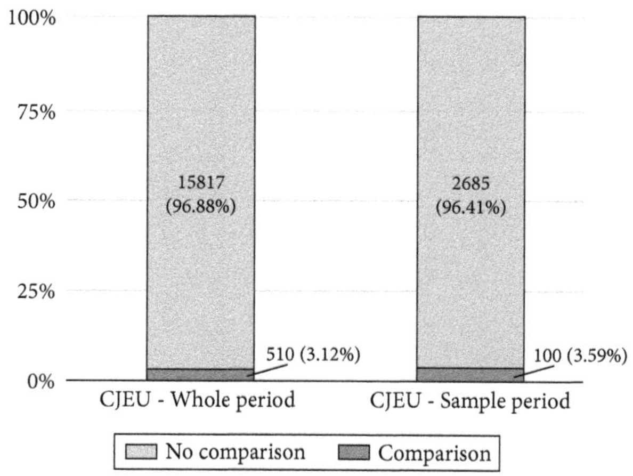

Figure 13.3 Proportion of explicit comparison in CJEU judgments (whole and sample periods).

full documents from the Court, including separate or dissenting opinions of judges. Out of a total of 163 cases retrieved through searches,[11] thirty-five were confirmed as referring to comparison. In turn, in sixteen of these cases, comparison was only found in separate or dissenting opinions. Therefore, there remained nineteen cases in which comparison is explicit, that is, 11.66 per cent of the total of 163 cases in the whole period (1947–2016): five cases of comparison in advisory opinions (19.23 per cent of twenty-six advisory proceedings) and fourteen cases of comparison in judgments

[11] Westlaw Next covers from 1947 until 2005 and additional opinions until 2010, including a total of 149 cases (123 contentious cases and 26 advisory proceedings). These results were double-checked and completed with searches in the ICJ's repository in particular: http://www.icj-ICJ.org/docket/index.php?p1=3&p2=2 (accessed 30 July 2016).

or orders (10.22 per cent of 137 contentious cases). The proportion of comparison is therefore significantly higher in the case of advisory cases.

If separate and dissenting opinions were included, cases of comparison would increase to thirty-four or 20.86 per cent of the total, including eleven in advisory proceedings (42.31 per cent of this subgroup) and twenty-three in contentious proceedings (16.79 per cent of the subgroup). While these opinions are relevant as an indication of when interpretative comparison was individually considered during the deliberations, they are treated separately for the sake of comparability if the comparison was not part of the Court's final decision.

In instances of comparison, 'text' by authentic language was by far the term most commonly used, in line with the terminology found in the VCLT. It is also worth noting that, in the case of the ICJ, comparisons might refer to the interpretation of bilateral or plurilateral treaties that are authentic in languages other than UN languages but brought to the Court in accordance with international law provisions in the UN languages. This was the case in four disputes: *Border and Transborder Armed Actions (Nicaragua v. Honduras)* of 1988 (disputed provision: Article II of the Pact of Bogota in English, French, Portuguese and Spanish); *Elettronica Sicula S.p.A. (ELSI) (U.S. v. Italy)* of 1989 (Article V (2) of the 1948 Treaty of Friendship, Commerce and Navigation in Italian and English); *Kasikili/Sedudu Island (Botswana/Namibia)* of 1999 (Article III of the Anglo German Treaty of 1 July 1890 in English and German); and *Sovereignty over Pedra Branca/Pulau Batu Puteh, Middle Rocks and South Ledge (Malaysia/Singapore)* of 2001 (involving Article IV of the 1891 Convention between Great Britain and the Netherlands in Dutch and English). Otherwise, the ICJ tends to focus on its working languages, English and French, when conducting comparison (see also Kuner 1991:957), especially on its own initiative. A breakdown of the specific languages compared in each case is beyond the scope of this study.

Finally, out of the 137 reports issued by the AB in the entire period (1995–2016),[12] thirty-seven, or 27.01 per cent of the total, included explicit comparison.[13] In fact, if we have a closer look at the cases and when the comparison is actually carried out by the AB and not only mentioned as part of the parties' argumentation, the frequency of comparison is significantly lower, down from thirty-seven to twenty-two cases (16.06 per cent of the total), as opposed to only three cases of comparison by a referring court or the parties not elaborated on by the CJEU (down to a total proportion of 3.48 per cent of comparison in the sample period) and two cases of this kind at the ICJ (and a proportion of 10.43 per cent of comparison) (see Section 4.4). The findings for the WTO are consistent with those obtained by Condon (2010: 204), who detected comparison in 22.1 per cent of the eighty-six reports issued by the AB until 7 October 2009, including a very marked increase of comparison practice between 2003 and 2005, also found in our corpus. The lower level of comparison in the past few years, after the 2003–5 peak (with comparison in more than 50 per cent of cases), explains the lower average for the period up to 2016 in this study.

Interestingly, at the WTO, 'version' was more frequently used than 'text' in instances of comparison, particularly in the case of French ('French version' found in seventeen

12 The period covers from 1 January 1995 until 15 July 2016.

13 Only three of the forty reports retrieved through the searches were excluded.

reports versus 'French text' in three reports) and, to a lesser extent, Spanish ('Spanish version' in twenty-four documents as opposed to 'Spanish text' in fourteen reports). This can be linked to the fact that English was the language indicated as 'original' at the beginning of all AB reports and the 'English text' (explicitly referred to in these terms in eight cases of comparison versus 'English version' in nine cases) tends to be used as the 'master' text to compare the Spanish and French texts. However, the fact that English is the working language of the AB and the main language of negotiations and original texts of the WTO's covered agreements does not mean that it is the authoritative language in the context of comparison.

At first sight, the above quantitative findings depict an almost perfect correlation between the number of official languages potentially considered and the frequency of explicit comparison of language versions in court proceedings. Applying the same methodology to all institutions, and regardless of the number of languages actually compared in each case, the result of 11.66 per cent of comparison at the ICJ (six official languages of UN law-making) roughly doubles in the case of the WTO, with half the number of official languages and a much more productive dispute settlement body. Inversely, the proportion found at the ICJ drops dramatically in the case of the CJEU, with exactly four times more official languages than the UN in the sample period, although, in instances of explicit comparison, these courts tend to focus on a few languages (most often those involved in divergence) and not all their official languages (as is more often the case at the WTO).

Another interesting finding is the higher proportion of comparison in advisory proceedings as opposed to contentious proceedings at the ICJ (almost double proportion) and the CJEU (four times higher proportion), whereas the outstanding proportion of comparison at the AB corresponds entirely to contentious cases and is marked by the abovementioned 2003–5 peak.

Do these results mean that the level of comparison is directly related to its practical feasibility depending on the number of languages? Our figures seem to point to that pattern. Nonetheless, the proportionality of the correlation may respond to multiple factors and raises new questions. Do CJEU judges conduct more 'routine' comparison without referring to it but tend to only address it explicitly in judgments when the case raises questions of possible divergence between language versions? In other words, does the CJEU follow the flexible approach set out in Article 33 of VCLT, adapting it to its own needs? Is there a connection between the level of comparison and the initiators of comparison by type of proceedings? To address these questions, we will focus on further analysis of two aspects: the explicit recourse to Article 33 of the VCLT and the initiators and motivation of comparison by type of proceedings.

4.3 References to Article 33 of the VCLT

This section examines the instances of comparison in which explicit reference was made to Article 33 since the VCLT entered into force on 27 January 1980 (a period that covers all cases of comparison of the corpus except for four instances at the ICJ). In this Court, four explicit references (26.67 per cent of cases of comparison) were found in *Military and Paramilitary Activities in and against Nicaragua (Nicaragua v. United States of America)*; *Elettronica Sicula S.p.A. (ELSI) (United States of America v. Italy)*; *LaGrand*

(Germany v. United States of America); and *Questions relating to the Obligation to Prosecute or Extradite (Belgium v. Senegal)*. The most prominent reference to Article 33 and the only one raised by the Court rather than a party or a judge is found in the *LaGrand* case, in which the Court compared the different texts and, since there was a difference of meaning, it resorted to the object and purpose of the Statute. It held that

> In cases of divergence between the equally authentic versions of the Statute, neither it nor the Charter indicates how to proceed. In the absence of agreement between the parties in this respect, it is appropriate to refer to paragraph 4 of Article 33 of the Vienna Convention on the Law of Treaties, which in the view of the Court again reflects customary international law.[14]

In WTO appellate proceedings, Article 33 of the VCLT or one of its paragraphs were cited in twelve reports or 32.43 per cent of cases of comparison, the highest proportion of the three contexts analysed. For instance, in *Canada – Renewable Energy / Canada – Feed-In Tariff Program* (WT/DS412/AB/R; WT/DS426/AB/R, 6 May 2013), the Panel's interpretation of the term 'governmental purposes' in Article III:8(a) of the GATT 1994 was called into question. The first explicit reference to Article 33(3) of the VCLT was made by the EU. It claimed that the terms in English, French and Spanish were not entirely identical and the provision had to be interpreted in light of Article 33(3) VCLT (ibid.: para. 2.125). The AB compared the three language versions and stated that the words *besoins* or *necesidades* could not be 'read harmoniously' with the definition of the term *purpose* as 'objectives' or 'aims' of the government, because 'neither the word *besoins* in French, nor the word *necesidades* in Spanish, encompasses the notion of an aim or objective' (ibid.: para. 5.67). To address the problem of interpretation, the AB resorted to the context of the provision. It examined another article of the GATT 1994 and also the immediate context of the terms (ibid.: para. 5.68).

Finally, we found only one case in which Article 33 of the VCLT was mentioned in CJEU case-law during the sample period,[15] *Kik v. OHIM*, but it was referred to by one of the interveners rather than by the Court: 'the Greek Government … points out that Article 33 of the [VCLT] of 23 May 1969 … establishes the general rule of equivalence for different language versions of treaties where the text is authentic in two or more languages.'[16] This lack of reference is not surprising, considering the autonomy of EU law and its case-law on the matter. Over the period 1998–2010, Kuijper (2011) found approximately forty cases in which the CJEU explicitly referred to the VCLT, mostly in connection with the interpretation of international agreements to which the EU is a party, as well as its founding treaties, which again is consistent with the distinction between applicable international customary law and the EU's own approach to the interpretation of its secondary legislation.

The above quantitative data (see Table 13.2) also corroborate the conclusions of previous studies on the international courts' explicit reliance on VCLT rules, particularly as regards the AB's tendency towards more systematic adherence to these rules. Isabelle

[14] *LaGrand (Germany v. United States of America)*, Judgment, I.C.J. Reports 2001, p. 502, para. 101.
[15] The sample period is also used for the rest of the quantitative analysis in this chapter.
[16] Case T-120/99, *Kik v. OHIM*, EU:T:2001:189, p. 2255, para. 43.

Table 13.2 Explicit references to Article 33 of the VCLT in cases of explicit comparison

	Cases including instances of comparison between languages (after the entry into force of the VCLT)	**Reference to Art. 33 of the VCLT**
ICJ	15	4 (26.67%)
AB	37	12 (32.43%)
CJEU	100	1 (1%)

Van Damme (2009) notes, however, that this trend, which was instrumental for the AB 'in making acceptable its early choice to function as a court and to build its judicial identity' (ibid.: 606), is on the decline. Likewise, Pauwelyn and Elsig (2012: 467) point to the need for legitimacy of 'young tribunals' like the early AB as a factor contributing to the more explicit sequencing of VCLT-based interpretative steps. The opposite trend was found by Torres-Bernárdez (1998) in the case of the ICJ, while Gardiner (2015) suggests that this trend has gradually changed into a more explicit interpretative approach. As regards references to Article 33, while our results on the ICJ are too limited to identify this kind of pattern statistically, two of the four instances found in those proceedings are from the shorter period that followed the first of the two studies.

4.4 Who resorts to comparison and why?

Three questions were posed in connection with the origin and agents of comparison: (1) who initiates comparison?; (2) why was comparison conducted?; and (3) when comparison is initiated by a referring court (in the case of the CJEU) or panel (in the case of the AB) or by the parties, do the international courts also compare?

We identified three groups of initiators: (a) the international courts (or judges or advocates general [AG] in the case of the CJEU); (b) the referring national courts (in CJEU proceedings) or panels (in AB proceedings); and (c) the parties. As reflected in Figure 13.4, in the ICJ and the CJEU, comparison was mostly initiated by the Court (in 78.95 per cent and 54 per cent of cases, respectively), while in the context of AB proceedings, it originated most often from the parties (54.05 per cent of cases, as opposed to 30 per cent in the CJEU and only 21.05 per cent in the ICJ). AB reports in which the dispute panel (the first instance dispute settlement body) is the initiator of comparison account for 10.81 per cent of cases at the WTO, whereas in the CJEU, referring national courts initiated comparison in 16 per cent of cases (or 24.62 per cent of the 65 cases of comparison in requests for a preliminary ruling). For example, in *Michael Timmel v. Aviso Zeta AG*, it was the referring court that highlighted a divergence 'between the various language versions of Article 14(2)(b) of the Prospectus Directive in relation to whether the obligation to make the prospectus available to the public' had to be 'performed at both the registered office of the issuer and the offices of the financial intermediaries or only at one of those two places'.[17]

[17] Case C359/12, *Michael Timmel v. Aviso Zeta AG*, EU:C:2014:325, para. 25.

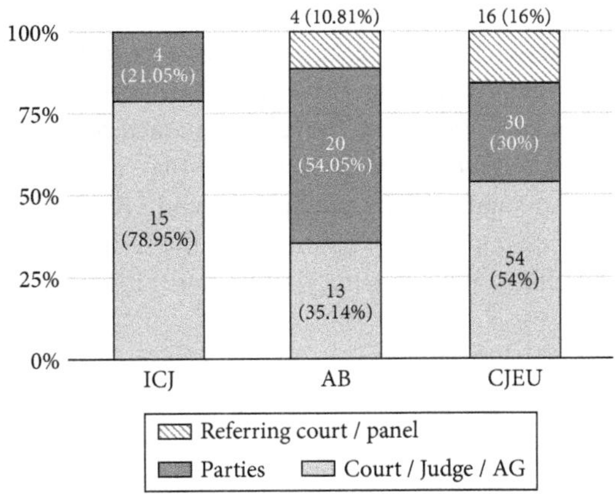

Figure 13.4 Who initiated comparison?

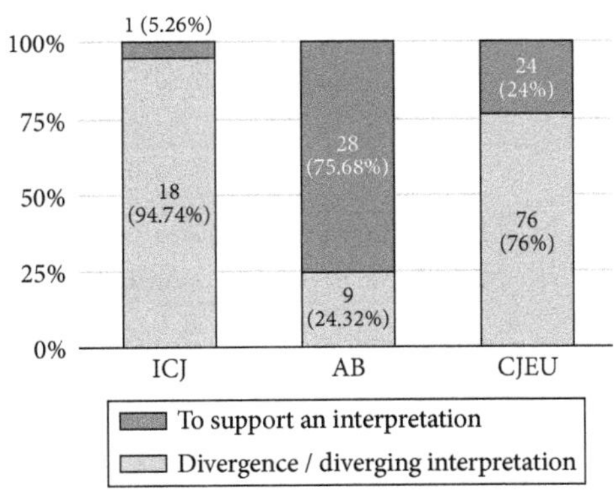

Figure 13.5 Motivation for comparison.

Table 13.3 Correlation between initiators and motivation of comparison

	Cases including comparison between languages	Comparison initiated by the Court	Comparison initiated by parties	Comparison initiated by referring court / panel	Divergence / diverging interpretations as reason for comparison	Comparison in support of interpretation
ICJ	19 (11.66%)	15 (78.95%)	4 (21.05%)	-	18 (94.74%)	1 (5.26%)
AB	37 (27.01%)	13 (35.14%)	20 (54.05%)	4 (10.81%)	9 (24.32%)	28 (75.68%)
CJEU	100 (3.59%)	54 (54%)	30 (30%)	16 (16%)	76 (76%)	24 (24%)

The results obtained regarding the motivation for comparison (see Figure 13.5 and Table 13.3) reveal a strong relationship with the most common initiators in each institution. In 94.74 per cent of cases at the ICJ and 76 per cent at the CJEU, comparison was initiated in connection with instances of divergence or diverging interpretations. This includes cases in which the parties argued that certain language versions would lead to different results, even if, strictly speaking, this was not referred to as divergence. However, in AB proceedings, the trend is exactly the reverse: comparison was primarily used to support an interpretation (in 75.68 per cent of cases). For instance, in *United States – Continued Suspension of Obligations in the EC – Hormones Dispute*, Norway submitted that 'a restrictive interpretation of "proceedings" is also supported by the Spanish and French versions of the DSU referring to the term "*actuaciones*" in Spanish and the term "*travaux*" in French, in accordance with Article 33 of the *Vienna Convention*'.[18] It is interesting to note that,

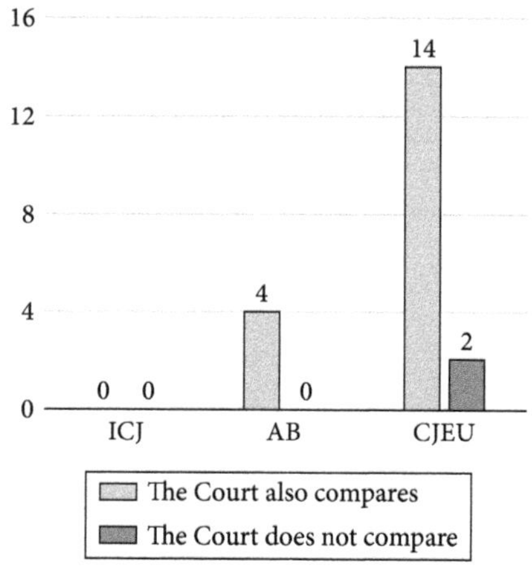

Figure 13.6 Comparison initiated by referring court or panel: consideration by the Court.

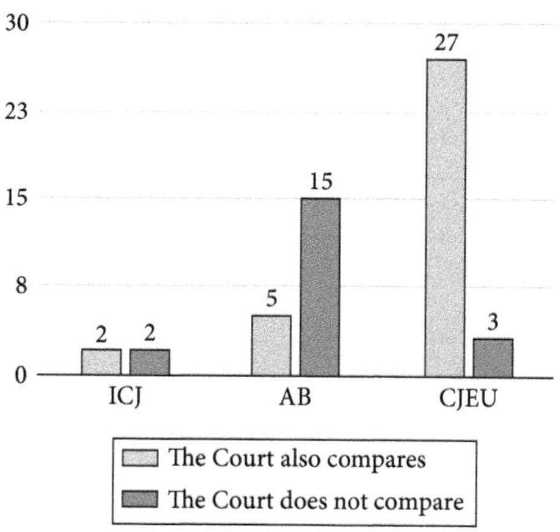

Figure 13.7 Comparison initiated by the parties: consideration by the Court.

[18] *United States – Continued Suspension of Obligations in the EC – Hormones Dispute*, WT/DS320/AB/R, 16 October 2008, p. 105, para. 255.

Table 13.4 Correlation between the Court's consideration of comparisons not initiated by it and the motivation for comparison

	Comparison initiated by the referring court / panel	The Court also compares	Divergence / diverging interpretations	To support an interpretation	The Court does not compare	Divergence / diverging interpretations	To support an interpretation
ICJ	–	–	–	–	–	–	–
AB	4	4	4	–	–	–	–
CJEU	16	14	14	–	2	1	1
	Comparison initiated by the parties	**The Court also compares**	**Divergence / diverging interpretations**	**To support an interpretation**	**The Court does not compare**	**Divergence / diverging interpretations**	**To support an interpretation**
ICJ	4	2	2	-	2	2	-
AB	20	5	1	4	15	3	12
CJEU	30	27	23	4	3	2	1

if we examine the total proportion of cases of divergence as percentage of each sub-corpus of case-law, it is not the AB (6.57 per cent of cases) but the ICJ (11.04 per cent) that presents the highest frequency of explicit challenges to semantic unity, with the EU showing the lowest proportion (2.73 per cent).

Finally, as regards the third question, that is, whether the Court also compares when comparison is initiated by a referring court (in CJEU proceedings) or a panel (in the case of the AB) or by the parties, the answer is positive in the first two scenarios (Figure 13.6), and we observe different patterns when comparison is initiated by the parties (Figure 13.7). In two of the four cases of comparison initiated by the parties in the ICJ, the Court does not find it relevant to address a potential divergence, and states: 'The Court does not find it necessary to resolve the controversy regarding the text … of this early treaty';[19] and 'the Court's reasoning does not require the resolution of the problem posed by this textual discrepancy, and it will therefore not rehearse all the arguments that have been put forward by the Parties'.[20] The CJEU does not compare in only three of the thirty cases of comparison that originated from the parties (10 per cent). This contrasts with 75 per cent of cases in AB proceedings (fifteen of twenty cases). These are generally cases in which the parties compare to support an interpretation but no other mention is made about comparison (Table 13.4), while the courts tend to systematically elaborate on the comparisons initiated by the referring court or panel to address divergences. This pattern aligns with the interpretative steps of the VCLT.

5 Discussion and implications for translation

This study has empirically confirmed significant variations in comparative interpretation of multilingual law in rulings of the ICJ, the AB and the CJEU, with the highest frequency of explicit comparison found in AB proceedings (27.01 per cent), the lowest in the CJEU (3.59 per cent) and the ICJ occupying the middle ground (11.66 per cent). This points to a correlation between the number of languages of each institutional language regime and the feasibility of comparison, particularly in the case of EU law, not only because it is the most multilingual and (in principle) the most exposed to comparison as directly-applicable law, but also because the CJEU's case-law itself has confirmed that comparison is mandatory as a tool for the uniform interpretation of EU law. However, this approach seems difficult to implement, particularly by national courts, as illustrated by our results: in only sixteen of sixty-five CJEU preliminary rulings featuring comparisons of language versions, these comparisons were initiated by the referring national court.

Further comparative analysis of references to Article 33 of the VCLT, and of the origin and purpose of comparison, has led to new correlations and provided a more nuanced understanding of the commonly held view that international courts do not systematically compare language versions. One important factor explaining

[19] *Western Sahara*, Advisory Opinion, I.C.J. Reports 1975, p. 12.

[20] *Border and Transborder Armed Actions (Nicaragua v. Honduras)*, Jurisdiction and Admissibility, Judgment, I.C.J. Reports 1988, p. 69.

comparison patterns is found in the correlation between the type of proceedings and the initiators and motivation of comparisons: the frequency of comparison is higher in advisory than in contentious proceedings in courts with this double function (almost double proportion in the ICJ and more than triple in the case of preliminary rulings as opposed to direct actions at the CJEU). In turn, these comparisons are more often initiated by the Court itself in connection with instances of divergence. The opposite applies to WTO dispute settlement, where parties are more often the initiators of comparison in order to support a particular interpretation, and these comparisons are frequently not further addressed by the AB itself. However, it is in this context that explicit references to Article 33 of the VCLT are the most frequent, as opposed to a marginal reference found in the CJEU.

These results are congruent with the interpretative approaches traditionally taken by the courts surveyed in this study, that is, a more textual orientation in the multilateral contexts of the ICJ and particularly the AB, and a more teleological autonomous approach at the CJEU. Nevertheless, in practice, all these courts seem to be consistent with VCLT rules and resort to comparison to resolve multilingual interpretation issues, even if VCLT provisions are not always explicitly mentioned.

The case of the ICJ is particularly telling, as the Court itself is the initiator of comparison in most cases (78.95 per cent) and deals with the highest proportion of divergences (94.74 per cent of cases of comparison and 11.04 per cent of all its case-law). If we consider instances of comparison as part of separate or dissenting opinions, it becomes apparent that comparative interpretation is not rare in the framework of ICJ deliberations (42.31 per cent of advisory proceedings, 16.79 per cent of contentious proceedings, and 20.86 per cent of total cases). This would be expected of a judicial organ of reference in international law, and can also be associated with the lower caseload of the ICJ. Yet, this Court refers to Article 33 of the VCLT in only 26.67 per cent of cases that include comparison.

Conversely, in AB proceedings, if we only consider cases of comparison actually elaborated on by the adjudicative body, the frequency of comparison drops from 27.01 per cent to 16.06 per cent of AB reports. Likewise, cases of divergence raised are less frequent than at the ICJ (6.57 per cent). It is the parties' argumentation in trade disputes that explains the high number of comparisons found in the AB sub-corpus. In the context of highly contentious disputes, where the issues at stake may have significant economic implications, it is not surprising to find that the parties scrutinize WTO agreements in their three authentic languages in search of support for their interpretations. As to the manner in which the comparisons are conducted, the AB's formalistic approach, including its more routine recourse to dictionary definitions, may partly respond to the general need to gain legitimacy as a young adjudicative body (Pauwelyn and Elsig 2012: 467).

Finally, the lower frequency of comparison and cases of divergence addressed in CJEU proceedings (3.49 per cent and 2.73 per cent, respectively, and up to 7.41 per cent of instances of comparison in preliminary rulings) must also be viewed in a holistic way. Apart from the reduced practicability of comparing a larger number of languages, other factors may contribute to explain the apparent contradiction between mandatory comparison (according to EU case-law) and proportionally low levels of explicit comparison. The first potential factor is the higher productivity of this Court.

The actual number of cases of comparison addressed at the CJEU in three years (100), albeit proportionally low, represented a volume almost three times higher than that of the AB in eleven years and five times higher than that of the ICJ in almost sixty years of existence. It would be justified to hypothesize that a certain threshold might naturally emerge in the detection of divergences depending on the volume and diversity of cases, the types of proceedings and the dynamics of different parties dealing with an ever-expanding body of law. In fact, the proportion of comparisons in CJEU case-law has remained remarkably stable according to our analysis of the overall and the sample periods of Court activity, which would support the idea of a certain historical threshold. These averages also suggest that the addition of languages may have two mutually counterbalancing effects: greater risk of divergence but lower feasibility of comparison.

Second, while more languages usually entail higher risk of divergence and more difficulties in detecting them, the Court's teleological approach itself may be less prone to highlighting differences of meaning between language versions unless it is absolutely imperative to address them. This does not necessarily mean, however, that the Court does not conduct more 'routine' comparative interpretation than explicitly mentioned in its decisions, even if the comparison does not involve all official languages. In other words, its conciliatory interpretative practice may well lead the CJEU to problematize textual differences less frequently than multilateral courts, and to deliberately adopt a less positivist stance on the intrinsic diversity of EU legal acts and the predictability of their meaning.

Last but not least, the linguistic limitations of national courts may also play a role. As mentioned above, they do not resort to comparison on a regular basis (see also Paunio 2007: 398 and Derlén 2009: 350), especially in contrast with the parties to WTO disputes. As pointed out by Advocate General Francis Jacobs (European Commission 2003) before the important 2004 enlargement, it is the national courts that actually interpret EU legislation most often. For him, it would be advisable that they follow the CJEU's purposive interpretative approach, as language divergence 'can rarely be resolved just by comparison of different versions' and it is 'a fiction to say that the legislature has considered all the language versions' in the first place (ibid.: 2). In the same vein, two decades earlier, Tabory (1980: 228) had referred to 'the inability of delegations to verify translations in several totally unfamiliar languages' in the context of the UN.

This kind of assertion can trigger other related questions: What are the limitations of effective multilingualism from a legal perspective? To what extent is equal authenticity truly respected in the way multilingual law is interpreted and applied? What are the best ways to ensure legal certainty in the integral development of multilingual law, from its conception to its interpretation? Can States and citizens rely on just one version of multilingual legal instruments?

The data and factors discussed in this chapter provide some preliminary replies on the multilingual character of interpretative patterns in the three courts through the lens of explicit instances of comparison. In order to answer more fully, further analysis would be required on the specific languages and problems examined in comparison, and on the hermeneutic techniques applied. Based on our analysis, it can be concluded that the English version is normally perceived as the leading text for the definition of the ordinary meaning of WTO agreements and for comparison with the other two official languages of this organization. As for the ICJ, the tendency is to focus on English and

French for the interpretation of international law provisions, but this Court might be required to resolve cases of divergence involving other non-UN languages of particular treaties (four cases detected in our corpus). Finally, proceedings at the CJEU are the most unpredictable in terms of languages of comparison, as the original language of the texts is not acknowledged and potential differences of meaning may arise between a wide myriad of language pairs. Nonetheless, the fact that most EU legislation is first drafted in English and that the CJEU itself uses French as internal working language places these languages in a prominent position. Scholars such as Derlén (2011) and Šarčević (2013) even argue for a more predictable interpretative approach to acknowledge this reality and reinforce legal certainty by keeping English and French as languages for mandatory consultation, together with the language of each case. This issue has attracted increasing attention in light of the dramatic increase in EU languages since 2004.

Regardless of the variations in language regimes and multilingual interpretation frequencies and approaches, one commonality is clear when it comes to reconciling multilingualism and legal certainty: the vital role of translation. Although interpretation problems cannot be totally prevented, the incidence of divergences between different language versions can be minimized by ensuring accuracy and interlinguistic concordance in processes of multilingual text production. From a systemic perspective, this entails acknowledging the time and expertise required for quality translation, the need for appropriate concordance control mechanisms and close cooperation between translators, legal drafters and other professionals involved in the production workflow. Furthermore, language experts can be key allies in assisting international and national courts with the comparative analysis of different language versions. This kind of cooperation can only be beneficial in the pursuit of institutional goals of quality multilingual communication: the translation process can help to spot and improve unclear passages or correct mistakes, and the multiple texts of an instrument can subsequently help to define its meaning, as illustrated by cases in which one or several versions were used to confirm a particular interpretation.

Of course, the above should be coupled with measures to update translation expertise and tailor it to the needs of each organization in various ways: by raising awareness of the relevance of coordinating solutions with other translators and drafters, and also, critically, by learning from hermeneutic practices and instances of divergence in the translator's language combination in order to better identify and handle similar problems of interpretation and reformulation in the future. This could contribute to enhancing the quality of multilingual texts, especially in terms of accuracy and ambiguity problem-solving. Translators of court documents are also expected to master the translation of texts in which definitions and semantic differences are discussed in languages beyond his or her language pairs as part of argumentation. In some cases, they deal with translation problems previously encountered in the translation of the disputed provisions. Translators of case-law thus tend to be the most sensitive to these matters. Translators of legislation and treaties would equally have an interest in learning from the courts' interpretation of the texts they translate. In short, all language professionals, from the early stages of law-making, can contribute to weaving a safety net based on the concordance of multilingual texts. This is a collective matter of quality that, albeit laborious, yields dividends in terms of legal certainty.

Bibliography

Abdallah, K. (2012). *Translators in Production Networks.* Joensuu: Publications of the University of Eastern Finland.

Abi-Saab, G. (2010). 'The Appellate Body and Treaty Interpretation'. In M. Fitzmaurice, O. Elias and P. Merkouris (eds), *Treaty Interpretation and the Vienna Convention on the Law of Treaties: 30 Years on*, 99–109. Leiden: Martinus Nijhoff.

Alonso, E. (2015). 'Analysing the use and Perception of Wikipedia in the Professional Context of Translation'. *The Journal of Specialised Translation* 23: 89–116.

APTIJ (2016a). *Complaint to the Spanish Ombudsman.* Available online: http://www.aptij.es/img/doc/Queja%20Defensor%20del%20Pueblo_web.pdf (accessed 20 September 2016).

APTIJ (2016b). *La APTIJ presenta una queja ante el Defensor del Pueblo.* Available online: http://www.aptij.es/index.php?l=es&s=n&c=68 (accessed 20 September 2016).

ASTM F2575-14 (2014). *Standard Guide for Quality Assurance in Translation.* West Conshohocken: ASTM International.

Azizi, J. (2011). 'Unveiling the EU Courts' Internal Decision-Making Process: A Case for Dissenting Opinions?' *ERA Forum* 12 (Suppl. 1): 49–68.

Baaij, C. J. W. (2012). 'Fifty Years of Multilingual Interpretation in the EU'. In P. Tiersma and L. Solan (eds), *The Oxford Handbook of Language and Law*, 217–31. Oxford: Oxford University Press.

Baisa, V., Michelfeit, J., Medveď, M. and Jakubíček, M. (2016). 'European Union Language Resources in Sketch Engine'. In *The Proceedings of tenth International Conference on Language Resources and Evaluation (LREC'16)*. European Language Resources Association (ELRA). Portorož, Slovenia. 2016. Available online: http://www.lrec-conf.org/proceedings/lrec2016/pdf/572_Paper.pdf (accessed 1 October 2016).

Baker, M. (1988). 'Sub-Technical Vocabulary and the ESP Teacher: An Analysis of Some Rhetorical Items'. *Medical Journal Articles, Reading in a Foreign Language* 4 (2): 91–105.

Baker, M. (1993). 'Corpus Linguistics and Translation Studies. Implications and Applications'. In M. Baker, G. Francis, E. Tognini-Bonelli (eds), *Text and Technology: In honour of John Sinclair*, 233–50. Amsterdam and Philadelphia: John Benjamins.

Baker, M. (1995). 'Corpora in Translation Studies: An Overview and Some Suggestions for Future Research'. *Target* 7 (2): 223–43.

Baker, M. (1996). 'Corpus-based Translation Studies: The Challenges that Lie Ahead'. In H. L. Somers (ed.), *Terminology, LSP and Translation. Studies in Language Engineering in Honour of Juan C. Sager*, 175–86. Amsterdam: John Benjamins.

Baker, M. (ed.) (1998). *Routledge Encyclopedia of Translation Studies.* London and New York: Routledge.

Barlow, M. (1995). 'ParaConc: A Concordancer for Parallel Texts'. *Computers & Texts* 10: 14–16.

Barlow, M. (2013). 'Individual Differences and Usage-based Grammar'. *International Journal of Corpus Linguistics* 18 (4): 443–78.

Bastarache, M. (ed.) (2004). *Language Rights in Canada* (Second edn.). Cowansville, Qc: Yvon Blais.
Bastarache, M. (2012). 'Bilingual Interpretation Rules as a Component of Language Rights in Canada'. In L. Solan and P. M. Tiersma (eds), *The Oxford Handbook of Language and Law*, 159–74. New York: Oxford University Press.
de Beaugrande, R. (1996). 'The "Pragmatics" of doing Language Science: The "Warrant" for Large-corpus Linguistics.' *Journal of Pragmatics* 25: 503–35.
Bédard, C. (1986). *La traduction technique – principes et pratique*. Montreal: Linguatech.
Bengoetxea, J. (2011). 'Multilingual and Multicultural Legal Reasoning: The European Court of Justice'. In A. L. Kjær and S. Adamo (eds), *Linguistic Diversity and European Democracy*, 97–122. Farnham: Ashgate.
Biber, D. and Jones, J. K. (2009). 'Quantitative Methods in Corpus Linguistics'. In A. Lüdeling and M. Kytö (eds), *Corpus Linguistics. An International Handbook*. Vol. 2. 1286–1304. Berlin: de Gruyter.
Biel, Ł. (2009) 'Corpus-Based Studies of Legal Language for Translation Purposes: Methodological and Practical Potential'. In C. Heine and J. Engberg (eds), *Reconceptualizing LSP. Online proceedings of the XVII European LSP Symposium 2009*. Available online: http://bcom.au.dk/fileadmin/www.asb.dk/isek/biel.pdf (accessed 10 October 2014).
Biel, Ł. (2014a). *Lost in the Eurofog. The Textual Fit of Translated Law*. Frankfurt am Main: Peter Lang.
Biel, Ł. (2014b). 'Phraseology in Legal Translation: A Corpus-Based Analysis of Textual Mapping in EU Law'. In L. Cheng et al. (eds), *The Ashgate Handbook of Legal Translation*, 177–92. Surrey: Ashgate.
Biel, Ł. (2017). 'Enhancing the Communicative Dimension of Legal Translation: Comparable Corpora in the Research-Informed Classroom'. *The Interpreter and Translator Trainer*, http://dx.doi.org/10.1080/1750399X.2017.1359761
Biel, Ł. and Engberg, J. (2013). 'Research Models and Methods in Legal Translation'. *Linguistica Antverpiensia, New Series – Themes in Translation Studies* 12, 1–11. Available online: https://lans-tts.uantwerpen.be/index.php/LANS-TTS/article/view/316/220 (accessed 1 October 2016).
Boas, H. C. (2013). 'Frame Semantics and Translation'. In A. Rojo and I. Ibarretxe-Antunano (eds), *Cognitive Linguistics and Translation: Advances in Some Theoretical Models and Applications*, 125–58. Berlin and Boston: De Gruyter.
Bocquet, C. (2008). *La traduction juridique: Fondement et méthode*. Brussels: De Boeck.
Borja Albi, A. (2013). 'A Genre Analysis Approach to the Study of the Translation of Court Documents'. *LANS-TTS*, a special issue on *Research Models and Methods in Legal Translation* 12(2013): 33–53. Available online: https://lans-tts.uantwerpen.be/index.php/LANS-TTS/article/view/235/202 (accessed 1 October 2016).
Borja Albi, A. and Prieto Ramos, F. (eds) (2013). *Legal Translation in Context. Professional Issues and Prospects*. Series *New Trends in Translation Studies*. Oxford: Peter Lang.
Borja Albi, A., Natividad, J. V., Ordóñez López, P. and Conde, T. (2014). 'A Genre-Based Approach to the Teaching of Legal and Business English: The GENTT Specialized Corpus in the LSP Classroom'. In E. Bárcena, T. Read and J. Arús (eds), *Languages for Specific Purposes in the Digital Era* (Educational Linguistics 19), 177–196. Cham: Springer.
Brady, H. (2014). *Twelve things everyone should know about the European Court of Justice*. London: Centre for European Reform. Available online: http://www.cer.org.uk/publications/archive/report/2014/twelve-things-everyone-should-know-about-european-court-justice (accessed 6 January 2017).

Brannan, J. (2013). 'Coming to Terms with the Supranational: Translating for the European Court of Human Rights'. *International Journal for the Semiotics of Law* 26(4): 909–25.

Brems, E., Meylaerts, R. and van Doorslaer, L. (2012). 'A Discipline Looking back and Looking Forward. An Introduction'. *Target* 24 (1): 1–14.

Breton, A. and Trebilcock, M. J. (2006). *Bijuralism: An Economic Approach*. Farnham: Ashgate.

Bridge, F. (1994). *Council of Europe French-English Legal Dictionary*. Strasbourg: Council of Europe.

Brown-John, C. L. and Pawley, H. (2004). *When Legal Systems Meet: Bijuralism in the Canadian Federal System*. Barcelona: Institut de Ciències Polítiques i Socials.

Buckingham, G. (2014). 'Outsourcing – from confrontation to influencing outcomes'. In *PEEMPIP – Shaping our common future*, 31 October 2014. Athens. Available online: https://www.youtube.com/watch?v=mZLMalYyrKo (accessed 20 September 2016).

Busse, D. (1987). *Historische Semantik: Analyse eines Programms*. Stuttgart: Klett-Cotta.

Busse, D. (2015). ''Juristische Semantik als Frame-Semantik'. In F. Vogel (ed.), *Zugänge zur Rechtssemantik. Interdisziplinäre Ansätze im Zeitalter der Mediatisierung*, 39–68. Berlin and Boston: de Gruyter.

Bybee, J. (2010). *Language, Usage, and Cognition*. Cambridge: Cambridge University Press.

Canadian Department of Justice (1995). *Policy on Legislative Bijuralism* (reproduced as appendix III in Wellington (2001)).

Cao, D. (2007). *Translating Law*. Clevedon, Buffalo and Toronto: Multilingual Matters.

Cayron, S. (2017). *Manual de traducción jurada de documentos notariales en materia de sucesiones entre los sistemas jurídicos francés y español. La Traductología Jurídica aplicada a la práctica*. Granada: Comares.

Chesterman, A. (2004). 'Hypotheses about Translation Universals'. In G. Hansen, K. Malmkjær and D. Gile (eds), *Claims, Changes and Challenges in Translation Studies. Selected contributions from the EST Congress, Copenhagen 2001*, 1–13. Amsterdam: John Benjamins.

Condon, B. J. (2010). 'Lost in Translation: Plurilingual Interpretation of WTO Law'. *Journal of International Dispute Settlement* 1 (1): 191–216.

Conway, G. (2012). *The Limits of Legal Reasoning and the European Court of Justice*. New York: Cambridge University Press.

Cornu, G. (2005a). *Linguistique juridique*. Paris: Montchrestien.

Cornu, G. (ed.) (2005b). *Vocabulaire juridique*. Paris: puf.

Cotterrell, R. (2012). 'What is Transnational Law?' *Law & Social Inquiry* 37 (2): 500–24.

Council of the European Union, Directorate Quality of Legislation (2015). *Manual of precedents for acts established within the Council of the European Union. SN 1250/6/10, rev 6.*

Court of Justice of the European Union (2016). *Annual Report 2015: Management Report*. Luxembourg: European Union. Available online: http://curia.europa.eu/jcms/upload/docs/application/pdf/2016-06/rapport_gestion_2015_en_version_web.pdf (accessed 6 January 2017).

Covacs, A. (1979). 'Bilinguisme officiel et double version des lois. Un pis-aller: la traduction. Une solution d'avenir: la corédaction'. *Meta: Translators' Journal* 24 (1): 103–8.

Creech, R. L. (2005). *Law and Language in the European Union. The Paradox of Babel 'United in Diversity'*. Groningen: Europa Law Publishing.

Crismore, A., Markkanen R. and Steffensen, M. (1993). 'Metadiscourse in Persuasive Writing: A Study of Texts Written by American and Finnish University Students'. *Written Communication* 10: 39–71.

Cronin, M. (2003). *Translation and Globalization*. London: Routledge.
Cronin, M. (2010). 'The Translation Crowd'. *Revista Tradumàtica* 8, Available online: http://www.fti.uab.es/tradumatica/revista/num8/articles/04/04central.htm (accessed 1 October 2016).
Crystal, D. (2010). *The Cambridge Encyclopedia of Language* (Third edn.). Cambridge: Cambridge University Press.
Cuerrier, M. (2007). 'Drafting Against a Background of Differing Legal Systems: Canadian bijuralism'. *The Loophole* July 2007: 50–8. Available online: https://www.opc.gov.au/calc/docs/Loophole_papers/Cuerrier_Jul2007.pdf (accessed 1 September 2016).
Dąbrowska, E. (2012). 'Different Speakers, Different Grammars: Individual Differences in Native Language Attainment'. *Linguistic Approaches to Bilingualism* 2 (3): 219–53.
Darbelnet, J. (1979). 'Réflexions sur le discours juridique'. *Meta: Translators' Journal* 24 (1): 26–34.
de Groot, G.-R. (1999). 'Das Übersetzen juristischer Terminologie'. In G.-R. de Groot and R. Schulze (eds), *Recht und Übersetzen*, 11–46. Baden-Baden: Nomos.
Decaux, E. (2000). 'Le Régime linguistique de la nouvelle Cour'. In J.-F. Flauss (ed.), *La mise en oeuvre du Protocole n° 11 : le nouveau Règlement de la Cour européenne des droits de l'homme*, 55–73. Brussels: Bruylant.
Dengler, P. (2010). 'Derecho de la UE y multilingüismo. El problema de las divergencias entre versiones lingüísticas'. In I. A. Araguás, J. B. Jalón and H. J. L. Campbell (eds), *Translating Justice*, 83–98. Granada: Comares.
Derlén, M. (2009). *Multilingual Interpretation of European Union Law*. Alphen aan den Rijn: Wolters Kluwer.
Derlén, M. (2011). 'In Defence of (Limited) Multilingualism: Problems and Possibilities of the Multilingual Interpretation of European Union Law in National Courts'. In A. L. Kjær and S. Adamo (eds), *Linguistic Diversity and European Democracy*, 143–66. Farnham: Ashgate.
Derlén, M. (2015). 'A Single Text or a Single Meaning: Multilingual Interpretation of EU Legislation and CJEU Case Law in National Courts'. In S. Šarčević (ed.), *Language and Culture in EU Law*, 53–72. Farnham: Ashgate.
DGT (2008a). *Report on the 2008 CAF Self-Assessment Exercise at DGT, Part 1: Results*, DGT S.4/JJ D(2008)23234.
DGT (2008b). *Action Tree, DGT 2008 CAF Self-Assessment Exercise Report Improvement Actions Reference Document* DGT S.4/JJ D(2008) 23367.
DGT (2009a). *Report on the 2008 CAF Self-Assessment Exercise at DGT, Part 2: Improvement Actions*, DGT.S.4/JJ D(2009) 24501.
DGT (2009b). *Programme for Quality Management in Translation – 22 Quality Actions*.
DGT (2014a). *Evaluation of DGT's translation management system after the 2013 reorganisation*. Ares(2015)171913.
DGT (2014b). *DGT Quality Management Framework*. Ares(2014)799428.
DGT (2014c). *Document versioning and its impact on DGT*.
DGT (2015a). *DGT Translation Quality Guidelines*. Ares(2015)5389770.
DGT (2015b). *How to write clearly*. Available online: https://bookshop.europa.eu/en/how-to-write-clearly-pbHC0215257/ (accessed 16 September 2016).
DGT (2016a). *DGT Guidelines for Evaluation of Outsourced Translation*. Ares(2016)3157529.
DGT (2016b). *DGT Outsourcing Framework 2016-2020*. Ares(2016)2986797.
DGT (2016c). *Strategic plan 2016-2020*. Available online: http://ec.europa.eu/atwork/synthesis/amp/doc/dgt_sp_2016-2020_en.pdf (accessed 20 September 2016).

DGT (2012). *Translation and Multilingualism*. Luxembourg: Publications Office of the European Union. Available online: http://bookshop.europa.eu/en/translation-and-multilingualism-pbHC3210532/ (accessed 1 September 2016).

Dollerup, C. (2004). 'The Vanishing Original'. *Hermes – Journal of Linguistics* 32: 185–99.

Drugan, J. (2013). *Quality in Professional Translation – Assessment and Improvement*. London: Bloomsbury.

EAGLES (1996). *Preliminary recommendations on Corpus Typology* (Version of May 1996). Available online: http://www.ilc.cnr.it/EAGLES/corpustyp/node20.html (accessed 15 September 2016).

Edo Marzá, N. (2009). *The Specialised Lexicographical Approach: A Step further in Dictionary Making*. Bern: Peter Lang.

Edward, D. (1995). 'How the Court of Justice Works'. *European Law Review* 20: 539–58.

Eisele, A. and Chen, Y. (2010). 'MultiUN: A Multilingual Corpus from United Nations Documents'. In D. Tapias et al. (eds) *Proceedings of the Seventh conference on International Language Resources and Evaluation. 2868-2872. La Valletta: European Language Resources Association (ELRA).*

EMT Expert Group of the European Commission Directorate-General for Translation (2009). Competences for professional translators, experts in multilingual and multimedia communication. Available online: http://ec.europa.eu/dgs/translation/programmes/emt/index_en.htm (accessed31 August 2016).

Engberg, J. (2009a). 'Methodological Aspects of the Dynamic Character of Legal Terms'. *Fachsprache* 31: 126–38.

Engberg, J. (2009b). 'Von der Rolle des institutionellen Verstehens für das professionelle Kommunizieren im Recht'. *Jahrbuch Deutsch als Fremdsprache 2008: Professionelle Kommunikation* 34: 97–111.

Engberg, J. (2013). 'Why Translators are not Lawyers. On Differences and Similarities of Interest and Knowledge'. In I. Alonso Araguás, J. Baigorri Jalón and H. J. L. Campbell (eds), *Translating the Law. Theoretical and Methodological Issues*, 23–32. Granada: Comares.

Engberg, J. (2015a). 'Autonomous EU Concepts – Fact or Fiction?'. In S. Šarčević (ed.), *Language and Culture in EU Law: Multidisciplinary Perspectives*, 169–82. London: Ashgate.

Engberg, J. (2015b). 'What does it Mean to see Legal Translation as Knowledge Communication? – Conceptualisation and Quality Standards'. *Terminology Science and Research* 25: 1–10.

Engberg, J. (2016). 'Conceptualising Corporate Criminal Liability: Legal Linguistics and the Combination of Descriptive Lenses'. In G. Tessuto, V. K. Bhatia, G. Garzone, R. Salvi and C. Williams (eds), *Constructing Legal Discourses and Social Practices: Issues and Perspectives*, 28–56. Newcastle upon Tyne: Cambridge Scholars.

European Commission (2003). *How to interpret legislation which is equally authentic in twenty languages*. Lecture by Advocate General Francis Jacobs as part of the Seminars on Quality of Legislation, Brussels, 20 October 2003. Summary report available online: http://ec.europa.eu/dgs/legal_service/seminars/agjacobs_summary.pdf (accessed 27 March 2017).

European Commission (2004). *Matching supply and demand for translation*. SEC(2004)638.

European Commission (2005). *Translation in a multilingual community – Managing supply and demand in the Commission in 2005 and beyond until the end of 2006*. SEC(2005)984.

European Commission (2006). *Translation in the Commission – Responding to the challenges in 2007 and beyond.* SEC(2006)1489.

European Commission (2016). *Translation as part of the Commission's decision-making process.* C(2016)2000.

European Commission Representation in Ireland (2016). *EU languages: Statement on behalf of the European Commission Representation in Ireland 27 June.* Available online: https://ec.europa.eu/ireland/news/statement-on-behalf-of-the-European-Commission-Representation_en (accessed 6 January 2017).

European Committee for Standardization (CEN) (2006). *EN 15038:2006 Translation services - Service requirements.*

European Court of Auditors (2006). *Special Report n° 9/2006 concerning translation expenditures incurred by the Commission, the Parliament and the Council.*

European Parliament, Committee on Budgetary Control (2006). *Working document on ECA's Special Report n° 9/2006 concerning translation expenditures incurred by the Commission, the Parliament and the Council.*

European Parliament, Council of the European Union and the European Commission (2000). *Joint Practical Guide for Persons Involved in the Drafting of Legislation within the Community Institutions.*

European Parliament, Council of the European Union and the European Commission (2016). *Joint Handbook for the presentation and drafting of acts subject to the ordinary legislative procedure.*

Felici, A. (2010). 'Translating EU Law: Legal Issues and Multiple Dynamics'. *Perspectives* 18 (2): 95–108.

Felici, A. (2015). 'Translating EU Legislation from a *Lingua Franca*: Advantages and Disadvantages'. In S. Šarčević (ed.), *Language and Culture in EU Law: Multidisciplinary Perspectives*, 123–40. Farnham: Ashgate.

Folkart, B. (1984). 'A Thing-bound Approach to the Practice and Teaching of Technical Translation'. *Meta* 29 (3): 229–46.

Frame, I. (2005). 'Linguistic Oddities in European Union Legislation: Don't Shoot the Translator'. *Clarity – Journal of the International Association Promoting Plain Legal Language* 53: 21–4.

Fujii, Y. (2013). 'The Translation of Legal Agreements and Contracts from Japanese into English: The Case for a Free Approach'. *Babel* 59: 421–44.

Gallas, T. (2001). 'Evaluation in EC Legislation'. *Statute Law Revue* 22: 83–95.

Gallas, T. and Guggeis, M. (2005). 'La traduction juridique dans l'expérience des juristes-linguistes du Conseil de l'Union européenne'. In J.-C. Gémar and N. Kasirer (eds), *Jurilinguistique: entre langues et droits – Jurilinguistics: Between Law and Language*, 491–503. Montréal; Bruxelles: Les Éditions Thémis; Les Éditions juridiques Bruylant.

Gallego-Hernández, D. (2015). 'The use of Corpora as Translation Resources: A Study Based on a Survey of Spanish Professional Translators'. *Perspectives: Studies in Translatology* 23 (3): 375–91.

Gallo, G. (2006). 'Organisation and Features of Translation Activities at the Court of Justice of the European Communities'. In B. Pozzo and V. Jacometti (eds), *Multilingualism and the Harmonisation of European Law*, 175–96. Alphen: Kluwer Law International.

Gambier, Y. (1995). *Le français dans les communications spécialisées: bilan mitigé.* In Y. Gambier (ed.), *Discours professionnels en français*, 35–62. Frankfurt am Main: Peter Lang.

Gärdenfors, P. (1993). 'The Emergence of Meaning'. *Linguistics and Philosophy* 16 (3): 285–309.

Gardiner, R. (2015). *Treaty Interpretation* (Second edn). Oxford: Oxford University Press.

Garner, B. (ed.) (2014). *Black's Law Dictionary* (Tenth edn). St. Paul: Thomson Reuters.

Gazzola, M. (2006). 'Managing Multilingualism in the European Union: Language Policy Evaluation for the European Parliament'. *Language Policy* 5 (4): 395–419.

Gémar, J.-C. (1979). 'La traduction juridique et son enseignement: aspects théoriques et pratiques'. *Meta: Translators' Journal* 24 (1): 35–63.

Gémar, J.-C. (1991). 'Terminologie, langue et discours juridiques. Sens et signification du langage du droit'. *Meta: Translators' Journal* 36 (1): 275–83.

Gémar, J.-C. (1995). *Traduire ou l'art d'interpréter – Langue, droit et société: éléments de jurilinguistique, Tome II: application*. Quebec: Presses de l'Université du Quebec.

Gémar, J.-C. (2013). 'Translating vs Co-drafting Law in Multilingual Countries: Beyond the Canadian Odyssey'. In A. Borja Albi and F. Prieto Ramos (eds), *Legal Translation in Context. Professional Issues and Prospects*, 155–79. Bern: Peter Lang.

Gentzler, E. (2003). 'Interdisciplinary Connections'. *Perspectives: Studies in Translatology* 11(1): 11–24.

Germain, C. M. (2014). 'CISG Translation Issues: Reducing Legal Babelism'. In L. A. DiMatteo (ed.), *International Sales Law: A Global Challenge*, 51–62. Cambridge: Cambridge University Press.

Glanert, S. (2014). 'Law-in-Translation: An Assemblage in Motion'. *The Translator* 20 (3): 255–72.

Glanert, S. (2015). 'Au lieu d'une langue commune, un discours commun? Le cas de l'Union européenne'. *International Journal for the Semiotics of Law* 28 (1): 73–90.

Gledhill, C. (1997). 'Les collocations et la construction du savoir scientifique'. *ASp* 15–18: 85–104. Available online: http://asp.revues.org/2989 (accessed 15 September 2016).

Göpferich, S. (2006a). 'How Comprehensible Are Popular Science Texts? The Use of Thinking-aloud Protocols and Log Files of Reverbalization Processes in Comprehensibility Research'. In M. Gotti and D. S. Giannoni (eds), *New Trends in Specialized Discourse Analysis*, 221–46. Frankfurt am Main: Peter Lang.

Göpferich, S. (2006b). 'How Successful is the Mediation of Specialized Knowledge? – The Use of Thinking-aloud Protocols and Log Files of Reverbalization Processes as a Method in Comprehensibility Research'. *Hermes. Journal of Language and Communication Studies* 37: 67–93.

Gotti, M. (2003). *Specialized Discourse. Linguistic Features and Changing Conventions*. Bern: Peter Lang.

Graff, D. (1994). *UN Parallel Text (Complete)*. Philadelphia: Linguistic Data Consortium.

Granger, S. (2003). 'The Corpus Approach: A Common Way Forward for Contrastive Linguistics and Translation Studies?' In S. Granger, J. Lerot and S. Petch-Tyson (eds), *Corpus-based Approaches to Contrastive Linguistics and Translation Studies*, 17–29. Amsterdam: Rodopi.

Grenon, A. (2014). 'Canadian Bijuralism at a Crossroad? The Impact of Section 8.1 of the Interpretation Act on Judicial Interpretation of Federal Legislation'. *Osgoode Hall Law Journal* 51(2): 501–41.

Griebel, C. (2013). *Rechtsübersetzung und Rechtswissen. Kognitionstranslatologische Überlegungen und empirische Untersuchung des Übersetzungsprozesses*. Berlin: Frank & Timme.

Guggeis, M. and Robinson, W. (2012). '"Co-revision": Legal-Linguistic Revision in the European Union "Co-decision" Process'. In C. J. W. Baaij (ed.), *The Role of Legal Translation in Legal Harmonization*, 51–81. Alphen aan den Rijn: Wolters Kluwer.

Halliday, M. A. K. (1978). *Language as Social Semiotic*. London: Arnold.

Halliday, M. A. K. and Martin, J. R. (1996). *Writing Science: Literacy and Discursive Power*. Pittsburgh: University of Pittsburgh Press.

Harmsen, R. and McAuliffe, K. (2014). 'The European Courts'. In J. M. Magone (ed.), *The Handbook of European Politics*, 263–79. London: Routledge.

Hartman, R. K. K. (ed.) (1986). *The History of Lexicography*. Amsterdam: John Benjamins.

Harvey, M. (2002). 'What's so Special About Legal Translation?'. *Meta: Translators' Journal* 47 (2): 177–85.

Heylen, K., Bond, S., de Hertog, D., Kockaert, H., Steurs, F. and Vulić, I. (2014). 'TermWise: Leveraging Big Data for Terminological Support in Legal Translation'. *Terminology and Knowledge Engineering*, June 2014, Berlin. Available online: https://hal.archives-ouvertes.fr/hal-01005842/file/TKE2014HeylenEtal.pdf (accessed 1 October 2016).

Higgins, R. (2016). 'The United Nations at 70 Years: The Impact Upon International Law'. *International and Comparative Law Quarterly* 65: 1–19.

Hindle, W. H. (1984). *A Guide to Writing for the United Nations*. New York: United Nations Department of Conference Services. Internal document (ST/DCS/3). Available online: http://www.un.org/Depts/OHRM/sds/lcp/English/docs/a_guide_to_writing_for_the_united_nations.pdf (accessed 31 August 2016).

Höfler, S. and Sugisaki, K. (2014). 'Constructing and Exploiting an Automatically Annotated Resource of Legislative Texts'. In *Ninth International Conference on Language Resources and Evaluation (LREC'14)*, Reykkjavik, 26 May 2014 – 31 May 2014, 175–80.

House, J. (2011). 'Using Translation and Parallel Text Corpora to Investigate the Influence of Global English on Textual Norms in Other Languages'. In A. Kruger, K. Wallmach and J. Munday (eds), *Corpus-Based Translation Studies. Research and Applications*, 187–207. London: Continuum.

House, J. (2013). 'Towards a New Linguistic-cognitive Orientation in Translation Studies'. *Target* 25 (1): 46–60.

http://curia.europa.eu/jcms/upload/docs/application/pdf/2014-02/rapport-c-255-en.pdf (accessed 6 January 2017).

http://curia.europa.eu/jcms/upload/docs/application/pdf/2016-06/rapport_gestion_2015_en_version_web.pdf (accessed 6 January 2017).

http://www.cer.org.uk/publications/archive/report/2014/twelve-things-everyone-should-know-about-european-court-justice (accessed 6 January 2017).

http://www.un.org/Depts/OHRM/sds/lcp/English/docs/a_guide_to_writing_for_the_united_nations.pdf (accessed 31 August 2016).

https://ec.europa.eu/ireland/news/statement-on-behalf-of-the-European-Commission-Representation_en (accessed 6 January 2017).

Hyland, K. (2005). *Metadiscourse: Exploring Interaction in Writing*. London: Continuum.

Ingels, M. (2006). *Legal English communication skills: introduction to writing skills and vocabulary acquisition for the legal profession*. Leuven: Acco.

ISO (2012). *ISO/TS 11669:2012, Translation projects – General guidance*.

ISO (2015). *ISO 17100:2015, Translation services – Requirements for translation services*.

Itzcovich, G. (2009). 'The Interpretation of Community Law by the European Court of Justice'. *German Law Journal* 10 (5): 537–60.

Jacobsen, U. C. (2012). *Knowledge Asymmetries. A situated inquiry in three sites of professional communication* (PhD), Aarhus University, Aarhus.

Jaroszyński, T. (2011). *Rozporządzenie Unii Europejskiej jako składnik systemu prawa obowiązującego w Polsce*. Warsaw: Wolters Kluwer.

Jedrzejowska, I. (2011). *Constitutional Terminology in Transition, The Drifting Semantics of the Supranational Discourse under Negotiation*. Berlin: Berliner Wissenschafts-Verlag (BWV).
Jopek-Bosiacka, A. (2013). 'Comparative Law and Equivalence Assessment of System-bound Terms in EU Legal Translation'. *Linguistica Antverpiensia* 12: 110–46.
Kang, J.-H. (2009). 'Institutional Translation'. In M. Baker and G. Sadanha (eds), *Routledge Encyclopedia of Translation Studies* (Second edn), 141–5. London: Routledge.
Kang, J.-H. (2014). 'Institutions Translated: Discourse, Identity and Power in Institutional Mediation'. *Perspectives: Studies in Translatology* 22 (4): 469–78.
Kastberg, P. (2011). 'Knowledge Asymmetries : Beyond to Have and Have Not'. *Fachsprache - International Journal of Specialized Communication* 34: 137–51.
Katz Cogan, J. (2015). 'The Changing Form of the International Law Commission's Work'. In R. Virzo and I. Ingravallo (eds), *Evolutions in the Law of International Organizations*, 275–90. Leiden: Brill/Nijhoff.
Kjær, A. L. (2004). 'Convergence of European Legal Systems: The Role of Language'. *Copenhagen Studies in Language* 29: 125–37.
Kjær, A. L. (2007) 'Legal Translation in the European Union: A Research Field in need of a New Approach'. In K. Kredens and S. Goźdź-Roszkowski (eds), *Language and the Law: International Outlooks*, 69–95. Frankfurt am Main: Peter Lang.
Kjær, A.L. (2014). 'New Challenges to the Theory of Legal Translation: Transnational Legal Communication and the Autonomization of International Law'. *The Translator* 20 (3): 430–6.
Kjær, A. L. (2015). 'Theoretical Aspects of Legal Translation in the EU: The Paradoxical Relationship between Language, Translation and the Autonomy of EU Law'. In S. Šarčević (ed.), *Language and Culture in EU Law: Multidisciplinary Perspectives*, 91–107. Farnham: Ashgate.
Kockaert, H. J. and Rahab, N. (2017). 'Introduction. Quality in Legal Translation'. *The Journal of Specialised Translation* 17: 2–9.
Kocourek, R. (2001). *Essais de linguistique française et anglaise. Mots et termes, sens et textes. Essays in French and English linguistic. Words and Terms, Meanings and Texts.* Leuven: Peeters.
Koole, T. and ten Thije, J. D. (1994). *The Construction of Intercultural Discourse – Team Discussions of Educational Advisers*. Amsterdam: Rodopi.
Kosař, D. (2015). 'Selecting Strasbourg Judges: A Critique'. In M. Bobek (ed.), *Selecting Europe's Judges*, 120–61. Oxford: Oxford University Press.
Koskinen, K. (2000). 'Institutional Illusions, Translating in the EU Commission'. *The Translator* 6 (1): 49–65.
Koskinen, K. (2008). *Translating Institutions. An Ethnographic Study of EU Translation*. Manchester: St Jerome.
Koskinen, K. (2014). 'Institutional Translation: The Art of Government by Translation'. *Perspectives* 22 (4): 479–92.
Koulaidis, V., Kostas, D. and Spyridoula, S. (2001). 'Analysing the Texts of Science and Technology: School Science Textbooks and Daily Press Articles in the Public Domain', Paper Presented at The Eighth International Literacy & Education Research Network Conference on Learning, *Learning for the future proceedings of the learning Conference*. Available online: https://www.upf.edu/pcstacademy/_docs/Learning_Conference1.pdf (accessed 15 September 2016).
Kuijper, P. J. (1998). 'The Court and the Tribunal of the EC and the Vienna Convention on the Law of Treaties 1969'. *Legal Issues of Economic Integration* 25 (1): 1–23.

Kuijper, P. J. (2011). 'The European Courts and the Law of Treaties: The Continuing Story'. In E. Cannizzaro (ed.), *The Law of Treaties Beyond The Vienna Convention*, 256–78. Oxford: Oxford University Press.

Kuner, C. (1991). 'The Interpretation of Multilingual Treaties: Comparison of Texts Versus the Presumption of Similar Meaning'. *International and Comparative Law Quarterly* 40 (4): 953–64.

Künnecke, M. (2013). 'Translation in the EU: Language and Law in the EU's Judicial Labyrinth'. *Maastricht Journal of European and Comparative Law* 20 (2): 243–60.

Kurzon D. (1997). '"Legal Language": Varieties, Genres, Registers, Discourses'. *International Journal of Applied Linguistics* 7 (2): 119–269. Available online: http://onlinelibrary.wiley.com/doi/10.1111/j.1473-4192.1997.tb00111.x/abstract (accessed 3 March 2017).

Labelle, A. (2000). 'La corédaction des lois fédérales au Canada. Vingt ans après: quelques réflexions'. In *Proceedings, Conference on Legal Translation, History, Theory/ies and Practice*. Geneva and Bern: ETI-ASTTI.

Labelle, A. (2002). 'La qualité de la législation: l'expérience canadienne'. Available online: http://ec.europa.eu/dgs/legal_service/seminars/ca_labelle_expose.pdf (accessed1 September 2016).

Labuschagne, J. M. T. (1999). 'Interpretation of Multilingual Treaties'. *South African Yearbook of International Law* 24: 323–9.

Lafeber, A. (2012). 'Translation Skills and Knowledge – Preliminary Findings of a Survey of Translators and Revisers Working at Inter-governmental Organizations'. *Meta: Translators' Journal* 57 (1): 108–31.

Lafeber, A. (2013). *The Search for (the right) Translators: Recruitment Testing at International Organizations*. Saarbrücken: LAP LAMBERT Academic Publishing.

Latour, B. (2010). *The Making of Law. An Ethnography of the Conseil d'État*. Cambridge: Polity Press.

Lenaerts K. and Gutiérrez-Fons, J. A. (2013). 'To say what the law of the EU is: methods of interpretation and the European Court of Justice'. European University Institute Working Papers AEL 2013/09. Available online: http://hdl.handle.net/1814/28339 (accessed 3 March 2017).

Lerat, P. (1995). *Les langues spécialisées*. Paris: puf.

Lerat, P. (2002). 'Vocabulaire juridique et schémas d'arguments juridiques'. *Meta: Translators' Journal* 47 (2): 155–62.

Letsas, G. (2004). 'The Truth in Autonomous Concepts: How to Interpret the ECHR'. *European Journal of International Law* 15 (2): 279–305.

Levert, L. A. (2011). 'Work Methods and Processes in a Drafting Environment'. *The Loophole* Special issue: 9 February 2011: 29–39.

Linderfalk, U. (2007). *On the Interpretation of Treaties. The Modern International Law as Expressed in the 1969 Vienna Convention on the Law of Treaties*. Dordrecht: Springer.

Loiacono, R. C. (2010). 'The Translation of Bilateral Agreements between Australia and Italy: Linguistic or Functional?'. In D. S. Giannoni and C. Frade (eds), *Researching Language and the Law: Textual Features and Translation Issues*, 245–62. Bern: Peter Lang.

Lönnroth, K.-J. (2008). 'Efficiency, Transparency and Openness: Translation in the European Union', 1–21. Available online: http:www.ec.europa.eu/dgs/translation/publications/presentations/speeches/20080801_shanghai_en.pdf (accessed 5 September 2016).

Lotman, J. M. (2009). *Die Innenwelt des Denkens*. Frankfurt: Suhrkamp.

Luttermann, K. (2010). 'Verständliche Semantik in schriftlichen Kommunikationsformen'. *Fachsprache. International Journal of LSP* 32: 145–62.

Lyons, J. (1995). *Linguistic Semantics: An Introduction*. Cambridge: Cambridge University Press.

Malinverni, G. (2000). 'Le régime linguistique de la procédure devant la nouvelle Cour européenne des droits de l'homme'. In P. de Fontbressin (ed.), *Les droits de l'homme au seuil du troisième millénaire*, 541–8. Brussels: Bruylant.

Marín, M. J. and Rea, C. (2014). 'Researching Legal Terminology: A Corpus-based Proposal for the Analysis of Sub-technical Legal Terms'. *ASp* 66: 61–82.

Mattila, H. E. S. (2013). *Comparative Legal Linguistics* (Second edn.). Aldershot: Ashgate.

Mattissek, A. (2010). 'Analyzing city images. Potentials of the "French School of Discourse Analysis"'. *Erdkunde* 64 (4): 315–26.

McAuliffe, K. (2011). 'Hybrid Texts and Uniform Law? The Multilingual Case Law of the Court of Justice of the European Union'. *International Journal for the Semiotics of Law* 24: 97–115.

McAuliffe, K. (2012). 'Language and Law in the European Union: The Multilingual Jurisprudence of the ECJ'. In P. Tiersma and L. Solan (eds), *The Oxford Handbook of Language and Law*, 200–16. Oxford: Oxford University Press.

McAuliffe, K. (2013a). 'Precedent at the Court of Justice of the European Union: The Linguistic Aspect'. In M. Freeman and F. Smith (eds), *Law and Language: Current Legal Issues*, vol. 15, 483–92. Oxford: Oxford University Press.

McAuliffe, K. (2013b). 'The Limitations of a Multilingual Legal System'. *International Journal for the Semiotics of Law* 26 (4):861–82.

McAuliffe, K. (2014). 'Translating Ambiguity'. *The Journal of Comparative Law* 9 (2): 49–70. Available online: http://www.ssrn.com/abstract=2594641 (accessed 5 September 2016).

McAuliffe, K. (2016). 'Hidden Translators: The Invisibility of Translators and the Influence of Lawyer Linguists on the Case-law of the Court of Justice of the European Union'. *Language and Law / Linguagem e Direito* 3 (1): 5–29.

McAuliffe, K. and Trklja, A. (2018). 'Superdiversity and the Relationship between Law, Language and Translation in a Supranational Legal Order'. In A. Creese and A. Blackledge (eds), *Handbook on Language and Superdiversity*. London: Routledge.

McEnery, T. and Hardie, A. (2012). *Corpus Linguistics. Method, Theory and Practice*. Cambridge: Cambridge University Press.

McEnery, T., Xiao, R. and Tono, Y. (2006). *Corpus-Based Language Studies. An advanced resource book*. London: Routledge.

Megale, F. (2015). 'Mondialisation de traduction juridique: nouveaux parcours de recherche'. *International Journal for the Semiotics of Law* 28 (1): 31–52.

MeLLANGE (2006). 'Corpora and e-learning questionnaire. Results summary'. Available online: http://mellange.eila.univ-paris-diderot.fr/Mellange-Results-1.pdf (accessed 1 October 2016).

Milian i Massana, A. (2002). 'Le principe d'egalité des langues au sein des institutions de l'Union européenne et dans le droit communautaire, mythe ou réalité? '. *Revista de llengua i dret* 38: 47–94.

Monjean-Decaudin, S. (2013). 'Réflexion sur l'*inflexion du signifié* dans la traduction juridique de Claude Bocquet'. *Parallèles* 25: 19–29.

Monzó Nebot, E. (2008). 'Corpus-based Activities in Legal Translator Training'. *The Interpreter and Translator Trainer* 2 (2): 221–51.

Morawski, L. (2006). *Zasady wykładni prawa*. Toruń: TNOiK.

Mossop, B. (1988). 'Translating Institutions: A Missing Factor in Translation Theory'. *TTR: traduction, terminologie, rédaction* 1 (2): 65–71.

Mossop, B. (2001). *Revising and Editing for Translators*. Manchester: St Jerome.
Mufwene, S. S. (2001). *The Ecology of Language Evolution*. Cambridge: Cambridge University Press.
Mulhall, S. (2008). *Wittgenstein's Private Language: Grammar, Nonsense, and Imagination in Philosophical Investigations*. Oxford: Oxford University.
Nord, Christiane (1997). *Translating as a Purposeful Activity. Functionalist Approaches Explained*. Manchester: St. Jerome.
Olohan, M. (2004). *Introducing Corpora in Translation Studies*. London: Routledge.
Orozco-Jutorán, M. (forthcoming). 'The TIPp project: developing technological resources based on the exploitation of oral corpora to improve court interpreting'. *InTRAlinea* 19.
Paltridge, B. (2006). *Discourse Analysis: An Introduction*. London and New York: Continuum.
Panel provided for by Article 255 of the Treaty on the Functioning of the European Union (2013). *Third activity report*. Available online: http://curia.europa.eu/jcms/upload/docs/application/pdf/2014-02/rapport-c-255-en.pdf (accessed 6 January 2017).
Pasteur, O. (2013). 'Technology at the Service of Specialized Translators at International Organizations'. In A. Borja Albi and F. Prieto Ramos (eds) *Legal Translation in Context. Professional Issues and Prospects*. Oxford: Peter Lang, 283–97.
Pattaro, E. (2007). *A Treatise of Legal Philosophy and General Jurisprudence a reappraisal of the reality that ought to be*. Dordrecht: Springer.
Paunio, E. (2007). 'The Tower of Babel and the Interpretation of EU Law'. In T. Wilhelmsson, E. Paunio and A. Pohjolainen (eds), *Private Law and the Many Cultures of Europe*, 385–402. Alphen aan den Rijn: Kluwer Law International.
Paunio, E. (2013). *Legal Uncertainty in Multilingual EU Law: Language, Discourse and Reasoning at the European Court of Justice*. Farnham: Ashgate.
Pauwelyn, J. and Elsig, M. (2012). 'The Politics of Treaty Interpretation: Variations and Explanations across International Tribunals'. In J. Dunoff and M. A. Pollack (eds), *Interdisciplinary Perspectives on International Law and International Relations: The State of the Art*, 445–73. New York: Cambridge University Press.
Pavel, S. and Nolet, D. (2001). *Handbook of Terminology/Precis de terminologie*. Ottawa: Minister of Public Works and Government Services of Canada.
Perfumi, C. (2013). 'Theory and Practice of Constructing a Common Contract Law Terminology'. In J. Devenney and M. Kenny (eds), *The Transformation of European Private Law: Harmonisation, Consolidation, Codification or Chaos?*, 131–47. Cambridge: Cambridge University Press.
Pescatore, P. (2007). *Vade-mecum: Recueil de formules et de conseils pratiques à l'usage des rédacteurs d'arrêts*. Brussels: Bruylant.
Peschl, M. F. and Fundneider, T. (2014). 'Designing and Enabling Interfaces for Collaborative Knowledge Creation and Innovation. From Managing to Enabling Innovation as Socio-epistemological Technology'. *Computers and Human Behavior* 37: 346–59.
Picton, A., Fontanet, M., Maradan, M. and Pulitano, D. (2015). 'Corpora in Translation: addressing the Gap between the Scholars' and the Translators' Point of View'. A conference presentation *Corpus Use and Learning to Translate (CULT)*, Alicante, Spain.
Piecychna, B. (2013). 'Legal Translation Competence in the Light of Translational Hermeneutics'. *Studies in Logic, Grammar and Rhetoric* 34 (47): 141–59.

Pommer, S. E. (2008). 'No Creativity in Legal Translation?'. *Babel* 54: 355–68.
Pommer, S. E. (2012). 'Interpreting Multilingual EU Law: What Role for Legal Translation?' *European Review of Private Law* 20: 5/6: 1241–54.
Pontrandolfo, G. (2012). 'Legal Corpora: an Overview'. *Rivista Internazionale di Tecnica della Traduzione* 14: 121–36.
Pontrandolfo, G. (2016). *Fraseología y lenguaje judicial. Las sentencias penales desde una perspectiva contrastiva*. Roma: Aracne.
Pool, J. (1996). 'Optimal Language Regimes for the European Union.'. *International Journal of the Sociology of Language* 121: 159–79.
Porup Thomasen, U. (2015). *Exploring the Communicative Dimensions of Knowledge-Intensive Innovation : An Ethnographic Insight into the Innovation Culture Initiative of Novo Nordisk*. Aarhus: Department of Business Communication, Aarhus University. Available online: https://pure.au.dk/ws/files/86923107/Exploring_the_Communicative_Dimensions_of_Knowledge_Intensive_Innovation.pdf (accessed 23 January 2017).
Poscher, R. (2012). 'Ambiguity and Vagueness in Legal Interpretation'. In P. Tiersma and L. Solan (eds), *The Oxford Handbook of Language and Law*, 128–44. Oxford: Oxford University Press.
Pozzo, B. (2012). 'English as a Legal *Lingua Franca* in the EU Multilingual Context'. In C. J. W. Baaij (ed.), *The Role of Legal Translation in Legal Harmonization*, 183–202. Alphen aan den Rijn: Wolters Kluwer.
Prieto Ramos, F. (2011). 'El traductor como redactor de instrumentos jurídicos: el caso de los tratados internacionales'. *The Journal of Specialised Translation* 15: 200–14.
Prieto Ramos, F. (2013a). 'Legal Translation at the World Trade Organization'. In A. Borja Albi and F. Prieto Ramos (eds), *Legal Translation in Context, Professional Issues and Prospects*, 263–81. Bern: Peter Lang.
Prieto Ramos, F. (2013b). '¿Qué estrategias para qué traducción jurídica?: por una metodología integral para la práctica profesional'. In I. Alonso Araguás, J. Baigorri Jalón and H. J. L. Campbell (eds), *Translating the Law. Theoretical and Methodological Issues / Traducir el Derecho. Cuestiones teóricas y metodológicas*, 87–106. Granada: Comares.
Prieto Ramos, F. (2014a). 'International and Supranational Law in Translation: From Multilingual Lawmaking to Adjudication'. *The Translator* 20 (3): 313–31.
Prieto Ramos, F. (2014b). 'Legal Translation Studies as Interdiscipline: Scope and Evolution'. *Meta: Translators' Journal* 59: 260–77. Available online: http://id.erudit.org/iderudit/1027475ar (accessed 3 March 2017). DOI: 10.7202/1027475ar.
Prieto Ramos, F. (2014c). 'Parameters for Problem-Solving in Legal Translation: Implications for Legal Lexicography and Institutional Terminology Management'. In A. Wagner, K.-K. Sin and L. Cheng (eds), *The Ashgate Handbook of Legal Translation*, 121–34. Farnham: Ashgate.
Prieto Ramos, F. (2015), 'Quality Assurance in Legal Translation: Evaluating Process, Competence and Product in the Pursuit of Adequacy'. *The International Journal for the Semiotics of Law* 28 (1): 11–30.
Prioux, R. (2006). 'Managing Quality in Translation Services of International Organisations' (handout from presentation held at IAMLADP meeting, 4.12.2006, Luxemburg).
Prioux, R. and Rochard, M. (2007). 'Economie de la révision dans une organisation internationale : le cas de l'OCDE'. *Journal of Specialised Translation* 8: 21–41.

Professional Interpreters for Justice (2013). Submission to UK Parliament's Justice Committee. Available online: http://www.publications.parliament.uk/pa/cm201213/cmselect/cmjust/645/645we20.htm; http://www.unitetheunion.org/how-we-help/list-of-sectors/community-youth-workers-and-not-for-profit/nupitnationalunionofprofessionalinterpretersandtranslators/nupitcampaigns/professionalinterpretersforjustice/ (accessed 16 September 2016).

Publications Office of the European Union (2016). *Interinstitutional Style Guide.* Available online: http://publications.europa.eu/code/en/en-000100.htm (accessed 20 September 2016).

Pym, A. (1992). 'Translation Error Analysis and the Interface with Language Teaching'. In C. Dollerup and A. Loddegaard (eds), *The Teaching of Translation*, 279–88. Amsterdam: John Benjamins.

Raffaelli, R. (2012). *Dissenting opinions in the Supreme Courts of the Member States.* Available online: http://www.europarl.europa.eu/document/activities/cont/201304/20130423ATT64963/20130423ATT64963EN.pdf (accessed 6 January 2017).

Raymond, J. (2000). 'The Limits of Logic in Legal Argumentation'. *ASTTI/ETI*, 309–27.

Robertson, C. (2012). 'EU Legal English: Common Law, Civil Law, or a New Genre?' *European Review of Private Law* 20 (5/6): 1215–40.

Robertson, C. (2016). *Multilingual Law: A Framework for Analysis and Understanding.* Abingdon: Routledge.

Rojo López, A. M. (2002). 'Applying Frame Semantics to Translation: A Practical Example'. *Meta: Translators' Journal* §47: 311–50.

Ronkes Agerbeek, F. (2015). Essential Guide to drafting Commission document on EU competition law. Available online: http://essentialguide.eu/ (accessed16 September 2016).

Rösler, H. (2012). 'Interpretation of EU Law'. In J. Basedow, K. J. Hopt and R. Zimmermann (eds), *Max Planck Encyclopedia of European Private Law*, 979–82. Oxford: Oxford University Press.

Rossene, S. (1983). 'The Meaning of "Authentic Text" in Modern Treaty Law'. In R. Bernhardt, W. K. Geck, G. Jaenicke and H. Steinberger (eds), *Festschrift für Hermann Mosler*, 759–84. Berlin and Heidelberg: Springer.

Sánchez Ramos, M. D. M. and Vigier Moreno F. J. (2016). 'Using Monolingual Virtual Corpora in Public Service Legal Translator Training'. In E. Martín-Monje, I. Elorza and B. García Riaza (eds), *Technology-Enhanced Language Learning for Specialized Domains: Practical applications and mobility*, 228–40. Abingdon: Routledge.

Šarčević, S. (1994). 'Translation and the Law: An Interdisciplinary Approach'. In M. Snell-Hornby, F. Pöchhacker and K. Kaindl (eds). *Translation Studies: An Interdiscipline*, 301–7. Amsterdam and Philadelphia: John Benjamins.

Šarčević, S. (1997). *New Approach to Legal Translation.* The Hague: Kluwer Law International.

Šarčević, S. (2000a). 'Creativity in Legal Translation: How much is too much? '. In A. Chesterman, N. Gallardo San Salvador and Y. Gambier (eds), *Translation in Context. Selected papers from the EST Congress, Granada 1998*, 281–92. Amsterdam et al.: John Benjamin's.

Šarčević, S. (2000b). 'Legal Translation and Translation Theory: A Receiver-Oriented Approach'. Available online: http://www.tradulex.com/Actes2000/sarcevic.pdf (accessed 3 March 2017).

Šarčević, S. (2001). 'Translation Procedures for Legal Translators'. In S. Šarčević (ed.), *Legal Translation: Preparation for Accession to the European Union*, 75–109. Rijeka: Rijeka Faculty of Law.

Šarčević, S. (2010). 'Creating a Pan-European Legal Language'. In M. Gotti and C. Williams (eds), *Legal Discourse across Languages and Cultures*, 23–50. Bern: Peter Lang.

Šarčević, S. (2012). 'Coping with the Challenges of Legal Translation in Harmonization'. In C. J. W. Baaij (ed.), *The Role of Legal Translation in Legal Harmonization*, 83–107. Alphen aan den Rijn: Wolters Kluwer.

Šarčević, S. (2013). 'Multilingual Lawmaking and Legal (Un)Certainty in the European Union'. *International Journal of Law, Language & Discourse* 3 (1): 1–29.

Šarčević, S. (2015). 'Basic Principles of Term Formation in the Multilingual and Multicultural Context of EU Law'. In S. Šarčević (ed.), *Language and Culture in EU Law: Multidisciplinary Perspectives*, 183–205. Ashgate: Surrey.

Šarčević, S. and Robertson C. (2013). 'The Work of Lawyer-linguists in the EU Institutions'. In A. Borja Albi and F. Prieto Ramos (eds), *Legal Translation in Context: Professional Issues and Prospects*, 181–202. Bern: Peter Lang.

Schäffner, C. (2003). 'Translation and Intercultural Communication: Similarities and Differences'. *Studies in Communication Sciences* 3 (2): 79–107.

Schilling, T. (2010). 'Beyond Multilingualism: On Different Approaches to the Handling of Diverging Language Versions of a Community Law'. *European Law Journal* 16 (1): 47–66.

Scollon, R., Scollon, S. W. and Jones, R. (2011). *Intercultural Communication: A Discourse Approach*. Oxford: Wiley-Blackwell.

Scott, J. (2012). 'Can Genre-Specific DIY Corpora Compiled by Legal Translators Themselves, Assist Them in "Learning the Lingo" of Legal Subgenres?'. *Comparative Legilinguistics* 12: 87–101.

Scott, M. (2008). *WordSmith Tools Version 5*. Liverpool: Lexical Analysis Software.

Sedley, S. (2011). 'Speaking in Tongues: The Dissemination of Human Rights Judgments'. In P. Titiun (ed.), *La conscience des droits : mélanges en l'honneur de Jean-Paul Costa*, 571–4. Paris: Dalloz.

Sekel, S. (2008). *United Nations Translators and Interpreters – silent partners in the diplomatic process*. Keynote Address delivered by Mr. Yohannes Mengesha, Assistant Secretary-General of the United Nations, at the 18th FIT World Congress, 4–7 August 2008 Shanghai, China. Posted on the intranet (staff-only) website of the United Nations Secretariat in September 2008.

Shabtai, R. (2007). *Essays on International Law and Practice*. Leiden: M. Nijhoff.

Sharma, R. S. (2004). *Applied Linguistics: Stylistics and Language Teaching*. New Delhi: Atlantic Publishers & Distributors.

Simonnaes, I. (2012). 'Zur korpusbasierten Erforschung von Fachübersetzungen bei der Nationalen Übersetzerprüfung in Norwegen'. *Meta: Translators' Journal* 57 (1): 132–44.

Sinclair, J. (1996). 'The Search for Units of Meaning'. *Textus: English Studies in Italy* 9: 75–106.

Sinclair, J. M. (1991). *Corpus, Concordance, Collocation*. Oxford: Oxford University Press.

Sinner, C. and Morales Tejada, B. (2015). 'Translatologische Perzeptionsstudien als Grundlage der Bestimmung gelungener Übersetzungen. ' *Lebende Sprachen* 60: 111–23.

Snell-Hornby, M. (1995). *Translation Studies: An Integrated Approach* (Revised edition ed.). Amsterdam: John Benjamin.

Snell-Hornby, M. (2012). 'From the Fall of the Wall to Facebook. Translation Studies in Europe twenty years later'. *Perspectives: Studies in Translatology* 20 (3): 365–73.

Solan, L. (2009). 'The Interpretation of Multilingual Statutes by the European Court of Justice'. *Brooklyn Journal of International Law* 34 (2): 277–301.

Somssich, R. et al. (2012). *Language and Translation in International Law and EU Law*. Availiable online: http://www.ec.europa.eu/dgs/translation/publications/studies/index_en.htm (accessed5 September 2016).
Soriano-Barabino, G. (2016). *Comparative law for legal translators*. Oxford: Peter Lang.
Sourioux, J.-L. and Lerat, P. (1975). *Le langage du droit*. Paris: puf.
Steinberger, R., Ebrahim, M., Poulis, A. et al. (2014) 'An Overview of the European Union's Highly Multilingual Parallel Corpora'. *Language Resources and Evaluation* 48: 679–707.
Stolze, R. (2002). 'The Hermeneutic Approach in Translation'. *Studia Anglica Posnaniensia* 37: 279–91.
Strandvik, I. (2015). 'On Quality in Multilingual Lawmaking'. In S. Šarčević (ed.), *Language and Culture in EU Law: Multidisciplinary Perspectives*, 141–65. Farnham: Ashgate.
Stubbs, M. (2004). 'Language Corpora'. In A. Davies and C. Elder (eds), *The Handbook of Applied Linguistics*, 106–32. Oxford: Blackwell.
Svejcer, A. (2004). 'Possibilities and Limitations of Linguistic Approaches to Translation'. In H. Kittel, A. P. Frank, N. Greiner, T. Hermans, W. Koller, J. Lambert and F. Paul (eds), *Übersetzung Translation Traduction*, vol. 1, 236–42. Berlin and Boston: de Gruyter.
Tabory, M. (1980). *Multilingualism in International Law and Institutions*. Alphen aan den Rijn: Sijthoff & Noordhoff International Publishers B.V.
TAUS (2012). Press release 'TAUS launches dynamic quality evaluation framework'. Available online: https://www.taus.net/think-tank/news/press-release/taus-launches-dynamic-quality-evaluation-framework (accessed20 September 2016).
TAUS (2015). *Dynamic Quality Framework Report* 2015. Available online: https://www.taus.net/think-tank/reports/evaluate-reports/dynamic-quality-framework-report-2015 (accessed 20 September 2016).
Terris, D., Romano, C. and Swigart, L. (2007). *The International Judge*, 71–9. Oxford: Oxford University Press.
Teubert, W. (2004). 'Language and Corpus Linguistics'. In M. A. K. Halliday, W: Teubert, C. Yallop and A. Čermáková (eds), *Lexicology and Corpus Linguistics*, 73–112. London: Continuum.
Thibault, P. (2004). *Brain, Mind and the Signifying Body: An Ecosocial Semiotic Theory*. London: Continuum.
Tomasello, M. (2009). *Constructing a Language: A Usage-Based Theory of Language Acquisition*. Cambridge: Harvard University Press.
Tomasello, M. (2014). *A Natural History of Human Thinking*. Cambridge, MA: Harvard University Press.
Torres-Bernárdez, Santiago (1998). 'Interpretation of Treaties by the International Court of Justice following the Adoption of the 1969 Vienna Convention on the Law of Treaties'. In G. Hafner et al. (eds), *Liber Amicorum: Professor Ignaz Seidl-Hohenveldern: In Honour of His 80th Birthday*, 721–48. The Hague: Kluwer Law International.
Torres-Hostench, O. and Bestué Salinas, C. (2015). 'Technology and e-resources for Legal Translators: The LAW10n project'. In P. Sánchez-Gijón, O. Torres-Hostench and B. Mesa-Lao (eds), *Conducting Research in Translation Technologies*, 285–305. Oxford: Peter Lang.
Tosi, A. (ed.) (2003). *Crossing Barriers and Bridging Cultures: The Challenges of Multilingual Translation for the European Union*. Clevedon, Buffalo, Toronto and Sydney: Multilingual Matters Ltd.
UNESCO (2005). *Guidelines for Terminology Policies. Formulating and Implementing Terminology Policy in Language Communities*. Paris: UNESCO.

United Nations (1965). *Yearbook of the International Law Commission, 1964*. Vol. I. New York: United Nations.
United Nations (1967a). *Yearbook of the International Law Commission, 1966*. Vol. I. New York: United Nations.
United Nations (1967b). *Yearbook of the International Law Commission, 1966*. Vol. II. New York: United Nations.
Van Damme, I. (2009). *Treaty Interpretation by the WTO Appellate Body*. Oxford: Oxford University Press.
van der Jeught, S. (2015). *EU Language Law*. Groningen: Europa Law Publishing.
Vanden Bulcke, P. (2013). 'Dealing with Deontic Modality in a Termbase: The Case of Dutch and Spanish Legal Language'. *Linguistica Antverpiensia, New Series – Themes in Translation Studies* 12, 12–32.
Vangehuchten, L. (2007). 'Identifying Phraseology in LSP: A "Spanish as a Foreign Language for Business and Economics" Perspective'. In K. Pelsmaekers and C. Rollo (eds), *Economically Speaking: Essays in honour of Chris Braeck*, 91–107. Anvers-Apeldoorn: Garant.
Varantola, K. (2002). 'Disposable Corpora as Intelligent Tools in Translation'. *Cadernos de Tradução IX – Tradução e Corpora* 1 (9): 171–89.
Venzke, I. (2014). *How Interpretation Makes International Law*. Oxford: Oxford University Press.
Verleysen, P. (2010). Opening address given at the JIAMCATT – International Annual Meeting on Computer-Assisted Translation and Terminology, Luxembourg, 28 April 2010. Available online: http://ec.europa.eu/dgs/translation/publications/presentations/speeches/20100428_jia mcatt_en.pdf (accessed May 2012).
Vismara, F. (2006). 'The Role of the Court of Justice of the European Communities in the Interpretation of Multilingual Texts.' In B. Pozzo and V. Jacometti (eds), *Multilingualism and the Harmonisation of European Law*, 61–8. The Hague: Kluwer Law International.
Vlachopoulos, S. (2013), 'The Translation of Legal Texts. To what Extent can Functionality be Creative?'. *Revue hellénique de droit international* 66: 471–86.
Volk, M., Graën, J. and Callegaro, E. (2014). *'Innovations in Parallel Corpus Search Tools'*. In Calzolari, N. et al. (eds), Proceedings of the Ninth International Conference on Language Resources and Evaluation (LREC'14), 3172–3178. Reykjavik: European Language Resources Association (ELRA). Available online: http://www.lrec-conf.org/proceedings/lrec2014/pdf/504_Paper.pdf (accessed 1 October 2016).
Wagner, E., Bech, S. and Martínez, J. M. (2002). *Translating for the European Union Institutions*. Manchester, UK & Northampton, MA: St. Jerome Publishing.
Wagner, E., Svend B. and J. Martínez. (2012). *Translating for the European Union Institutions* (Second edn). Manchester: St Jerome.
Walker, D. (2001). *The Scottish Legal System: An Introduction to the Study of Scots Law*. Edinburgh: Thomson, Sweet & Maxwell.
Weiler, J. H. H. (2010). 'The Interpretation of Treaties – a Re-examination'. *European Journal of International Law* 21 (3): 507.
Wellington, L. M. (2001). 'Bijuralism in Canada: Harmonization Methodology and Terminology'. In *The Harmonization of Federal Legislation with the Civil Law of the Province of Quebec and Canadian Bijuralism*. Second Publication, booklet 4. Ottawa: Department of Justice. Available online: http://publications.gc.ca/collections/Collection/J2-176-4-2001E.pdf (accessed 1 September 2016).

Westerdiek, C. (1998). 'Practices developed by the Commission: Its use of Languages'. In M. de Salvia and M. Villiger (eds), *The Birth of European Human Rights Law*, 365–73. Baden-Baden: Nomos Verlagsgesellschaft.

Weston, M. (1988). 'The Role of Translation at the European Court of Human Rights'. In F. Matscher and H. Petzold (eds), *Protecting Human Rights: The European Dimension*, 679–89. Köln: Heymann.

Weston, M. (2005). 'Characteristics and Constraints of Producing Bilingual Judgments: The Example of the European Court of Human Rights'. In J.-C. Gémar and N. Kasirer (eds), *Jurilinguistics: between Law and Language*, 445–59. Brussels: Bruylant.

Weston, M. (2010). 'Speaking unto Nations: The Language Dimension of the Court's Work'. In J. Sharpe (ed.), *The Conscience of Europe: 50 years of the European Court of Human Rights*, 77–9. London: Third Millennium Publishing.

White, J. B. (1989). *Heracles' Bow: Essays on the Rhetoric and Poetics of the Law. Rhetoric of the Human Sciences*. Madison: University of Wisconsin Press.

White, J. B. (1994). *Justice as Translation: An Essay in Cultural and Legal Criticism*. Chicago: University of Chicago Press.

Williams, M. (1989). 'The Assessment of Professional Translation Quality: Creating Credibility out of Chaos'. *TTR : traduction, terminologie, redaction* 2 (2): 13–33.

Wood, M. J. B. (1996). 'Drafting Bilingual Legislation in Canada: Examples of Beneficial Cross-Pollination between the Two Language Versions'. *Statute Law Review* 17 (1): 66–77.

Wright, S. (2016). 'The Language of the Law in Multilingual contexts – Unpicking the English of the EU Courts' Judgments'. *Statute Law Review* 37 (2): 156–63.

Zanettin, F. (2012). *Translation-Driven Corpora. Corpus Resources for Descriptive and Applied Translation Studies*. Manchester: St. Jerome.

Zaretskaya, A., Corpas Pastor, G. and Seghiri, M. (2015). 'Translators' Requirements for Translation Technologies: A User Survey'. In *Proceedings of the AIET17 Conference New Horizons in Translation and Interpreting Studies*. Malaga, Spain. Available online: https://www.academia.edu/13708082/Translators_Requirements_for_Translation_Technologies_a_User_Survey (accessed 1 October 2016).

Zhao, X. and Cao, D. (2013). 'Legal Translation at the United Nations'. In A. Borja Albi and F. Prieto Ramos (eds), *Legal Translation in Context, Professional Issues and Prospects*, 203–20. Bern: Peter Lang.

Ziemski, M., Junczys-Dowmunt, M. and Pouliquen, B. (2016). 'The United Nations Parallel Corpus v1.0'. In *Language Resources and Evaluation (LREC'16)*, Portorož, Slovenia, May 2016. Available online: http://conferences.unite.un.org/UNCorpus/Content/Doc/un.pdf (accessed 1 October 2016).

Zweigert, K. and Kötz, H. (1996), *Einführung in die Rechtsvergleichung* (3. Auflage). Tübingen: J.C.B. Mohr.

Index

www.ingramcontent.com/pod-product-compliance
Ingram Content Group UK Ltd.
Pitfield, Milton Keynes, MK11 3LW, UK
UKHW020935310326
469516UK00005B/37